D0215433

W. H. Auden: 'The Language of Learning and the Language of Love'

AUDEN STUDIES 2

W. H. AUDEN

'The Language of Learning and the Language of Love'

821.91
Au23Le

WITHDRAWN

UNCOLLECTED WRITING, NEW INTERPRETATIONS

Auden Studies 2

EDITED BY KATHERINE BUCKNELL AND
NICHOLAS JENKINS

CLARENDON PRESS · OXFORD
1994

LIBRARY ST. MARY'S COLLEGE

Oxford University Press, Walton Street, Oxford OX2 6DP
Oxford New York
Athens Auckland Bangkok Bombay
Calcutta Cape Town Dar es Salaam Delhi
Florence Hong Kong Istanbul Karachi
Kuala Lumpur Madras Madrid Melbourne
Mexico City Nairobi Paris Singapore
Taipei Tokyo Toronto
and associated companies in
Berlin Ibadan

Oxford is a trade mark of Oxford University Press

Published in the United States
by Oxford University Press Inc., New York

Editorial matter © Katherine Bucknell and Nicholas Jenkins 1994
Text © The several contributors 1994
All previously unpublished material by W.H. Auden is © 1994 by
the Estate of W.H. Auden. Not to be reprinted without permission

All rights reserved. No part of this publication may be reproduced,
stored in a retrieval system, or transmitted, in any form or by any means,
without the prior permission in writing of Oxford University Press.
Within the UK, exceptions are allowed in respect of any fair dealing for the
purpose of research or private study, or criticism or review, as permitted
under the Copyright, Designs and Patents Act, 1988, or in the case of
reprographic reproduction in accordance with the terms of the licences
issued by the Copyright Licensing Agency. Enquiries concerning
reproduction outside these terms and in other countries should be
sent to the Rights Department, Oxford University Press,
at the address above

British Library Cataloguing in Publication Data
Data available
ISBN 0–19–812257–8

Library of Congress Cataloging in Publication Data
Auden, W. H. (Wystan Hugh), 1907–1973.
The language of learning and the language of love: uncollected writings,
new interpretations / W.H. Auden; edited by Katherine Bucknell and Nicholas Jenkins.
(Auden studies; 2)
Includes bibliographical references and index.
Contents: School writings—Uncollected songs and lighter poems—Gerhart Meyer
and the vision of Eros / David Luke—Whatever you do don't go to the wood / Richard
Bozorth—Everything turns away / David Pascoe—Persuasions to rejoice / Stan Smith—The
achievement of Edward Upward / Katherine Bucknell—Interviews, dialogues, and conversations
with W.H. Auden: a bibliography / Edward Mendelson.
I. Bucknell, Katherine. II. Jenkins, Nicholas, 1961– .
III. Title. IV. Series.
PR6001.U4A6 1994 811'.52—dc20 94–18393
ISBN 0–19–812257–8

1 3 5 7 9 10 8 6 4 2

Set by Hope Services (Abingdon) Ltd.
Printed in Great Britain
on acid-free paper by
Biddles Ltd.
Guildford & King's Lynn

PREFACE

THIS new volume of *Auden Studies*, the second in the series, centres on the first decade of Auden's literary career, and in particular on his roles as a teacher and dramatist. The book also explores some of the tensions and drives at work behind Auden's public faces—for instance, his battles with literary fathers, his private experience of love, and his attempt to devise a rhetoric that could adequately express his homosexual feelings. Three different kinds of work are presented here: original material by Auden including poems and songs (most of them previously unpublished, or printed only in now scarce magazines); literary-critical essays; and bibliography.

The volume begins with two small editions of Auden's poems and prose. These pieces reflect the side of Auden's literary persona that wished to communicate with a specific audience, to be part of a tightly knit circle. Each edition is accompanied by an introductory essay describing the character and significance of the material and, wherever necessary, the texts are annotated. The first group of texts, introduced by Auden's new biographer Richard Davenport-Hines, includes poems, songs, and a travel piece, all written while Auden was working as a schoolmaster in the 1930s; the second group, prepared by the Benjamin Britten scholars Donald Mitchell and Philip Reed and by Nicholas Jenkins, brings together scattered lyrics Auden offered to Britten to be set as cabaret songs, longer versions of songs written for the Auden–Isherwood plays, and songs Auden intended for children. Reed and Mitchell have also contributed a sketch of the singer Hedli Anderson for whom Auden and Britten wrote several of these cabaret pieces.

The editions of Auden's own work are followed by new literary-critical essays. The first, by Auden's friend and colleague at Christ Church, David Luke, combines scholarship and reminiscence to examine Auden's personal idea of love. This is followed by Richard Bozorth's study of the homosexual stylistics of *The Orators*, by David Pascoe's account of Auden's attitude towards the Surrealist movement, and by Stan Smith's intertextual account of Auden's struggle to assimilate and transcend the influence of the poetry of Yeats. After these Katherine Bucknell reassesses the career of Auden's contemporary and friend Edward Upward.

The last third of the book is devoted to an extensive supplement by Edward Mendelson to the second edition of Bloomfield and Mendelson's *Bibliography*. This supplement, part of Mendelson's work-in-progress for the third edition of the *Bibliography*, lists every known Auden interview, reported conversation, and fictional portrait.

K.B.

N.J.

ACKNOWLEDGEMENTS

ONCE again, our thanks are due to the Estate of W. H. Auden and to Edward Mendelson, Auden's literary executor, for permission to print the unpublished material by Auden that appears in this volume. We would also like to thank Don Bachardy for permission to quote from correspondence exchanged between Christopher Isherwood and Edward Upward, to quote from a letter from Auden to Isherwood, and to print the texts of songs and poems by Auden now in his possession; the British Library for permission to quote from letters and manuscripts in the Upward Papers; and Edward Upward for permission to quote from his unpublished letters and manuscripts. The Henry W. and Albert A. Berg Collection of The New York Public Library (Astor, Lenox, and Tilden Foundations) has allowed us to print poems and songs in its collection; excerpts from Auden's 1929 journal; excerpts from Auden's letters to Benjamin Britten, Nevill Coghill, Rupert Doone, Naomi Mitchison, Hedwig Petzold, John Pudney, Arnold Snodgrass, and Monroe K. Spears; and excerpts from a letter from Chester Kallman to Auden. Also, the Library's Rare Book Room has allowed us to print an Auden poem in its collection. The Bodleian Library, Oxford, has again permitted us to print excerpts from Auden's letters to E. R. and A. E. Dodds in the Dodds Bequest (MS Eng. lett. c. 464), and the Trustees of the Britten–Pears Foundation have shared the texts of songs by Auden in the possession of the Britten–Pears Library at the Red House, Aldeburgh, Suffolk. The Dartington Trust Archives have allowed us to quote from correspondence between Auden and Dorothy Elmhirst. At Oxford University Press, Frances Whistler and Vicki Reeve have been exceptionally patient and encouraging, while closer to home we have received devoted help and understanding from Siri Huntoon, Bob Maguire, and Sally Whitaker. John Fuller, Samuel Hynes, Frank Kermode, and Edward Upward have given us generous advice for which we are greatly in their debt. Finally, this volume of *Auden Studies* would not have been possible without the continued personal enthusiasm of Edward Mendelson; we thank him for his energy and sagacity.

CONTENTS

ABBREVIATIONS

Works by Auden Cited in this Volume

CP91   *Collected Poems*, ed. Edward Mendelson, 2nd edn. (New York and London, 1991).

DBS   *The Dog Beneath the Skin or Where Is Francis?*, with Christopher Isherwood (London and New York, 1935).

DM   *The Double Man* (New York, 1941), American edn. of *NYL*.

EA   *The English Auden: Poems, Essays and Dramatic Writings 1927–1939*, ed. Edward Mendelson (London, 1977; New York, 1978).

FA   *Forewords and Afterwords*, selected by Edward Mendelson (New York and London, 1973).

LFI   *Letters from Iceland*, with Louis MacNeice (London and New York, 1937).

Libretti   *Libretti and Other Dramatic Writings 1939–1973*, with Chester Kallman, ed. Edward Mendelson (Princeton, NJ, 1993).

LS   *Look, Stranger!* (London, 1936).

NYL   *New Year Letter* (London, 1941), British edn. of *DM*.

O^3 *The Orators: An English Study*, 3rd edn., 1st American edn. (London, 1966; New York, 1967).

P30   *Poems* (London, 1930).

PD   *The Prolific and the Devourer*, in *Antaeus*, 41 (Summer 1981), 4–65.

PDW   *Plays and Other Dramatic Writings 1928–1938*, with Christopher Isherwood, ed. Edward Mendelson (Princeton, NJ, 1988; London, 1989).

SW   *Secondary Worlds* (London, 1968; New York, 1969).

For works by Auden printed in *EA* and *CP91*, page references are given only to *EA*. For works appearing in *PDW* as well as in *EA* or *CP91*, references are given only to *PDW*.

Some Other Abbreviations Used in this Volume

Ansen   Alan Ansen, *The Table Talk of W. H. Auden*, ed. Nicholas Jenkins (Princeton, NJ, 1990; London, 1991).

AS1   Katherine Bucknell and Nicholas Jenkins, eds., *W. H. Auden: 'The Map of All My Youth': Early Works, Friends, and Influences*, Auden Studies 1 (Oxford, 1990).

ASN   *The W. H. Auden Society Newsletter*.

BBLFL   Donald Mitchell and Philip Reed, eds., *Letters from a Life: The Selected Letters and Diaries of Benjamin Britten 1913–1976*, vol. 1: 1923–1939, vol. 2: 1939–1945 (London, 1991).

Bibliography B. C. Bloomfield and Edward Mendelson, *W. H. Auden: A Bibliography 1924–1969*, 2nd edn. (Charlottesville, Va., 1972).

Carpenter   Humphrey Carpenter, *W. H. Auden: A Biography* (London and New York, 1981).

C&HK   Christopher Isherwood, *Christopher and His Kind 1929–1939* (London and New York, 1979).

Cunningham   Valentine Cunningham, *British Writers of the Thirties* (Oxford, 1988).

Early Auden   Edward Mendelson, *Early Auden* (New York and London, 1981).

Farnan   Dorothy J. Farnan, *Auden In Love* (New York and London, 1984).

Haffenden   John Haffenden, ed., *W. H. Auden: The Critical Heritage* (London, 1983).

Hynes   Samuel Hynes, *The Auden Generation: Literature and Politics in England in the 1930s* (London, 1976; New York, 1977).

Lions   Christopher Isherwood, *Lions and Shadows: An Education in the Twenties* (London, 1938).

SE   Sigmund Freud, *The Standard Edition of the Complete Psychological Works of Sigmund Freud*, trans. and ed. James Strachey, in collaboration with Anna Freud, assisted by Alix Strachey, Alan Tyson, Angela Richards, 24 vols. (London, 1953–74).

Smith   Stan Smith, *W. H. Auden* (Oxford and New York, 1985).

Spears   Monroe K. Spears, *The Poetry of W. H. Auden: The Disenchanted Island* (New York, 1963).

Spiral   Edward Upward, *The Spiral Ascent: A Trilogy of Novels* (London, 1977) containing *In the Thirties* (London, 1962), *The Rotten Elements* (London, 1969), and *No Home But the Struggle*.

WWW   Stephen Spender, *World Within World* (London and New York, 1951).

British and American editions are distinguished, where necessary, by the suffixes '(UK)' for books published in the United Kingdom and '(US)' for books published in the United States.

Libraries and Institutions

Berg   The Henry W. and Albert A. Berg Collection, New York Public Library (Astor, Lenox, and Tilden Foundations).

Bodleian   The Department of Western Manuscripts, Bodleian Library, Oxford.

HRC   Harry Ransom Humanities Research Center, The University of Texas at Austin.

PRO   Public Records Office, London.

Except where otherwise indicated, all letters are in the possession of their recipients or the heirs of their recipients.

School Writings

INTRODUCTION BY RICHARD DAVENPORT-HINES

Auden and Boarding Schools: A Background

THE nine items published here are all examples of Auden's school writings. After returning from Berlin, Auden spent the autumn of 1929 working as a tutor in London. During that time he visited Sedbergh School, a boys' boarding school run on spartan lines and set in magnificent high moorland near the border of Westmorland and the West Riding of Yorkshire: he once described Sedbergh to A. L. Rowse as in every respect his idea of 'paradise'.[1] An offer of a teaching job at Sedbergh was too tentative for him to rely on, and from April 1930 until the summer of 1932 he taught English and French at Larchfield Academy (now called Lomond School), a boys' school at Helensburgh, Dumbartonshire, Scotland. From the autumn of 1932 until the summer of 1935 he worked near the boundaries of Herefordshire and Worcestershire as a master at the Downs School, Colwall ('I teach English, Arithmetic, French, Gym and Biology', he told Naomi Mitchison).[2]

These schools differed in character. Larchfield had some resemblance to Sedbergh: its regime gave emphasis to sports. 'I teach rugger here', he wrote to Spender. 'Every day I rush about in shorts telling people not to funk'.[3] The Downs, by contrast, he described to Nevill Coghill as 'a posh liberal quaker school financed by chocolate, good kind people dependant [sic] on usury, which muddles them, poor things'.[4]

There were pedagogic traditions on both sides of his family. His great-uncle, the Rev. Thomas Auden, had been headmaster of Wellingborough Grammar School; a maternal great-uncle, the Rev. Henry Birch, was tutor to King Edward VII when Prince of Wales; and another Birch great-uncle, Augustus, had been master of a house

[1] Interview with Dr A. L. Rowse, 28 Oct. 1992.
[2] Naomi Mitchison, *You May Well Ask* (London, 1979), 123.   [3] *AS1* 61.
[4] ALS, n.d., ? Jan. 1933 (Berg); The 'chocolate' reference is to Cadbury family money.

at Eton, 'called the House of Lords because of the great number of noblemen who boarded there'.[5] Auden, though, approached teaching with attitudes shaped by the eleven years which he spent as a boarding schoolboy. He had left home at the age of seven in 1914. 'For the first time I came into contact with adults outside the family circle and found them to be hairy monsters with terrifying voices and eccentric habits, completely irrational in their bouts of rage and good-humour, and, it seemed, with absolute power of life and death', he recalled in *The Prolific and the Devourer*. 'Those who deep in the country at a safe distance from parents spend their lives teaching little boys, behave in a way which would get them locked up in ordinary society'.[6]

Financial exigencies forced him to teach. The spoilt or captious behaviour of contemporaries who could afford not to take jobs but wasted their opportunities was exasperating to him. 'As the one who has to have the job, *I* am naturally jealous of you and Christopher who can do as you please', he wrote to Spender from the Downs School in 1933. 'I dont think you know all the humiliations and exploitation of ones weakness that a job like mine involves, how hard it is to preserve any kind of integrity. If I ever sound complacent about it, it is because as compensation I exaggerate its occasional exquisite moments of satisfaction'.[7]

Nevertheless he did not repine. The world of British boarding schools enriched his imagination. Its images abound in his early poetry. 'Amid rustle of frocks and stamping feet', he wrote in a poem of March 1930, 'They gave the prizes to the ruined boys.'[8] The following year, in October 1931, he published in T. S. Eliot's *Criterion* his glorious 'Speech For A Prize-Day',[9] later part of *The Orators*. He took a close interest in educational theory. In 1932 he asked Gerald Heard to arrange a visit to Dartington Hall in Devon, where Dorothy and Leonard Elmhirst had opened a progressive school in the 1920s. 'I am much looking forward to seeing what I keep hearing of, and hearing nothing but praise', he wrote when Mrs Elmhirst's invitation arrived.[10] His admiration for schools like Dartington or Bedales was

---

[5] James Brinsley-Richards, *Seven Years at Eton 1857–1864* (London, 1883), 52. Auden, who enjoyed hearing campy female nicknames for his male acquaintances, might have relished the fact that the other baptized name of his Victorian uncle Henry was Mildred.

[6] *PD* 12.   [7] *ASI* 62.   [8] *EA* 47.   [9] *Criterion*, 11.42 (Oct. 1931), 60–4.

[10] Dorothy Elmhirst to Auden, 5 Mar. 1932; Auden to Dorothy Elmhirst, 11 Mar. 1932 (both in Dartington Trust Archives, Totnes, Devon).

inconstant, however. By 1936, in 'Letter to Lord Byron', he had decided that

> my bad old Adam is
> Pigheadedly against the general trend;
> And has no use for all these new academies
> Where readers of the better weeklies send
> The child they probably did not intend,
> To paint a lampshade, marry, or keep pigeons,
> Or make a study of the world religions.[11]

His memories of school were adapted to his new circumstances as a teacher. 'The primitive tribe ruled by demons which had terrified and fascinated the small boy, now appeared to the employee in a more prosaic light as a private business enterprise operating under a laissez-faire capitalism, a shop in which, as in all other kinds of shop, success depended upon our ability to be more attractive to customers than our competitors', he wrote of himself in 1939. 'A private school is an absolute dictatorship where the assistant staff play, as it were, Goering Roehm Goebbels Himmler to a headmaster Hitler. There are the same intrigues for favour, the same gossip campaigns, and from time to time the same purges'.[12]

From September 1932 until the following summer he wrote a series of essays and reviews on educational theory and practice. Reviewing *The Dark Places in Education* by Willi Schohaus for *The Criterion* in 1933, he noted that

an excessive interest in child welfare, like an obsession about cruelty to animals, is not a symptom of a healthy society; a preoccupation of those with small independent incomes, it is often a propitiation of the feelings of guilt at not attacking the fundamental abuses of a society, in which an unsatisfactory educational system is one of many results, not a cause.

Remembering the lunacy of his teachers during his own boyhood, he found it 'topsy-turvy' that although pupils at teacher training colleges were taught the rudiments of child psychology,

they learn nothing about their own, are given no sort of insight whatever into themselves, which, in a profession where adults are expected . . . to profess official opinions on every subject of importance, to lead the private life of a clergyman, where a mask is essential, sets up a strain that only the long

---

[11] *LFI* 207; repr. in *EA* 193.   [12] *PD* 15.

holidays of which other professions are often so jealous, safeguard from developing into a nervous breakdown.[13]

Auden believed that the only ways to survive in boys' boarding schools were either to 'possess some special talent' or to be 'the licensed Buffoon critic'. To some extent in these school writings he is playing the part of a buffoon critic: they are boisterous fun, but some of their absurdities are obscurely subversive. As he wrote of himself:

A teacher soon discovers that there are only a few pupils whom he can help, many for whom he can do nothing except teach a few examination tricks, and a few to whom he can do nothing but harm. The children who interested me were either the backward, i.e. those who had not yet discovered their real nature, the bright with similar interests to my own, or those who, like myself at their age, were school-hating anarchists. To these I tried, while encouraging their rebellion, to teach a technique of camouflage, of how to avoid martyrdom.[14]

Auden's School Writings: Recitation and Subversion

'The last five years, with the wireless and the talkies, have witnessed a revival in the use of the spoken word', Auden wrote in 1932 in a draft of his essay 'Writing, or the Pattern Between People' for Naomi Mitchison's *An Outline for Boys and Girls and Their Parents*. He welcomed this revival, and felt that oral traditions had advantages in smaller communities. 'Generally speaking, the *feeling* meaning is transmitted with extraordinary accuracy, as the gestures and tone of voice which go with the words are remembered also'.[15]

This belief in the value of the spoken word had been stimulated when Auden was a pupil at Gresham's School in the early 1920s. More than thirty years later he was still impressed by 'the magnificent reading voice' of the senior classics master there; but more importantly, Frank McEachran (the Gresham's teacher whose importance to Auden has been convincingly argued by John Bridgen) built his brilliantly stimulating teaching techniques around his collection of 'Spells'. These 'Spells' were an eclectic and provocative collection of extracts from the great literature of several cultures—chiefly but not exclusively poetry—which he would recite, or make his boys recite

---

[13] *Criterion*, 12.48 (Apr. 1993), 537–8. For an examination of Auden's shifting attitudes to education, see *Early Auden*, 128–31, 257–9, 286–95, and *passim*.

[14] *PD* 16.

[15] 'Writing', *AS1* 44–5. Mrs Mitchison published a revised version of this essay in her *Outline*.

while standing on chairs, as a way of showing the glory of words and of celebrating his own love of poetry. The 'Spells' were a compelling teaching aid, unforgettable to his brighter pupils, and impressive even in the dry form in which they were later published.[16]

McEachran's emphasis on recitation may have influenced Auden's own teaching methods, and certainly contributes to our understanding of some of the feelings and meanings which underlie the school writings. Of these 'A School Song' (item 4) was first published in 1936 in *Spur*, the magazine of Raynes Park School, of which the headmaster was John Garrett (1902–66). It was with Garrett, whom he had probably met through Nevill Coghill and who was perhaps briefly a lover, that Auden had collaborated in compiling the anthology of poetry for use in schools, *The Poet's Tongue*, published in 1935. Their introduction to that anthology was another declaration in favour of the spoken word. 'Of the many definitions of poetry, the simplest is still the best: "memorable speech"', Auden and Garrett wrote.

That is to say, it must move our emotions, or excite our intellect, for only that which is moving or exciting is memorable, and the stimulus is the audible spoken word and cadence, to which in all its power of suggestion and incantation we must surrender, as we do when talking to an intimate friend. We must, in fact, make exactly the opposite kind of mental effort to that which we make in grasping other verbal uses, for in the case of the latter the aura of suggestion round every word through which . . . it becomes ultimately a sign for the sum of all possible meanings, must be rigorously suppressed and its meaning confined to a single dictionary one. For this reason the exposition of a scientific theory is easier to read than to hear. No poetry, on the other hand, which when mastered is not better heard than read is good poetry.[17]

The poems in their anthology are chosen to make the point that good poetry is best when recited to listeners. The selection, it is crucial to remember, was undertaken by two men who were both working at the time as schoolmasters: many of the poems, when read aloud to schoolchildren, have a gratifying impact. *The Poet's Tongue* is one of those rare books that can show children that poetry is exciting, teasing stuff which can upset habits of thought or unsettle old assumptions. Its contents are meant to have a liberating but not a didactic

---

[16] 'Frank McEachran (1900–1975)', *AS1* 118, 120 ff. Laurence Le Quesne's introduction to Frank McEachran, *A Cauldron of Spells* (East Horrington, Somerset, 1992), xv and *passim*; information from Peter Davenport, Aug. 1992. The widest selection is McEachran's *Cauldron* drawn from his *Spells* (Oxford, 1955), *More Spells* (London, 1970), and *Spells for Poets* (London, 1974).

[17] W. H. Auden and John Garrett, *The Poet's Tongue* (London, 1935), v.

effect. As Auden and Garrett wrote, 'Poetry is not concerned with telling people what to do, but with extending our knowledge of good and evil, perhaps making the necessity for action more urgent and its nature more clear, but only leading us to the point where it is possible for us to make a rational and moral choice'.[18] The necessity of personal choice, its value and attendant griefs, always provided some of Auden's profoundest preoccupations as a poet and thinker; but the dilemma of choice seems to have been notably explicit in his association with Garrett: his 'Song' for Garrett's school, for example, concludes,

> Boys and cities, schools and nations,
>> Though they change like you and me,
> Do not simply grow and happen:
>> They are what they choose to be.

The outlook of *The Poet's Tongue* is the outlook with which these school writings should be approached. With two exceptions, all of these pieces were first published in school magazines (mainly *The Badger* of the Downs School). They were addressed to a readership predominantly composed of schoolboys. Some—such as 'A School Song' written for John Garrett—were explicitly written to be spoken, chanted, or sung. All of them are improved by it. Recitation aloud was key to understanding Auden. Gabriel Carritt recalls that when he was an undergraduate at Christ Church in the late 1920s, he would go to bed, closing the outer door of his rooms and wanting to sleep, but that Auden would come along, sit outside in the corridor, and recite his latest poems loudly through the shut door.[19]

As his ideas about his audiences changed, he was drawn to write light verse for children. The first of these school poems was written by Auden in a jotting book kept by Norman Wright, a Larchfield pupil. Wright himself 'was not greatly impressed' by Auden as a teacher. As a Scot he found Auden's English pronunciation hard to understand, he later wrote,

---

[18] W. H. Auden and John Garrett, *The Poet's Tongue* (London, 1935), ix. His preoccupation with choice is discernible in his play of the same year, *The Dog Beneath the Skin*: 'You are fighting your own nature, which is to learn and to choose' (*PDW* 286); 'Choose . . . that you may recover' (*PDW* 289).

[19] Gabriel Carritt in conversation with Katherine Bucknell, Nov. 1992. Stephen Spender recalls that Auden 'had an excellent verbal memory and could recite poems with an intonation which made them seem obscure, and yet significant and memorable. He had the power to make everything sound Audenesque' (*WWW* (UK), 51).

and, frankly, his reasoning was beyond me. I believe he was the first adult I had met who bit his nails and smoked heavily. I did not admire the habits. He seemed rather aloof and not very companionable. Not a person in whom we could confide. He did accompany us to games but his appearance on the rugby pitch was a bit of a giggle. He wasn't endowed for such sport.[20]

Resurrected by Stan Smith and first published in 1988,[21] 'Listen, Norman Wright' is an irregularly scanned piece of doggerel; its rhymes and syntax seem poor if read to oneself, but are more rollick-ing if read aloud. It is the earliest, least significant of these school writings. To take another example, 'Lament', the first of Auden's writings to be published in *The Badger*, in the autumn of 1933, appears strained and dull until it is read aloud, with noisy inflexions, to schoolchildren. Its refrain 'Miss Royster!' is comparable to 'The Akond of Swat!' in Edward Lear's poem (anthologized in *The Poet's Tongue* and gleefully received by children when read aloud with the right degree of hamminess).

There are other influences in the poems: 'To Robert Russell' (item 5) is Betjemanesque; 'Johnny' (item 7) is indebted to Hilaire Belloc's *Cautionary Tales*; and the influence of Lewis Carroll was never long suppressed when Auden was travelling.

Enunciation remained important for Auden. His response to his mother's death was to write his Christmas oratorio 'For the Time Being' (1944). He wrote librettos for Britten, Stravinsky, Hans Werner Henze, and Nicolas Nabokov, translated the libretto of Mozart's *Magic Flute*, and in the 1960s composed several songs intended for a Broadway production (called *Man of La Mancha*) about the life of Don Quixote. He was excited by the challenge of writing stirring or devotional or witty, fast-paced lyrics that com-manded attention yet were well-matched with the music of such dif-ferent composers. The precocious child who learnt that words could be used to elicit approval, admiration, and laughter—who 'appalled his aunts by talking like a professor of geology'[22]—developed into an adult with a lifelong fascination with creating 'memorable speech'. His success in reciting his work at poetry readings was another manifesta-tion of this: by the early 1940s he was recognized in the USA as a superb performer; later his platform performances made him the 'mascot' of the Poetry International festivals held in London from

[20] Quoted in Carpenter, 112.
[21] 'A Manuscript Poem to Norman Wright', *ASN*, 1 (Apr. 1988), 3–4.
[22] *PD* 11.

1967.[23] His work yielded new meanings and richness when recited by others too. This was recognized, sometimes instinctively, by his peers. When E. M. Forster in 1963 experimented to see if 'reading a poem aloud to myself' would revive his creativity, he chose Auden for the trial: 'no success, though the poet was Auden—his threnody on Freud—and the emotions congenial', he reported. The choice of Auden was not casual. As Forster sensed, he is a poet for recitation.[24]

In 'The Chase', the play written by Auden in 1934 while he was teaching at the Downs School, the reactionary General Hotham fulminates against 'young people' and underdogs. 'The greatest injury we did them', Hotham declares,

> Was teaching them to read and write
> To imagine that a smattering of knowledge
> Puts reverence and duty in the shade
> Books have debauched them as the trader's gin
> Degrades the savage
> · · · · ·
>   I am a soldier
> And I know why private soldiers are admired.
> It is obedience makes them beautiful
> Take that away as in a panic
> And in the instant squalor rushes back.[25]

Auden's opinions by 1934 were the antithesis of this. He wanted the young to read books (or hear poetry) as a way of losing mindless obedience. The only 'danger' in children reading, he had written in 1932, was 'when we only read what encourages us in lazy and crude ways of feeling and thinking; like cheap company'.[26] Yet as shown by his jibes against Dartington, or people excessively interested in protecting children, he was repelled by those who tried to perfect children, or idealize their existence.

> I hate the modern trick, to tell the truth,
>   Of straightening out the kinks in the young mind,
> Our passion for the tender plant of youth,
> Our hatred for all weeds of any kind.
>   Slogans are bad: the best that I can find
> Is this: 'Let each child have that's in our care
> As much neurosis as the child can bear'.

---

[23] William Carlos Williams, *Autobiography* (New York, 1951), 310; Charles Osborne, *Giving It Away* (London, 1986), 198.

[24] Mary Lago and P. N. Furbank, eds., *Selected Letters of E. M. Forster 1921–1970* (London, 1985), 283.

[25] *PDW* 146–7.   [26] Auden, 'Writing', *AS1* 50.

. . . . .
Goddess of bossy underlings, Normality!
    What murders are committed in thy name!
Totalitarian is thy state Reality,
    Reeking of antiseptics and the shame
    Of faces that all look and feel the same.
Thy Muse is one unknown to classic histories,
The topping figure of the hockey mistress.[27]

These school writings have a small but significant part in the development of his ideas about his audience. The obscurity of *The Orators*, which Auden completed in 1931, exemplified Cyril Connolly's retrospective complaint a decade later: 'the tragedy of our civilisation is that a specialized education has segregated an advanced artistic minority from the main body as with a tourniquet'.[28] In the months after completing *The Orators*, Auden, who was aged only 24, determined to loosen this tourniquet. Katherine Bucknell has analysed this process meticulously.[29] He wanted to be read and remembered: he strove for greater accessibility and less obscurity: he recognized too that children were not only the least scary of readers, but offered a chance to influence posterity. As he wrote early in 1932,

People write in order to be read. They would like to be read by everybody and for ever. They feel alone, cut off from each other in an indifferent world where they do not live for very long. How can they get in touch again; how can they prolong their lives. Children by their bodies, live on in life they will not live to see meet friends they will never know, and will in their turn have children, some tiny part of them too living on all the time.[30]

Ambivalent about the possibility of personal fulfilment or change, he began seeking 'emotional sustenance less in private, sexual relations and more in public, social ones'.[31] Under the influence of Gerald Heard, he hoped to find satisfaction in group life. 'We're all sex-obsessed today because there isn't any decent group life left', he wrote to John Pudney on 28 July 1932. 'The whole value of a group is that its constituents are as diverse as possible, with little consciously in common. Plurality is unity'.[32]

What was Auden's experience of group life after 1930? For almost five years he lived in British boarding schools. In the early 1940s he

---

[27] *LFI* 206–7 repr. in *EA* 193.
[28] Cyril Connolly, *The Condemned Playground* (London, 1945), 287.
[29] 'Auden's "Writing" Essay', *AS1* 17–18.   [30] 'Writing', *AS1* 48.
[31] Bucknell, *AS1* 17–18.   [32] ALS (Berg).

lived semi-communally in a house in Brooklyn Heights, though it is not clear that the household had much in common with his ideas of group life: its occupants were too much his own kind, and at times their emotional life was cannibalistic. Teaching at small American colleges similarly contained few elements of group life. The nearest to it (before his final unhappy move to Christ Church in 1972) was provided by the gay resorts of Fire Island and Ischia, where he had holiday homes. For all the dissatisfactions of schoolmastering, Larchfield and the Downs provided him with the fullest model of group life that he knew.

Travel Writing

'In Search of Dracula', the sixth of these items, is the only prose work. It is a deliciously mischievous travel journal recounting a holiday which Auden took in the summer of 1934 with two former Downs pupils, Michael Yates and Peter Roger (the latter then working as a gardener at the school). Meeting in London on 14 August, they travelled by boat and car through Belgium to Germany, 'which is being run by a mixture of gangsters and the sort of school prefect who is good at Corps' (16 August). Presumably armed with an introduction from Nevill Coghill, they stayed (19–20 August) at Schloss Eisenberg with Coghill's Anglo-Irish first cousin, formerly Gillian Somerville of Drishane House, Castletownshend, but since 1924 the wife of Maximilien-Erwin Marie Joseph Anton de Padoue Henri Thomas, 10th Prince of Lobkowicz and Duke of Raudnice (1888–1967). The Prince was a blackleg among European nobility— 'what the French would call un déséquilibré et un irresponsible', as the Duke of Portland had decried him to Lord Curzon in 1920, 'the *only member* of the Austrian Aristocracy who is a *Bolshevist* [and] who has the reputation of being completely mad'.[33] The Prince had left the Hapsburg army in protest at the treatment of Czechs, afterwards held various posts at the Czech Legation in London, and at the time of Auden's visit was Czech representative on the League of Nations Commission for German refugees.

From Schloss Eisenberg Auden's party crossed Czechoslovakia, but their intention of exploring the Carpathians was frustrated: 'Peter suffering from gardener's leg . . . so magnanimously decided to give Dracula a miss' (23 August). They returned through the Tyrol and

---

[33] Duke of Portland to Marquess Curzon of Kedleston, marked 'Secret', 8 Aug. 1920, FO 371/4720, PRO.

Switzerland, visiting Auden's beloved former landlady in Kitzbühel, Hedwig Petzold (31 August), before reaching London and the shop-talk of Gerald Heard (4–5 September).

This short journal fills one with regret that Auden disliked letter-writing.[34] Written just after 'The Chase', parts of which it resembles in tone, 'In Search of Dracula' is an attractive piece of the Auden canon, with its fast, extemporaneous activity, facetious distortions, jaunty misanthropy and sense of continuous but fleeting personal triumphs over a world that is variously silly, sordid, or sinister. It stimulated the passages of European travelogue incorporated into *The Dog Beneath the Skin* (1935), and has interesting points of comparison with his longer ventures at travel writing, *Letters from Iceland* (1937) and *Journey to a War* (1939), compiled jointly with MacNeice and Isherwood respectively.

Travel writing was a popular but mixed genre for the British. Early travel writers accumulated vast numbers of ethnographic and geographic facts. They were followed by a few heroic adventurers, whose example was then cautiously imitated by impecunious hacks fulfilling publishers' commissions. Another pattern of travel writing was epistolary, exemplified by the Marquess of Dufferin and Ava's account of his visit to Iceland, *Letters from High Latitudes* (1857), which Auden rightly admired. In the 1930s a younger generation of travellers started a new trend in literary journeying by developing the epistolary tradition into an altogether more personal and introspective pursuit. Patrick Leigh Fermor, for example, made his famous journey on foot from England to the Balkans in the same year as Auden's search for Dracula. Like Wilfred Thesiger, Laurens van der Post, Lawrence Durrell, and later Bruce Chatwin, Leigh Fermor was to transform the higher class of travel literature into literary questing for a sense of self as well as a sense of place. In all types of the genre, premeditation masqueraded as serendipity. As Auden realized, travel writers were drearily formulaic even when they pretended to be spontaneous.

He created his own version of travel writing, which played up the hilarious unreality of what other people thought concrete or important; he mixed the epistolary with the personal quest but avoided all the more strained contrivances of the genre. There are long passages

---

[34] 'As a correspondent I'm the shit', Auden to Rupert Doone, ALS, 28 July 1932 (Berg; quoted in *PDW* 490); 'I'm the worst letter writer in the world', TLS to Hedwig Petzold, n.d. [Jan. 1938] (Berg); 'At answering letters . . . I'm very slack' (*LFI* 203; repr. in *EA* 190).

in *Letters from Iceland* (1937) which read like a verse rendering of the mood of 'Dracula' in 1934:

> Louis read George Eliot in bed
> And Michael and I climbed the cliff behind Hraensnef
> And I *was* so frightened, my dear.
> And we all rowed on the lake and giggled because the boat leaked
> And the farmer was angry when we whipped his horses
> And Louis had a dream—unrepeatable but he repeated it—
> And the lady at table had diabetes, poor thing
> And Louis dreamt of a bedroom with four glass walls
> And I was upset because they told me I didn't look innocent
> (I liked it really of course)
> And the whaling station wouldn't offer us any coffee
> And Michael didn't speak for three hours after that
> And the first motor-boat we hired turned back because of the weather
> 'A hot spot' he said but we and the vice consul didn't believe him
> And that cost an extra ten kronur.
> And it was after ten when we really got there and could discover a landing
> And we walked up to the farm in the dark
> Over a new mown meadow, the dogs running in and out of the lamplight
> And I woke in the morning to hear Louis vomiting.[35]

'Dracula' is not a respectable piece of writing, or written by a respecter of persons. The 'occasional exquisite moments of satisfaction' which Auden told Spender he experienced as a schoolmaster, when he 'tried, while encouraging . . . rebellion, to teach a technique of camouflage, of how to avoid martyrdom', may have been aroused in publishing 'In Search of Dracula'. It has subversive touches and is surprisingly explicit for the magazine of a school where 'those who loiter in the lavatories are not much thought of'.[36] The 'Fairy Ring in Piccadilly' which Auden visited, for example (4 September), is surely the homosexual 'meat-rack' that existed until the 1980s on the corner of Glasshouse Street and Regent Street: the reference, however camouflaged, in a school magazine is defiant. The 'meat-rack' incidentally was only a few yards from the Regent Palace Hotel, which Auden had earlier described as 'the Yids' home in Regent Street' (14 August). This rare anti-semitic jibe by Auden seems to have been provoked by the clientele of the hotel (owned by the Salmon and Gluckstein families): a novel (published four years earlier) set in the hotel (with its name Regent Palace thinly disguised) opened with a reference to 'that

[35] *LFI* 224–5.   [36] Auden to Rupert Doone, ALS, [19 Oct. 1932] (Berg).

peculiarly detestable brand of Jew-boys which the Piccadilly Palace
lounge seems to attract like flies to sugar, smarmed and stinking of
cheap scent'.[37] Auden later described himself as 'a Gentile inheriting
an O-so-genteel anti-semitism',[38] but his meeting with Chester
Kallman in 1939 cured this vice.

'In Search of Dracula' is full of treasures: autobiographical fragments ('"Your god is your belly", my aunt used to tell me'—14
August) and throw-away lines which remind us of the slapstick talents
of his early plays ('Ordered Bubbly which . . . made us feel very on-
the-Continong'—21 August). There are Audenesque disputations
('Argument about the scenery cult. Personally give me a good hotel
and a petrol pump or city streets in a fog'—18 August) alongside his
political revulsion from Nazism (17–18 August) and his aesthetic dislike of Belgians ('A dingy race with too many large cars fitted with
trumpets which they blow continuously'—16 August). We find images
of obscure menace that could come straight from one of his poems
('Went in the evening to see strong man run over by a motor car and
stood upon by the local Fatty Arbuckle'—23 August). At least one
phrase in the journal was later adapted for a poem: 'inspected the
new railway they are building. Very pansy' (25 August) was re-
worked into the November 1934 version of 'A Bride in the 30's'.
There the poet who travels through 'the sixteen skies of Europe|
And the Danube flood' encounters a 'new pansy railway'.[39] In other
ways his Dracula trip contributed to the revisions of *The Chase* which
resulted in the best moments of the picaresque in *The Dog Beneath
the Skin*.

Community Writing in America

At the end of the 1930s Auden was still preoccupied with educational
matters, but his speech to the New Education Fellowship at
Hoddesdon in Hertfordshire (27 October 1938) reflected the deterio-
rating political situation in Europe: its sentiments were harder and
grimmer than the group ideals of Gerald Heard with which he had
earlier toyed.[40] His views on the corruption of political language had
become Orwellian, as shown by his article published on 25 November

[37] Anthony Berkeley, *The Piccadilly Murder* (London, 1929), 8.   [38] Farnan, 65.
[39] *LS* 50; 'strategic' was substituted for 'pansy' in later versions with meagre success. See also Graham Martin, 'Pansy Railway', *ASN*, 4 (Oct. 1989), 4–5 and John
Whitehead's 'Pansy Railway: A Reply', *ASN*, 5 (Aug. 1990), 5.
[40] 'Democracy's Reply to the Challenge of Dictators', *New Era in Home and School*,
20 (Jan. 1939), 5–8; *Birmingham Post*, 28 Oct. 1938, 13.

in a radical Birmingham newspaper, *The Town Crier*. After contrasting educational aims in tyrannies and democracies, he deplored the deficiency of English-language teaching in Britain because 'the basis of a general education' for democratic citizens should be 'training in the use of one's own language'. The fact that 'language and understanding are alike vague' among pupils was 'a hindrance' to 'political understanding'. These defects he attributed 'to the domination of English teaching by the teaching of English literature, the learning about and imposed appreciation of great books which, after all, have mostly been written by adults about adults for adults'.[41]

Three months later he left for the USA. The two final examples of school writings both date from May or June of 1939, when (through the intervention of the poet Richard Eberhart) Auden taught for four or five weeks at St Mark's School, Southborough, Massachusetts— 'the Eton of America', as he described it to Benjamin Britten.[42] 'He seemed amazing to me', Eberhart has recalled. 'He looked like a clown but talked like a sage . . . He enchanted the boys by his teaching'.[43] He had also recently met Chester Kallman and was 'mad with happiness' as he told Britten in the same letter about St Mark's. Their separation was frustrating to them both. 'Darling', Kallman wrote on 13 May 1939 from New York, '*I* love you, I *love* you, I love *you* . . . I w[h]ile away time imagining you teach some student French in bed'.[44] Auden's reply has not survived, except in the form of 'Love Letter' (item 8), which he wrote at St Mark's:

> O but I was mad to come here, even for money:
> To put myself at the mercy of the postman and the daydream,
> That incorrigible nightmare in which you lie weeping or ill
> Or drowned in the arms of another.
>
> To have left you now, when I know what this warm May weather
> Does to the city; how it brings out the plump little girls and
> Truculent sailors into the parks and sets
> The bowels of boys on fire.

Another poem, 'Calypso', which he wrote in the same month and first published in *Another Time*, is on a similar theme. Travelling back

---

[41] 'The Teaching of English', *The Town Crier*, NS 999 (25 Nov. 1938), 2.
[42] ALS, n.d. [1939] (Berg).
[43] 'A Tribute to W. H. Auden', *Harvard Advocate*, 108 (1974), 30. See also Joel Roache, *Richard Eberhart, the Progress of an American Poet* (New York, 1971), 102–6 and Eberhart's poem 'To Auden on his Fiftieth': *Collected Poems 1930–1976* (London, 1976), 238–9.   [44] ALS (Berg).

down the Springfield line, he is impatient to arrive at Grand Central Station:

> For thére in the míddle of thát waiting-háll
> Should be stánding the óne I love best of áll.
>
> If he's nót there to méet me when Í get to tówn,
> I'll stand on the síde-walk with téars rolling dówn.[45]

'Love Letter' and 'Calypso' are light poems, but their theme of separation is neither obscure nor trivial; the Springfield experience is universal.

If 'Dracula' was unexpectedly explicit for a school magazine, then parts of 'Love Letter' seem brazen for publication in 1939 in Kenyon College's *Hika*. The two pieces have a similar tendency to encourage young people to be insubordinate and to test how much exposure to neurosis they can bear. The St Mark's 'Ode' is another celebration of community life and a fitting conclusion to this sequence. Its adolescent larkiness and sympathies as well as its roistering rhythms and mockery resemble some of the earlier British school writings; yet it is also arguable that some of his later pieces, written to give pleasure to Kallman's circle, like 'The Queen's Masque, by Bojo the homo' performed in Michigan in 1943,[46] are comparable to his school writings as attempts at community writing.

[45] *CP91* 266—I owe this reference to Christopher Phipps.
[46] The Queen's Masque, by Bojo the homo, 'to be presented at 803 South State Street on January 7th 1943 by Kallman's Klever Kompanions' (*Libretti*, 422–9).

Poems and Prose

W. H. AUDEN

Edited by
Richard Davenport-Hines and Nicholas Jenkins

These poems by Auden are taken from printed sources, most of which are now difficult to obtain. No changes have been made here in the punctuation, but obvious spelling errors have been corrected. The house-style of *The Badger* has been retained both in order to preserve the period look of the poems and prose first printed there and also because it probably accurately reflects details of Auden's original manuscripts.

[1]

Listen, Norman Wright
Do you want a fight
That you've just taken a bite
Out of my ear—not slight
For you held on tight
With all your might.
I'm in a terrible plight
My ear looks like a kite
Do you think it right
That a boy of your height
Should so delight
In casting a slight?
If I catch you to-night
I'll shoot at sight
So you'd better take flight
To the Isle of Wight.

[MS in Auden's hand, dated '8.11.30', in Norman Wright's jotting book. First published in 'A Manuscript Poem to Norman Wright', introduced by Stan Smith, *ASN*, 1 (April 1988), 3–4, quoted in 'Peterborough', *Daily Telegraph*, 28 April 1988; reprinted in full in Donald MacLeod, 'Recollections that Throw an Ironic Light on Auden', *Scotsman*, 21 June 1988, p. 13; and quoted again in Christie, Manson & Woods, Mediaeval and Illuminated Manuscripts . . . [catalogue], London, 7 December 1988, p. 127.]

[2] Lament[1]

The day of dawn had scarce broke through
When 'long the corridor there flew
A boy who could not find his tie,
What did he do? Oh, naught, but cry
    'Miss Royster!'

Then at long break another came,
Not quite so big (you know his name),
'My running-shoes have gone astray,
Where can they be since yesterday
    Miss Royster?'

Then after lunch as sure as fate
Along they'd come in greater spate,
Some big, some wee, some short, some tall,[2]
And all emitting that shrill call,
    'Miss Royster!'

So on it goes from morn till night,
Till oft I wake from sleep in fright,
Haunted by running-shoes and ties,
Shrieking with most blood-curdling cries,
    'Miss Royster!'

[First printed in *The Badger*, 1.2 (Autumn 1933), 34, signed 'Anon'.]

---

[1] The first of the poems written for his pupils at the Downs School in Colwall.

[2] Cf. Auden's most famous poem written at the Downs School, 'Out on the lawn I lie in bed': 'The moon looks on them all: | The healers and the brilliant talkers, | The eccentrics and the silent walkers, | The dumpy and the tall' in *EA* 137.

[3] In Search of Dracula[3]

Tuesday, 14th.[4]—Arrived with Michael at 12.30 to find Peter rocking a cradle[5] outside the Lodge.[6] Lunch beautifully hot but missed Mr. Pup's carving.[7] Mr. Booge,[8] a good samaritan as usual, helped us to tie on our stores, tents, theodolites, sleighs, reindeer food, etc. Photographs of the doomed heroes were taken, babes and sucklings held up.

Raced a quartet of beauties in dinky scarves as far as the Watford bypass. Dropped Peter to say good-bye to his parents—sneaking into

[3] Auden conceived the idea of going to visit Dracula's castle. In an ALS [?Spring 1934], to Naomi Mitchison (Berg) he wrote: 'I'm off to the Carpathians this summer stimulated I believe by childish memories of Dracula. I hope we get interned [interred?].' Auden had been at his parents' cottage in Wescoe immediately before the trip. He picked up the Old Downian Michael Yates from the Yates's family home, Broadlands, in Lime Grove, Manchester, before they motored down to Colwall to pick up Peter Roger, another Old Downian who was then back at the school working as a gardener. This information, and a few details of the trip in the notes that follow, have been gleaned from recollections offered by Michael Yates in a conversation during the 1970s with Edward Mendelson. These details are marked in the notes by '(MY)'.

[4] August 1934.

[5] An allusion to 'The hand that rocks the cradle | Is the hand that rules the world' in the poem 'The Hand that Rules the World' by William Ross Wallace (1819–81).

[6] Emended from 'the lodge' in the *Badger* text. This is where the bachelor masters at the Downs lived.

[7] In his history of the Downs, E. J. Brown writes, 'Throughout the G. H. era [Geoffrey Hoyland's headmastership from 1920 to 1940] and for some years afterwards, the Downs hummed with nicknames. G. H. was an adept at choosing unusual though apt ones and a large number of boys were known by them, the rest by their surnames. Rarely were Christian names used. The staff were frequently referred to by their nicknames, the traditional "Mr." being inserted if safety and the occasion demanded it' (*The First Five: The Story of a School* [Colwall, Malvern, 1987], 15; hereafter referred to as 'Brown'). Hoyland himself was referred to, and addressed, as 'G. H.', 'Pup' was F. M. Day, the Latin master and a devout Anglican. (He was known as 'Pup' because when a master who had taught him at the Dragon School, Oxford, saw him appear with his own team of Downians, the master greeted him as 'Puppy-dog Day'.) 'Pup' taught at the Downs from 1921 to 1951 (Brown, 15, 44, 46). For more on 'Pup', see also 'Epilogue' (p. 30 and n. 64) and 'Johnny' (p. 38 and n. 78).

[8] Usually spelt 'the Booj', the name the boys gave to the Second Master at the Downs, E. C. Coxwell, apparently after The Boojum in Carroll's *The Hunting of the Snark* (1875–6). (According to Michael J. Sidnell, Coxwell acquired this nickname when he played 'the part of "Booge" in an earlier Downs sing-song' (*PDW* 505).) Coxwell, who was born in Rhodesia, taught PE, mathematics, carpentry, cricket, and swimming at the Downs from 1920 to 1938. But above all he was a rugger enthusiast. He left the school in 1938 to take holy orders (Brown, 15, 16, 43–4). For other references to him, see: 'Epilogue' (p. 30, n. 62), 'Johnny' (p. 38, n. 77) and the 'Hobbies' song that Auden wrote for the Downs School's December 1934 Sing-Song: 'With chairs on which Mr Booge has sat' (*PDW* 506).

his drive like an assassin. Found a bed at the Yids' Home in Regent Street.[9] Dinner at Boulestin's.[10] Must remember not to go there again unless invited by an elderly literary admirer. Still, it was worth an unemployed family's country holiday. 'Your god is your belly' my aunt used to tell me.

Went to see 'Men In White'.[11] Good slick acting and quite a nice set, but the usual American wickedness about germs, the don't-kiss-your-baby-on-the-mouth lie. Dropped into the Café Royal to have coffee but were driven out by two art-bores.[12]

Wednesday, 15th.—Breakfast in bed. Talked to toothless chambermaid about Brighton. P. arrives and we set off, throwing cigarettes to lorry drivers, exchanging hats and yelling like idiots. Lunch at the Falstaff at Canterbury.[13] Loathsomely genteel. Arrived at Dover about 2 and flirted with policeman till 4 when we managed to get on to the quay. New boat, the *Prince Baudouin*, very posh. Mutual photography. Went first-class out of bravado and to look at the splendid people in their soup plates. Sea calm unfortunately as I was looking forward to seeing Peter sick over a cocktail bar. St. Anne of Cleves or someone was having a feast in Ostende so all hotels full.[14] Drove out in the dark to Gistelle, Peter very excited about driving on the right, followed by a bore on a motor bike who continued his conversation in a thieves' kitchen. Food rotten; beds hard; sanitation none. Peter had nightmares about losing his passport.

Thursday, 16th.—Agree entirely with Baudelaire's opinion of the Belgians.[15] A dingy race with too many large cars fitted with trumpets

---

[9] The Regent Palace Hotel; see Introduction, pp. 12–13.

[10] A small, expensive basement restaurant in Southampton Street between the Strand and Covent Garden. Noted for its opulent murals, it attracted a slightly theatrical clientele. Le Boulestin closed in 1994.

[11] A Hollywood melodrama of 1934 in which Clark Gable played an ambitious young doctor in love with a society beauty (Myrna Loy) who resented his dedication to duty.

[12] Cf. *DBS*: 'club-houses for the golf-bore' (*PDW* 191).

[13] An inn just outside the city walls at West Gate.

[14] Anne of Cleves (1515–57) was the fourth wife of Henry VIII, but she was never canonized. The Roman Catholic Feast of the Assumption of the Virgin Mary is on 15 August. Presumably this festival had filled Ostende.

[15] Baudelaire lived miserably in Belgium from April 1864 to July 1866. In his *Journals*, he wrote of 'minds born servile, Belgian minds, which can only think collectively' (*Intimate Journals*, tr. Christopher Isherwood, first pub. in London, 1930, and repub. in Hollywood in 1948 with an introd. by Auden; see p. 63). Baudelaire also

which they blow continuously. Michael is beginning to despise the Morris and call it a hearse. Peter hoots all the time. Ghent, Bruxelles, Louvain. Visited nothing. Thank goodness Peter only shows slight tendencies to be a tourist and Michael none at all. I once went to Yugoslavia with father and wished I was dead.[16] German frontier at tea. Officials politer than the English but rather like Stainless[17] to explain anything to. Pestered in Aachen by a German scoutmaster, probably a spy. Reached Cologne and went to a Christian boarding house. First row with Peter about money. Sat in the Café am Dom all evening delivering a message about the Good Life while Peter and Michael gorged themselves on sickly cake and ices.

Friday, 17th.—All rather subdued this morning and no wonder in this country which is being run by a mixture of gangsters and the sort of school prefect who is good at Corps. Voting for the Reichskanzler on Sunday.[18] Every house waves a flag like a baby's rattle.[19] Private yachts for the flagmakers. Each shop has pasted a notice, 'We are all going to vote yes'. Slogans hang screaming above the cobbled streets of tiny hamlets, 'One Folk: One Leader: One Yes'. Photographs of the circus manager followed by a multitude of men and women showing their uvulas are pasted on the walls of barns, together with the information, 'The voting is absolutely free. Do YOUR DUTY.' Tea near Marburg where there were hornets. In a furious temper for some reason or other (O, Mr. Censor), skidding round corners on two wheels through pretty wooded hills. Reached Eisenach, Bach's birthplace, thinking of the Rector and Superbos.[20] Talked to hotel proprietor who suddenly stopped and rushed to open the window. The Labour Corps were passing and one must be keen. After they had gone he closed it with a sigh of relief. Sat in a café in the market square

---

began a blistering satire, *Pauvre Belgique*, which contains the lines: 'One becomes a Belgian through having sinned. | A Belgian is his own hell.'

[16] This was in the summer of 1927 (see Carpenter, 73).

[17] A pupil called Stephen Marriage, whose nickname came from 'Stainless Stephen', a famous thirties comic character of obscure origin. (Auden mentioned Marriage again in the Downs School 'Revue' of December 1934; see *PDW* 509.

[18] The German President, Field-Marshal von Hindenburg, died on 2 August 1933. The Nazis instantly combined the Presidency with the Chancellorship, and transferred all presidential functions to Hitler, the Chancellor. A plebiscite was called for 19 August to confirm Hitler's assumption of these offices.

[19] Cf. *DBS*: 'Black flags hang from each window-sill' (*PDW* 212).

[20] Auden was a member of the Downs' 'Bach Choir' (Brown, 35; see also n. 66 below).

listening to Hitler shouting from Hamburg.[21] Sounded like a Latin lesson.[22] Peter ate an ice out of his handkerchief.

Saturday, 18th.—Weimar, Leipsig, Dresden. Roadmending, that mask of bankruptcy, everywhere, but the roadmender's singlet or nothing a pleasant contrast to the English workman's waistcoat and stiff collar. Peter getting impatient for his mountains. Argument about the scenery cult. Personally give me a good hotel and a petrol pump or city streets in a fog. Reached Dresden for tea. Very beautiful Varogne buildings ruined by flags, and the only nice church bell I have ever heard. Michael went off to photograph and I took Peter to be inoculated by a stage German doctor who took half an hour to sterilize his instruments, peering over the top of his spectacles and grunting like a gas engine. Flicks after dinner. Film 'A Man wants to Return to Germany', about a German colonial officer who escapes from internment camp and the wiles of a non-Aryan temptress.[23] Every time he said 'I must do my duty', which was every 20 feet of film, he made a face as if he had swallowed the cap of his fountain pen. The old faithful retainer comic relief which shows how much Socialism[24] we are to expect. Came home feeling rather sick.

Sunday, 19th.—Peter rather seedy after inoculation. Pleasant drive over Erzgebirge reaching a doll's house frontier village for lunch. Thank God we're out of the sight of flags at last. Waiter intrigued to see Peter drinking chlorodyne and water. A man with false teeth leant over from the next table to whisper in my ear a warning about the temptations of Prague and fell off his chair.

Stopped in Bruch to ask the way from two garage attendants looking, acting and dressed like Tweedledum and Tweedledee down to the school caps. Reached Schloss Eisenberg, a seventeenth century building the size of the Malvern Girls' School, armed with letters of introduction to Princess Lobkovics (provincial papers please

[21] According to the British diplomat Sir Victor Perowne, 'this was Hitler's most important speech in the whole [plebiscite] campaign' (minute of 28 Aug. 1934, FO 371/17768, PRO). The Hamburg speech was a long harangue during which Hitler boasted that his ideas had already 'demanded the blood and freedom of many', warned 'we have evil enemies in the world', and ended with the messianic screech, 'only one thought, so help me God, has dominated and ordered me—Germany.'

[22] Cf. the Leader's speech through a picture in *DBS* (*PDW* 228–9).

[23] *Ein Mann will nach Deutschland* (usually known in English as *A Man Must Return to Germany*), set during World War I and directed by Paul Wegener, was released in 1934. It depicted the British as worthy and honourable adversaries.

[24] i.e. in a National Socialist regime.

copy).[25] Albert the butler, flat-footed and terrifying, inspected my trousers and Peter's social credit shirt[26] with his dolphin's eye but finally led us to our respective suites. Michael had left his rucksack in the car which I asked Albert to send for. The footman brought up the tents and the stove.[27] Temperature low. A fine collection of pictures, including a magnificent Breughel. Michael caught opening a chest in the hall. Temperature arctic. Prince,[28] Princess and American friend returned at last. Explored estate after tea. Lovely dinner. Albert apparently has a grudge against the greyhound which he keeps surreptitiously kicking. Played Battle, a game with billiard balls which excites the worse passions and smashes the Louis Quinze chairs. Peter, determined not to miss anything, had a whiskey and soda but didn't look as if he liked it. Talked about Hölderlin and the Prince gave a marvellous imitation of Hitler. Peter is getting off with Henny-Penny, the American.

Monday, 20th.—The Princess and Henny-Penny went to have their hair done, so off to Karlsbad where those who are afraid of weighing machines go. All pansied up in helmets, goggles and fur coats. Bought a new coat to placate Albert and inspected improper post-cards, but forgot Mr. Day[29] until too late.[30] Drove back through the Pilsner hop fields.

[25] Auden had a letter of introduction to the Anglo-Irish Princess Lobkowicz, probably either from a Mr France, a master at the Downs School (MY) or from Nevill Coghill's cousin Gillian Somerville (see Introduction, p. 10).

[26] Just as supporters of Jimmy Maxton's Independent Labour Party wore red shirts and members of Sir Oswald Mosley's British Union of Fascists wore black shirts, the followers of Major Clifford Douglas (1879–1952) and his social credit policy for international economic recovery wore green shirts.

[27] The footman at Schloss Eisenberg saw the camping gear in the car, silently took it in, and divided it between their three rooms (MY).

[28] An intelligence report from Prague on the Prince, dated 16 July 1920, was sent to the head of the British secret service, Sir Basil Thomson. It read in part, 'During the war Max Lobkowicz suffered a great deal morally from the discipline and brutality of the Austrian General Staff and from the horror and devastation of the war . . . Of high intellectual standing he is an extreme idealist and inclined to fantastic and theoretical political judgments . . . He is highly educated, without prejudices, with very artistic gifts, and a gentleman in the true sense of the word. He speaks Czech, German and French perfectly, and English and Polish well' (FO 371/4720, PRO). Although he impressed intelligence sources as an intellectual, when he was appointed head of the exiled Czech Legation in London in 1941, he was described variously as a 'bonehead' and 'very slow and something of a bore' (William Strang, minute of 28 Aug. 1941, and F. K. Roberts, minute of 29 Sept. 1941, FO 371/26415, PRO).

[29] See n. 7 above and 'Epilogue' (p. 30): 'all good schools, like dogs, must have their Day.'

[30] The trip to Carlsbad, which also included the Prince, was made in the Prince's

Partridges for dinner. Played Battle again which brings that dangerous light to Peter's eye which we all know so well. To bed, worrying
about tips.

Tuesday, 21st.—Very hot. Settled tipping question, and arrived in
Prague for lunch in the courtyard where the diplomats go incognito.
Peter and Michael went off to bathe in the Elbe and I went to bed
with a detective story. Dinner on a restaurant boat. Ordered Bubbly
which didn't suit our clothes but made us feel very on-the-
Continong.[31]

Wednesday, 22nd.—Drove steadily all day through Brod and Jihlava
but then lost the road and beached in a field. O Mummy. Started to
sing 'Now the Day is Over', until Peter suggested getting out of the
car and we managed to get her off again, careering like Puck over hill
and dale till we found a road and reached Ur Hradista in the dark.
Good and cheap but camera stolen.

Thursday, 23rd.—Hills at last but Peter suffering from gardener's leg.
Over the Bile Carpathians to Trencin and thence through Salvator
Rosa gorges to Poprad[32] near the Tatras. Gardener's leg very bad so
magnanimously decided to give Dracula a miss and stay here for two
days. Town full of peasants with their leathery everlasting faces.
Went in the evening to see strong man run over by a motor car and
stood upon by the local Fatty Arbuckle.[33]

Friday, 24th.—To-day according to the others we are going to camp.
I don't see why we can't make up that part. Bought a sausage as big
as a Michelin tyre and a bottle of local red wine tasting like sanitary
fluid, and set off for the Tatras. Real tourist resort, full of Tyrolese
hats and peaks.[34] Poured with rain so returned to hotel and cooked
eggs in our bedroom.[35] Went to see Conrad Veidt in the 'Wandering

---

large car, not Auden's Morris. Auden bought a jacket in order to look more respectable
(MY).

[31] Cf. 'The south of England before very long | Will look no different from the
Continong' in 'Letter to Lord Byron' (1936), repr. in *EA* 176.

[32] For Poprad, and, later on, Basel and Bar-le-Duc, see 'Prologue at Sixty' in *CP91* 831.

[33] A reference to the obese film star Roscoe Arbuckle (1887–1933), who in 1921 was
acquitted of murdering a woman during sexual rough-play.

[34] Emended from 'peeks' in *Badger* text.

[35] Auden was glad when it rained and so they couldn't actually use their camping
equipment (MY).

Jew', a sad come-down from his Student-of-Prague days[36] and then got off with the hotel band who by request played Hungarian music into the small hours, which always makes me feel like the exiled lover pulling on his snow boots in the middle of Siberia. To bed a little tiddley. 'Why am I a Schoolmaster?' I asked Peter, but he was asleep so now I shall never know.

Saturday, 25th.—Through mist-hidden forests to the Dobsina Ice Caves. Guide's[37] information and delivery a fit subject for a Sherlock Holmes monograph. Suppose people were once really interested in that kind of thing and it survives like mediaeval latin in prep. schools. Went our first and last walk after lunch and inspected the new railway they are building. Very pansy.[38] Returned in a violent hailstorm which the hood is designed to concentrate on the driver's neck. Band very inquisitive and thirsty. The school where I teach, I told them, is the most aristocratic in England. The headmaster never appears except in spurs and on an Arab stallion and the games master lives on the raw flesh of freshly killed stags.[39]

Sunday, 26th.—Very wild country to Lucenec where we met a private detective who showed us his photograph. On reflection have decided it was Mr. Telfer[40] in disguise. Hungarian frontier doubted my Englishman's word and said we ought to have visas and must buy them in Budapest.[41] Steering very peculiar since we met Mr. Telfer. One skid and two punctures before we got to Budapest which we had

[36] A British film released in 1933 about a Jew who is condemned to perpetual life but dies in the Spanish Inquisition. *Der Student von Prag* (1926), directed by Herbert Galeen and starring Veidt, was a film of the supernatural with startlingly hellish visual effects and characterization.

[37] Emended from 'Guides' in *Badger* text.

[38] Cf. 'Easily, my dear, you move, easily your head', *EA* 152: 'Lucky to Love the new pansy railway.' The parallel is made in Carpenter, 169. See also Introduction, p. 13 and n. 39.

[39] Probably a reference to E. C. Coxwell (see n. 8 above). Cf. *DBS*: 'Used to breakfast at midnight on champagne and raw beef' (*PDW* 217).

[40] Mr Telfer was a science master, a part-time employee, who came over from Malvern to teach.

[41] The party had a money crisis in Hungary after being forced to pay a fee at the border. Auden recovered it at the police station later on (MY). On 5 Jan. 1934 Auden and Isherwood had experienced the tyrannic powers of immigration officials when Isherwood's boyfriend Heinz was refused entry to Britain at Harwich, but these experiences in Hungary nine months later perhaps also lie behind the lines in the chorus in *DBS* about 'frontier officials . . . in whom private terrors breed a love of insult and interference' (*PDW* 224).

to pay to enter.[42] Found a garage run by a sinister old lady on a couch, and a cod-fish. Peter very suspicious indeed and for once rightly. Went to Café Hungaria[43] in the evening to see and be seen by those who matter.

Monday, 27th.—BLACK MONDAY. Went to see Cod who was full of praises but no performance. After two hours of waiting, I tore off my pearls in the street and stamped on them. The Cod burst into tears but gave up the car after I had paid a king's ransom. Returned to hotel to find the Police Station closed till 4. Went to Bank which charged 20 per cent. for the privilege of having their beastly pengos.[44]

Michael has bought himself a pair of brown and white shoes, which means I shall have to go to the bank again to-morrow. Walked in a blistering sun for miles with the local Deadly Nightshade to find the police station, only to be told that I was quite right and needn't have come. In the middle of the night Michael had an acute attack of indigestion. Am in no mood to be a member of the League of Nations Union.[45]

Tuesday, 28th.—Shook the dust off our feet but lost our way. Much weeping but ran over a hen and felt better. Reached Vienna in a thunderstorm.[46] Went to the theatre to see a Viennese light opera 'The Princess on the Ladder'; good. Had to speak to Peter very severely for pulling feathers out of the wrap of the lady in front.

Wednesday, 29th.—Peter off to see museums. Michael and I on a charabanc tour of the city. Trip out improved by an English spinster with a face like a horse, a voice like a spoilt little girl in a hotel, and a flat enthusiasm like stale Vichy water. Michael's shoes put her off, but not enough. Free time after lunch so mooched about. Went to flicks in the evening to see Bela Lugosi in 'The White Zombie'.[47]

---

[42] Cf. the final chorus of the Dec. 1934 Downs School Sing-Song: 'Paris | Or Budapest | Munich | And all the rest' (*PDW* 509).

[43] A smart rendezvous in the Erzsébetváros district.

[44] The unit of currency is a pengö.

[45] A British society formed in 1918 to support the work of the League of Nations and to secure permanent international peace. It organized the Peace Ballot of 1934, in which 11½ million people endorsed disarmament or pacifist sentiments.

[46] Three days before, on 25 July, the Nazis in Austria had attempted a daring *coup d'état*. In Vienna the Chancellor, Dr Englebert Dollfuss, had been shot while trying to escape from his Chancellery by a Nazi ex-sergeant named Otto Planetta.

[47] A superior American horror film of 1932 about Haitian zombies working in a sugar-mill.

Thursday, 30th.—Wobbled to Salzburg.[48] Too poor to make whoopee, so played Bogey Bogey in the lounge.

Friday, 31st.—Stopped at Kitzbuhel to see Hedwig but found she was lunching at a Schloss near by.[49] Peter's trouser buttons missing so he had to change in the road. Owner of Schloss a real treasure. Very fat, quite buttonless, he lives on snails, keeps lions, and says things to the ladies at table in an Austrian dialect which I cannot possibly repeat here. Stopped for the night at a little gasthouse[50] beyond Innsbruck, all beams and swallows. Caught after supper by a schoolmaster belonging to the Vaterland Front. The Pope has blessed our revolvers.

Saturday, September 1st.—Over the Arlberg which was covered in snow and through part of Switzerland to Pfäffikon on Lake Zurich. Hate Switzerland. Cooking rotten and architecture hideous. Tormented Peter by hiring a concertina player to play just behind him.

Sunday, 2nd.—Zurich, Basel, and here are the titchy little Frenchmen of the Première Année.[51] Steering much worse and Peter driving like a fireman. Reached Bar-le-Duc and had an epic meal.[52] Champagne very cheap. Peter eclipsed all previous efforts.

Monday, 3rd.—Started at 6 a.m. Peter started to sing but was dissuaded. He must have the worst repertoire of songs of any man in Europe. The coffee at Rheims exceeded even that of the Winter Gardens, Malvern, in rankness and horror. Contretemps at Frontier about the store and Peter very upset at having his clothes inspected. Through the battlefields which were full of girl guides to Ostende,

[48] Stephen Spender was also in Salzburg around this time. Sheila Grant Duff wrote from Salzburg on 25 Aug. 1934 to Adam von Trott zu Solz, 'Stephen is here . . . writing a long poem about the Viennese troubles . . . full of despair about Central European politics' (quoted in Klemens von Klemperer, *A Noble Combat* (Oxford, 1988), 43).

[49] Hedwig Petzold, whom Auden had met when he and his father stayed with her in Kitzbühel in the summer of 1925.

[50] An anglicization of the German for guest house.

[51] Possibly a reference to the French Revolutionary calendar introduced in 1793 (i.e. the French Constitution of 1795 was known as the Constitution of Year III).

[52] For Basel and Bar-le-Duc, see n. 32.

the hood behaving like the baby in 'Alice in Wonderland'.[53] Pa has come up to scratch and sent a fiver. Spent the evening hating the other English guests.

Tuesday, 4th.—Having lost a document had to pay a tax which leaves us penniless. Only sandwiches for lunch, and situation not improved by forgetting to wait for eight bob's worth of change at Dover. Telephoned to friends but all were out. Very unhappy. Spent all but fourpence on dinner, and rang up again. Managed to raise £8 in return for promises of post-dated cheques. Sent Peter and Michael in a taxi for five of it, and went to the Fairy Ring in Piccadilly[54] to collect the remaining three from the half-wit brother of a friend.[55] Stayed at Hotel Russell. Too respectable.

Wednesday, 5th.—Called on Gerald[56] to hear the latest news about the Dinosaurs. Apparently they suffered from arthritis. Then past the new factories on the Great West Road, past the Old College, to Colwall. Dropped Peter in the road and turned north.[57]

[First published in two parts in *The Badger*, 2.4 (Autumn 1934), 21–4, and *The Badger*, 3.5 (Spring 1935), 16–18. 'Apologia', the editor's remarks (probably written by Auden or by the Downs' headmaster Geoffrey Hoyland) in the Autumn 1934 *Badger*, notes: 'Two members of the staff, together with an O.D., disappeared into the mist of Central Europe in a Morris (more vocal than dependable) during the Summer holidays. Something of what they did may be gathered from "In Search of Dracula"—to be continued in our next' (p. 1). The travelogue was broken between the entries for 21 and 22 August. Both parts are signed: 'By W. H. A.']

[53] The trench warfare battlefields of the First World War. The baby in Lewis Carroll's *Alice in Wonderland* (1865) sneezed incessantly until it turned into a pig.
[54] See Introduction, p. 12.
[55] Perhaps Richard Bradshaw-Isherwood.
[56] Gerald Heard. This refers to William Swinton's *The Dinosaurs* (London, 1934), enthusiastically popularized in Heard's *The Source of Civilization* (London, 1935), 71–2.
[57] Auden presumably turned north because he was driving Michael Yates back to his parents' home in Manchester (see n. 3 above). He then seems to have spent a few days after the trip with his own family in Harborne, Birmingham.

[4] Epilogue

Now is the time when all our spirits mount;
When grubby thumbs and blackboard figures count
The hours between us and the railway station,
The two more Latins and the last Dictation:
Careless the sentences but rare the bate.
The boys wake early and the staff sleep late.
A school year ends for some; but to a score
An epoch closes to return no more.
So we who leave, our packing done, must now
Our farewell speeches make and farewell bow.

To you, sir,[58] first who daily to each one
Have been the guide, philosopher and sun,
Who in the study like a rock have stood
To gas[59] the erring and approve the good
Our thanks; and may all those who take our places
Have sharper intellects and nicer faces,
As naughty certainly, for who indeed
Would wish without a struggle to succeed?
It is not angels that your talents want,
Clean and obedient from the christening font,
But boys like —— and ——. O may you, yes
With stuff more stubborn have the more success.

And, Madam,[60] you whose thoughtful loving care
Has made domestic the scholastic air,
Who when the measles struck us or sore throat
Calmed the hot mamma with [a][61] soothing note.

[58] The Downs' headmaster Geoffrey Hoyland, the dedicatee of 'A Summer Night' (see Brown, 15 and n. 7 above).

[59] Cf. 'Johnny' Part III (p. 37). Morris Marple, *Public School Slang* (London, 1940), says that 'gas' is a derogative word for talk, as in 'Shut up gassing' or 'What's all this gas?' (p. 87). Brown adds that in Downs School vernacular 'gas' meant 'a talk, usually describing the Sunday evening sermon' (Brown, 42). From the two instances in the present poems, though, it seems that to 'gas' someone also meant to talk sternly to them or to lecture them on bad behaviour.

[60] Probably the headmaster's wife, Dorothea Hoyland, a Cadbury heiress (Brown, 15, 50–3).

[61] The indefinite article, missing from the *Badger* text, is required by the metre.

O may you still, when bearded we return,
Stiffen the altos and dispense the urn.

Next you with bull voice and with torso huge
By wife called Edward and by boys called Booge,[62]
To whom what power we have, we owe,
To hold the high catch and to tackle low,
Long be your presence here and near the day
When you shall cast your crutches far away.

And you, Miss Freeman, may you never fail
To chivvy for his marks the careless male,
Still help lame boys across the gallic stiles,
Still keep the letters and the beauteous files.[63]

A long life also, Mr. Pup, to you
The Old Boys' genial barman whom we, too,
Shall visit in a year or so from now
To hear the great laugh and to milk the cow.[64]
From Iceland to Penang[65] the people say
That all good schools, like dogs, must have their Day.

Nor you, Miss Woodhams, shall we soon forget.[66]
Our clumsy fingers to the keys you[67] set
And taught the tone-deaf to relax the throat,
To sing more clearly and to get the note.

[62] E. C. Coxwell. See 'In Search of Dracula' (p. 19, n. 8) and 'Johnny' (p. 38, n. 77).

[63] Miss Freeman taught French to the Upper Forms and was also the School's secretary and accountant. She was a stern and practical woman (Brown, 46).

[64] For Mr Day the Latin master, see also 'In Search of Dracula' (p. 19 and n. 7) and 'Johnny' (p. 38 and n. 78). One Old Downian remembered Day's 'beaf-steak of a laugh' (quoted in Brown, 44). Day also took a special interest in the old boys and when they returned on visits he often dispensed glasses of beer to them (Brown, 46).

[65] Cf. *The Chase*: 'In the boiler rooms of liners from Vancouver to Penang' (*PDW* 115).

[66] Hilda Woodhams taught music at the Downs from 1916 to 1943. Geoffrey Hoyland viewed music as 'on the whole, the most important single factor in the life of a preparatory school' (quoted in Brown, 35) and Miss Woodhams organized individual lessons on instruments, an orchestra, and later a group called 'the Bach Choir' in which Auden sang (Brown, 35, 50). During his time at the Downs Auden tried, and failed, to teach Miss Woodhams to drive (see Maurice Feild, 'Wystan Auden—1907–1973', *The Badger*, 47 (Autumn 1974), 33).

[67] *The Badger* reading was 'we'.

May you each year a better treble find,
His range more wide, his timbre more refined
For solo anthems, and on Mondays still
Soften the basses and control the trill.

Last, to the others who we have no time
To specify in this heroic rhyme,
We wish you freedom from financial cares,
Attire more startling, luck in your affairs
In reading shockers or in playing Handel,
In drinking, spooning, or in talking scandal.

O you, our small successors who next year
Shall take the late mark and shall shed the tear,
Terrors of nurseries, you must shortly learn
To answer meekly and to wait your turn;
Your books to study and your sins to shun.
Remember this, 'The building MUST be done.'[68]

July 1935

[First printed in *The Badger*, 3.6 (Autumn 1935), 46–7, signed 'W. H. Auden'. Auden himself left the Downs at the end of the summer term.]

[68] The Downs School motto, chosen by Geoffrey Hoyland, was 'AEDIFICANDUM EST'. Hidden behind the moral ideal, there is probably a school joke about the substantial amount of new construction undertaken by Hoyland during his early years as headmaster (for details, see Brown, 15–26).

[5] A School Song

Time will make its utter changes,
  Circumstance will scatter us,
But the memories of our schooldays
  Are a living part of us.

  Chorus

  So remember then when you are men
    With important things to do,
  That once you were young and this song have sung
    For you were at school here too.

Daily we sit down in form rooms,
  Inky hand to puzzled head:
Reason's Light and Knowledge Power;
  Man must study till he's dead.

  Chorus

Man has mind but body also
  So we learn to tackle low,
Bowl the off-breaks, hit the sixes,
  Bend the diver's brilliant bow.[69]

  Chorus

Man must learn to like his neighbour
  For he cannot live alone;
Friendships, failures and successes,
  Here we learn to make our own.

  Chorus

Tractors grunt where oceans wandered,
  Factories stand where green grass grew;
Voices break and features alter,
  We shall soon be different too.

---

[69] Cf. 'the diver's brilliant bow' in 'No trenchant parting this' and 'As I walked out one evening' (*EA* 21, 228).

Chorus

Boys and cities, schools and nations,
    Though they change like you and me,
Do not simply grow and happen:
    They are what they choose to be.

Chorus

[Written summer 1936? Auden's friend John Garrett was the headmaster of Raynes Park School (see Introduction, p. 5). Published as 'Raynes Park School Song' in the school magazine, *Spur*, 1.1 (October 1936), [p. 1] and as 'A School Song', signed 'Very Anon' in *The Badger*, 5.10 (Autumn 1937), 73–4.]

[6] Johnny[70]

(A Cautionary Tale by Request)

Part I

His name was John, a charming child,
Whose ways were neither rude nor wild,
He never argued with his mother.
He never pinched his little brother;
Despite his rather tender years
He always washed behind the ears.
He never had a sulky mood,
Nor was he captious with his food
But finished up the lumps of fat;
And better still, supposing that
The pudding was a chocolate cream,
An ice or some delicious dream,
He did not gobble like a beast;
He did not hurry in the least,
Or even whine or pant or yelp
Or ogle for a second help
To show that he was interested,
But waited till one was suggested.
Good manners also were his forte
For he was neither shy nor haughty:
For instance, if his Auntie Lil
Said, 'How you've grown!' (as Aunties will)
He did not blush at all or scowl,
'Oh buzz off quick, you tiresome fowl,'
But even offered to assist
And put his face up to be kissed.
Yes, he was handsome, brave and clever.

[70] A poem, like many by Auden from 1937, written under the influence of Hilaire Belloc's 'cautionary' tales. 'Johnny' is especially reminiscent of Belloc's 'Lord Lundy' and 'Charles Augustus Fortescue' (see Belloc, *Complete Verse*, ed. W. N. Roughead (London, 1970), 205–7, 270–1). There is a slightly earlier mention of Auden's fondness for Belloc's *Cautionary Tales* in 'Letter to Lord Byron', *EA* 172.

I could go on like this for ever;
He was the almost perfect boy,
Like you, or young Lord Fauntleroy.
His life might well have been plain sailing,
But—O alas—he had one failing
That brought him to a horrid fate:
Our hero, John, was always late.
If breakfast was at eight-fifteen
Johnny was nowhere to be seen,
But might turn up at nine or ten;
And not on Sundays, even then.
If one was time for dinner, he
Might just arrive in time for tea;
And as for supper time, that might
Be any hour before mid-night.
His father stormed, his mother cried,
'You could be punctual if you tried.'
But John, that aggravating child,
Just said, 'Oh, am I late?' and smiled.

Part II

You know in England it's the rule
That every child must go to school,
So Johnny's parents had to face
The question of the proper place
For John to get the education
To fit him for his rank and station.
They asked their friends, they asked their neighbours,
They asked the boy who brought the papers,
The man who came to mend the bells.
They looked at volumes in hotels.
They asked their banker, asked their rector,
They even asked their rate collector,
But all replied, 'I cannot say,
John is a good boy in his way
Of course, but then that little kink,
I mean to say, it makes you think,
You couldn't send him anywhere.'
His parents both were in despair,

Till one night in the drawing room
As they were sitting wrapped in gloom
His father smote his thigh, cried, 'Zounds!
But why not send him to The Downs?
Cousin Bertie's dreadful son
Who shot the Bishop with a gun,
Aunt Janet's beastly little brat
Who put a hedgehog in my hat,
And Dick, who stoned the farmer's geese
(They hushed it up with the police),
And William, who made rude grimaces
And stole and betted at the races,
Were all packed off to Colwall, and
Were taken seriously in hand.
Look at them now—there's William (strange!)
A credit to the Stock Exchange,
There's Dick a rising barrister,
And Janet's Marmaduke a "sir",
While Bertie's brilliant Algernon
Is shortly to become a don.
Why that's the place to send John to,
Other schools just will not do,
That fellow Hoyland is the man,
If he can't cure him, no one can.'
So that was that. The choice was made,
The first term's cheque was signed and paid,
The trunks were found, the clothes were bought.
At length a large saloon car brought
Young Johnny to the Downs front door,
As cars have brought young boys before,
And left him, shivering and small,
A trifle weepy in the hall.

Part III

At first he made a good impression,
Both out of school and in a lesson.
His winning ways, his cheerful laugh
Enchanted both the boys and staff,
But soon both boys and staff, I fear,

Began to doubt the little dear
As rumours gathered rapidly
About his unpunctuality.
His guardian[71] was the first to find
This curious kink in Johnny's mind.
He tried cajolery at first,
Then gassing[72] till he nearly burst.
Perhaps he wasn't very clever,
But Johnny was as late as ever.
The weeks went by, and every day
More latenesses came Johnny's way.[73]
Tribe Councils met on Sunday nights[74]
To try to put the thing to rights.
They sat for hours, goodness knows,
And argued till they came to blows,
For each one had his patent plan
To cure the little gentleman.
They tried them all. They gave him lines:
They took his bank away in fines:
They took away his marmalade:
They had him out on nips' parade:
They sent him down to roll the pitch:
And tried ingenious tortures, which
Jones I,[75] I fancy, had invented,

[71] For the first couple of weeks, new boys were given junior and senior 'Guardians', the former to offer everyday help, the latter 'to keep a fatherly eye that all was well generally' (Brown, 42).

[72] Cf. 'Epilogue', p. 29 and n. 59.

[73] There were few punishments at the Downs, but the quest to instil punctuality seems to have been something of a mania during Geoffrey Hoyland's early years. A 'lateness' was originally a black mark specifically for tardiness. It was recorded on a board. However latenesses were soon being given for offences that had little to do with punctuality (Brown, 17–18). Latenesses were often discussed and individual cases debated at Tribe Councils (see n. 74 below).

[74] The Downs as a whole became known during Hoyland's reign as the 'Tribe'. It was divided into a number of sections called 'Packs', each run by a boy called a 'Leader'. The 'Tribe Council' consisting of all the Leaders and the members of staff met in the Headmaster's study, usually after Sunday evening service. At these meetings everything connected with school life from discipline to food was discussed. Both boys and masters were free to contribute their views (see Brown, 17–18, and Auden's 4 Oct. 1932 letter to Iris and Alan Sinkinson, quoted in Carpenter, 142).

[75] i.e. the eldest of the Joneses: an English public-school way of differentiating boys with the same surname.

Though Mr. Frazer H. dissented.[76]
They tried that last resort, the cane:
But Johnny smiled; it was in vain.
It got on everybody's nerves,
Poor Mr. Booge[77] lost all his curves,
And Mr. Pup[78] could eat no kippers
But sat and gnawed his carpet slippers,
And Mr. Brown[79] shaved his moustache,
And Grassy's colour schemes grew harsh,[80]
And things were getting past a joke
When even Wizz forgot to smoke.[81]
Then Mr. Hoyland shook his head,
'We can't go on like this,' he said,
'We all have done our best, I'm sure,
But we must try one method more.'
So striding into tea next day
He rang the bell, as is his way,
And looking his most serious
Addressed the hushed assembly thus:

'Boys, until some future date
John cannot be counted late;
You must not bother him to hurry;
If he's not there you must not worry.
Report his absence, no more,
But such delinquencies ignore.'

---

[76] Geoffrey Hoyland's brother, Frazer Hoyland, who succeeded him as headmaster in 1940. He taught English to the Upper Forms (Brown, 59, 69).

[77] See 'In Search of Dracula', p. 19 and n. 8, and 'Epilogue', p. 30 and n. 62.

[78] See 'In Search of Dracula', p. 19 and n. 7, and 'Epilogue', p. 30 and n. 64.

[79] E. J. Brown came to the Downs School as a science master in 1933, where he lived in the Lodge, the building where Auden also had rooms for a while. He became Headmaster in 1970 (Brown, 107).

[80] One of Auden's closest friends amongst the Downs staff, Maurice Feild, taught art at the school from 1928 to 1955. His nicknames were 'Pars', 'Parsy', and sometimes 'Grassy'. He was an admirer of Impressionist painters, and particularly Pissarro (Brown, 36–8).

[81] One Old Downian remembers Auden's 'companion box of 100 cigarettes from which he was never separated' (Brown, 50).

Part IV

Now shortly after this event
One afternoon young Johnny went
Onto Brockhill[82] to take the air
All by himself, and spying there
A splendid tree—a lofty ash—
The thought came to him in a flash,
And he began to climb the tree
To see if he could see the sea.[83]
At first the branches bore him well,
But then one broke, he slipped and fell.[84]
But not so far. A splintered stump,
Some five feet down, just missed his rump,
And catching firmly in his coat
It left him hanging like a stoat
Or owl in some gamekeeper's larder.
It made the situation harder
To feel that he was safe and sound,
For he was ten feet off the ground.
He wriggled: shouted: no one heard,
Except perhaps a casual bird.
The sun went down in seas of flame,
The stars shone out, but no one came,
For back at school they were so used
To Johnny's habits, they refused
To bother, and had quite forgot
To think if he was there or not.
Or if a sudden undesigned
Thought *did* by chance cross some boy's mind,
'I wonder now where Johnny is
He's never been as late as this?'
He put the thought by hurriedly

---

[82] Brown spells it 'Brock Hill', an area of woods and meadows, rich in fossil deposits, that was part of the school's generous holdings of land (Brown, 22).

[83] The mouth of the River Severn and the opening of the Bristol Channel lie roughly 25–30 miles SSW of the Downs School.

[84] Cf. the early poem 'Elegy' ('A wagtail splutters in the stream'), written in May 1925: 'The rotten branches bore him well, | For he had reached it [the squirrel's drey] when he fell' W. H. Auden, *Juvenilia: Poems 1922–1928*, ed. Katherine Bucknell (Princeton, NJ and London, 1994), 90.

Remembering what was said at tea.
And not till several years had passed
Was our poor Johnny found at last,
When some one going for a stroll
Saw, hanging high up on the bole
Of a tall ash, a skeleton,
And thought, 'Dear me, that must be John.'

[Written June or July 1937? Published in *The Badger*, 5.10 (Autumn 1937), 68–73, signed 'Rather Anon'.]

[7]

When a little older, Robert,[85]
  Owner of a Kozy-Kot
Somewhere in the jolly Cotswolds,
  Will you write a lot?

At the fumed-oak writing-table,
  Bought on the instalment plan,
Will you still be writing Tiny[86]
  Sentiments that scan?

Looking out into the garden
  Where the quaint stone rabbits sit,
Will you think about your boyhood,
  And the beaks who ruined it?

Will you, when my ashes scatter
  Past your Tudor bungalow,[87]
Will you still screw up your features
  As you used to? I hope so.

[Probably written Dec. 1937. MS in a copy of John Betjeman, *Continual Dew* (London, 1937), given at Christmas 1937 to Robert Russell and now in the Rare Book Room, New York Public Library. The poem is written immediately after the autograph inscription 'To Robert Russell | with best wishes for Xmas 1937 | from | Wystan Auden'. First printed in W. H. Auden, *Three Unpublished Poems* (New York, 1986), [p. 8].]

[85] Nothing is known about Robert Russell, the subject of this poem.
[86] Auden probably meant to write 'tiny'. However, he may possibly be referring to a person: 'Tiny' is the name of Paul Bunyan's daughter.
[87] Fake 'Tudor' buildings are a common part of Auden's early vision of suburban England. See, for example, in *The Orators*: 'In the neo-Tudor club-house the captains frown' (*EA* 104); in 'Modern Poetic Drama': 'the romantic sham-Tudor' (*Listener*, 11.278 (9 May 1934), 808); in *DBS*: 'Tourists to whom the Tudor cafés | Offer Bovril and buns' (*PDW* 192) and 'We come from brick rectories and sham-Tudor villas' (*PDW* 262); in 'New Year Letter': 'YE OLDE TUDOR TEA-SHOPPE [stands] for | The folly of dogmatic law' (*CP91* 227).

[8] Love Letter

The movies and the magazines are all of them liars
Pretending that love has anything to do with pleasure,
With the bland Horatian life of culture and wines
    And conversational friendship.[88]

For love has a puritanical loathing of art and
Food, and even of sensible average people
Who are glad to tell him the time: for spiders and men
    Love is a destroyer of cities.[89]

Now when my work is over, I sit at the window,
The senses huddled like cattle, observing nothing,
Or run to the lavatory; in the net of the ribs
    The heart flails like a salmon.

O but I was mad to come here, even for money:
To have put myself at the mercy of the postman and the daydream,
That incorrigible nightmare in which you lie weeping or ill,
    Or drowned in the arms of another;

To have left you now, when I know what this warm May weather
Does to the city: how it brings out the plump little girls and
Truculent sailors into the parks[90] and sets
    The bowels of boys on fire.

When, after all, what reason have you to love me,
Who have neither the prettiness and moisture of youth, the
                          appeal of the baby,
The fencing wit[91] of the old successful life,
    Nor brutality's fascination?

---

[88] Cf. 'Christmas 1940': 'The bland Horatian life of friends and wine' (*EA* 460).

[89] Cf. 'In Memory of Sigmund Freud': 'sad is Eros, builder of cities' (*CP91* 276).

[90] Cf. 'Spring leads the truculent sailors into | The parks, and the plump little girls', from 'Prologue', (*DM*, repr. in *EA* 457).

[91] Cf. 'XII' (called 'Vocation' in *DM*) in 'The Quest': 'Women and books would teach his middle age | The fencing wit of an informal style' (*CP91* 291).

Some say there's a treasure in all; but, in some, to find it
Takes an anthropologist's patience: grown-up in a prison,
The heart shrinks back from the visitor's hand like a child
   That only knows how to be punished.[92]

Have you really the wish to endure the boredom of healing
What without you will never get well? O never leave me.
Never. Only the closest attention of your mouth
   Can make me worthy of loving.

[Written May 1939? There is a TS in McFarlin Library, University of Tulsa and a carbon copy in HRC. Published in *Hika* (Kenyon College), 6 [*sic*, for 5].8 (June 1939), 9 and reprinted in John Fuller, ed., *The Chatto Book of Love Poetry* (London, 1990).]

---

[92] Cf. 'VI' ('The First Temptation' in *DM*) in 'The Quest': 'And when Truth met him and put out her hand. | He clung in panic to his tall belief | And shrank away like an ill-treated child' (*CP91* 288).

[9] Ode

The vacation at last is approaching
  And the end of the term is in sight;
Though a few may require extra coaching
  In the sums they can never get right,
For the rest it's a period of leisure
  That will last until late in the Fall,
When one has the unparalleled pleasure
  Of doing just nothing at all.
Now slates,[93] recitations and duties
  Disappear from our lives with a swish,[94]
And Moore may cast glances at beauties,[95]
  And Randy cast cowdung at fish.[96]

Happy Days when life in the groove is!
  When the Torch is burning in Maine,[97]
And Woof rushes into the movies[98]
  Again and again and again,
When the Egg is absorbing a palmy
  Hospice de Beaune of '15,[99]

---

[93] 'Serving slate' was a school punishment. Marks were scratched up for offenders on a slate, and, when a sufficient number had been accumulated, the boy involved had to perform such chores as raking leaves and sawing wood. (The notes to this poem rely on three main sources: Benjamin C. Bradlee *et al.*, eds., *The St. Mark's Lion* (Southborough, 1939), the yearbook of the Class in 1939; Henry Whitney Munroe, ed., 'St. Mark's School Class of 1939: 50th Reunion Class Report', a privately printed pamphlet, distributed to members of the Class of 1989; recollections generously offered by many members of the Class of 1939, in particular, by Dr David Baldwin, Henry Whitney Munroe, Edward Patterson, Robert W. Perkins, and Robert Sturgis.)

[94] A 'swish' was 1930s slang for an effeminate gay man. See Robert L. Chapman, *New Dictionary of American Slang* (New York, 1986), 426.

[95] William Scoville Moore, a handsome, bashful boy, known by his classmates to be particularly fond of a female cousin.

[96] David S. Randolph, an enthusiastic fisherman.

[97] 'The Torch' was Dr Francis Parkman (1898–1990), the school's headmaster. He was very tall and in his youth had had flaming red hair, hence his nickname. Parkman spent his summers in Northeast Harbor, Maine.

[98] Wilfred T. Grenfell, a master who sometimes coached the rowing crew, got his nickname by running along beside the boat barking out to the boys like a dog.

[99] Probably George B. Fernald, a short, bald (hence, 'egg-headed') teacher. He was a gourmet, fond of spending his summers in France, after which he would come back and regale the boys with details of the food and wine he had savoured there.

And the Beau of the beach at Miami
  Is butch, (if you know what I mean)[100]
And the Moth[101] and the small mountain Daisy[102]
  Garibaldi[103] and Minnie[104] and Spike[105]
And Muzzey[106] and Dreamy[107] are lazy,
  All doing whatever they like.

All the best to the Sixth who now leave us
  For Harvard and Princeton and Yale;[108]
e.g. Potter who works like the beavers,[109]
  And Tess the American Male.[110]
May none of them flunk in their courses,
  And may even Patterson smile,[111]

[100] 'Butch' was the nickname of Roland D. Sawyer, Jr., a master who was also the school's football coach.

[101] Philip Eaton, an ancient bachelor on the staff. (His nickname was a play on 'moth-eaten'.)

[102] Probably George D. Braden (the pun is on 'daisy braid'), the school's business manager, who also worked part-time as a master. (Some class members suggest that 'Daisy' might refer to Chauncy L. Parsons, a prissy English master, usually known to the boys as 'Pansy'.)

[103] Frederick C. Baldy, St Mark's senior master.

[104] Melvin W. Mansur, a master with a high-pitched, squeaky voice which made him sound like Minnie Mouse.

[105] Several class members suggest Charles B. Saunders, a master who was also baseball coach.

[106] Frederick W. Hackett, the assistant headmaster, taught American history. He was passionately fond of referring to a textbook by the prolific David Saville Muzzey— probably *The American Adventure* (1927) or *History of the American People* (1933)—and would often declare to his classes, 'Let's see what Muzzey says'.

[107] Probably the poet Richard Eberhart, who taught English and History and was known as 'Dreamy Dick' (but possibly Dr John R. Suydam, an absent-minded teacher, or the baseball coach Saunders, see n. 105 above).

[108] Of the thirty-nine members of the St Mark's class of 1939, sixteen went on to Harvard, eight to Princeton, and seven to Yale.

[109] Robert S. Potter, a popular, hard-working boy. The *Lion* in a free-verse acrostic (one was written for every member of the class) noted his 'Ever-present pained expression' (33).

[110] Robert W. Perkins, a bright, shy boy, one of the youngest in the class. He explains: 'I got the horrible name [of Tess, or Tessy] almost immediately upon arriving at school, because I was very small, very scared, hopeless at any sport, heavily spectacled and quite pedantic'.

[111] Edward Patterson, who, his classmates say, smiled a lot but also frowned often. The *Lion*, in the acrostic on his name, expanded 'wa' to 'WORRY | Apologetic' (32).

May Tuckerman win on his horses,[112]
　　And Harvey wear clothes with a style;[113]
May Munroe be a noise on the fiddle,[114]
　　And Swell[115] be a swell in the team,
May there never be pitchers to diddle
　　Our Ham[116] or our Peaches-and-Cream.[117]

So let's skip like the rams in the Bible,[118]
　　And sing like the wrens and the larks
Or a debutante after a highball,
　　Because we were sent to St. Mark's;
And not, *Gott sei dank*, sent to Groton[119]
　　Where the Masses must go *faute de mieux*,
And the baseball, they tell me, is rotten,
　　And the *ton*, so I hear, is *affreux*;[120]
Or worse, just imagine, to Eton[121]
　　Where in spite of Debrett on their shelves
The boys who won't work are well beaten,[122]
　　And the faculty eat by themselves.[123]

---

[112] Herbert Sears Tuckerman, whose father owned a racing stable, frequented the track.

[113] Eldon Harvey, Jr. Some of his fellow pupils remember him liking to dress in unusual, not always successful, clothing combinations. According to Mr Harvey himself, he just liked wearing old clothes and looked a mess.

[114] Henry W. Munroe played the violin in the school orchestra.

[115] Herbert G. Wellington, Jr., captain of the school football team. Mr Wellington says that his nickname came from a time when 'Sawyer [see n. 100 above] pointed a ruler at [a] person he wanted to recite, then named him. I sat next to Walker Stuart [another boy], who was asleep. Sawyer pointed at Stuart, went "SSSSSSWELLINGTON", switching to me. I became "Swellington"'.

[116] Charles B. Armour, from the family that owned the Armour Ham Co. He played a lot of baseball at school.

[117] George Q. Palmer, the school's main baseball pitcher. A blond boy whose complexion prompted the nickname 'Peaches and Cream'.

[118] Psalm 114: 'The mountains skipped like rams, and the little hills like lambs.'

[119] The school that was St Mark's main rival.

[120] Cf. 'Democracy Is Hard' in *Nation*, 149.15 (7 Oct. 1939), 386: 'I am sure that Mr. Barzun personally knows as well as I do that faith in democracy is an enthusiastic, disreputable, and ascetic faith. Its *ton*, as Madame du Deffand would say, is *affreux*.'

[121] However, in several letters written while he was there, Auden privately referred to St Mark's as the 'American Eton'.

[122] Corporal punishment had virtually been abolished at St Mark's by the mid-thirties.

[123] The faculty members at St Mark's sat at either end of the long form tables in the dining hall and ate with the boys early in the evening.

To you all, may I say what an honour
    I feel it to be, to be here,
When one half of Europe's a gonner,
    (And the other decidedly queer):
Dear genuine Dems. (if they're any),
    And even Dear hardened Repubs.,[124]
(Who remind me of Home and our many
    Old fossils asleep in their clubs);[125]
May it be your own feet that you drop on,
    Or, if you can't take it, velour,
And may each of us find $\tau\grave{o}\nu$ $\epsilon\overset{\prime\prime}{v}\tau o\pi o\nu$[126]
    Et le vert paradis des amours.[127]

THE FEATHER MERCHANT[128]

[Written late May or early June 1939? Published in *Vindex*, Southborough, Mass., 63.6 (June 1939), 174–5.]

---

[124] St Mark's was then a stiff, WASP school with great social pretensions and a fierce cadre of Republican parents.

[125] Cf. 'A Communist to Others': 'fade away like morning dew | With club-room fossils' (*EA* 123).

[126] 'Ton eutopon' in Greek 'the Good Place', a region of ideal happiness. The word 'Eutopia' was first used by Sir Thomas More or Peter Giles in the preface to More's *Utopia* (1516). (There is a pun on the word Utopia, 'No-place'.)

[127] Baudelaire, 'Moesta et errabunda' in *Les fleurs du mal* (1857): 'le vert paradis des amours enfantines | L'innocent paradis, plein de plaisirs furtifs'.

[128] 'Feather merchant' was part of the St Mark's dialect. 'The Feather-Merchants' was the generic name given by the Class of 1939 to the Class of 1940, which was shortly to take over the positions of seniority at the school (see *Lion*, 17); the term comes from a group of small, parasitic characters called 'feather merchants' in the 'Barney Google' comic strip. Several ex-pupils suggest that Auden must have picked the name during the open-houses that he held in his school suite most evenings, when students were invited to come and drink tea and talk, but no one remembers Auden himself being called 'The Feather Merchant' by the boys. There are further, probably relevant, connotations of 'feather merchant' that may well have been current in pre-war America, even though slang dictionaries list them as Second World War terms. The *New Dictionary of American Slang*, ed. Robert L. Chapman (New York, 1986), for instance, defines 'feather merchant' as meaning in wartime a civilian, especially one who evades military service; or (citing the 'Barney Google' characters) a Navy phrase meaning a sailor who has a desk job.

Uncollected Songs and Lighter Poems, 1936–40

INTRODUCTION BY NICHOLAS JENKINS

I

In the thirties Auden theorized that verse had begun with the exhilaration of the primitive group: the first verses were rapturous chants welling up almost involuntarily as a tribe faced a common enemy or prey. Over time that situation had been internalized so that a poet writing verse 'excites the words and makes them fall into a definite group, going through definite dancing movements, just as feeling excites the different members of a crowd and makes them act together.'[1] With his 'daydream of a large audience',[2] Auden looked around his own stratified society for enclaves that might generate similar group-feelings, places where there was a sense of closeness and rapport between a poet and his listeners, and where art could be the 'product of a community united in sympathy, sense of worth, and aspiration'.[3] He found something approximating to his ideal in Berlin's boy bars, in the hot-house of the English public school, and in the collaborative ethic of the Group Theatre. And at the same time he experimented, playfully but not unseriously, with the anti-Romantic, anti-modernist rhetoric of light verse and popular song, the kinds of writing that depend for their effects (of punchline, put-down, and helpless lament) on a world-view shared by speaker and listeners.[4] He enjoyed the brio of these genres—in April 1939 he shocked a left-wing audience in New York by enthusiastically reciting Kipling's 'The Gods of the Copybook Headings'[5]—and he found that he could adapt these kinds of writing to his own purposes.

The poems printed below are reflections of Auden's fascination

[1] See 'Writing' (1932), repr. in *AS1*, 45–6. In his description, Auden is careful to call the powerful excitement of words in metre 'verse' and not 'poetry'.
[2] ALS to Monroe K. Spears, 11 May [1963] (Berg).
[3] Introduction to *The Poet's Tongue* (1935), repr. in *EA* 329.
[4] Auden wanted to call his Oxford anthology *The Oxford Book of Light and Popular Verse* but OUP demurred (Carpenter, 231).
[5] See Bernard Knox, 'W. H. Auden', *Grand Street*, 1.2 (Winter 1982), 22.

with these frowned-on, secondary traditions of popular song, cabaret, light verse, and nonsense writing. For all their 'lightness', these conservative, relatively static kinds of literature carried a real current of feeling for him: 'laughter', he once explained to Isherwood, 'is the first sign of sexual attraction.'[6] Exempt from modernist burdens of complexity, indirection, and originality, as well as being, in Auden's politico-anthropological amalgam, 'communistic'[7] in their allegiances, popular styles appeared to offer access to a vast underworld of common experience. Anyone reading Auden's 'Writing' essay of 1932 is bound to be struck by the discrepancy between his aloof tone of certainty and the powerful sense of loneliness underlying his arguments. For him, as for Housman, who made a similar use of hymns, these lyrics represented one possible ground of reconciliation between the inner divisions of the psyche and the outer divisions of class, intellect, and age. All are ostensibly open, public poems without a 'creepered wall'[8] of allusions and in-jokes—though some of the love lyrics obviously hint at meanings that were less than acceptable in the thirties.

As he toyed with these buoyant, playful types of popular poetry, Auden hoped he might narrow the gulf between the poet and society and produce what Eliot had described as 'the collaboration of the audience with the artist which is necessary in all art'.[9] More covertly, anxious about what he considered his unfeeling sense of distance and detachment, Auden dreamed that this everyday world could 'give back to | the son the mother's richness of feeling,'[10] redeeming him from his sense of sexual and intellectual isolation and infusing his poems with the emotional charge which he felt that his virtuosity and intellect were always threatening to eradicate. Auden told his old schoolmate John Pudney that, without a group to be a part of, poets 'have no material, must split their emotions into ever finer and finer hairs'[11] and his use of the word 'finer' suggests that he connected an increasing aesthetic sophistication with the danger of triviality.

But in the end, these kinds of popular poetry were to remain for him just one more available mask rather than a viable alternative to his bourgeois sense of self-consciousness and separateness. Auden quickly realized this; none of the poems below was ever re-printed in

[6] *Lions*, 189.   [7] 1929 Journal printed in *EA* 298.
[8] 'Out on the lawn I lie in bed' (1933), repr. in *EA* 137.
[9] In 'Marie Lloyd' (1922) repr. in *Selected Prose of T. S. Eliot*, ed. Frank Kermode (New York, 1975), 174.
[10] 'In Memory of Sigmund Freud' (1939), repr. in *CP91* 276.
[11] ALS, 28 July 1932 (Berg).

his collections, some were never printed at all. A restlessness stirs just below the geniality and very few are free from ironic strains: their fictions of wholeness and integration are at most savoured daydreams, as literary as an Elizabethan poet's pastoral visions of the countryside. The songs' notes of detachment and ambivalence are the reflexes of an individualism that Auden could wish away at moments but did not want to destroy. Unlike Brecht, he could never 'go over' to the working class completely, not even in poetry.

II

Probably under the stimulus of *Die Dreigroschenoper* and of Berlin cabaret, Auden began to explore popular forms, and particularly popular song, at least as early as 1929, the year he wrote 'It's no use raising a shout'.[12] The parodic public odes in *The Orators* (1932) developed this interest.[13] His involvement continued with the collage of popular forms in *The Dance of Death* (1933), before opening out around 1936 and 1937 during the first phase of his collaboration with Benjamin Britten. Auden had already mixed in hymns and light verse amongst canonical literature in *The Poet's Tongue* (1935), the egalitarian anthology he compiled with John Garrett. In the second half of 1937 he amassed large numbers of anonymous and popular ballads for his polemical *Oxford Book of Light Verse* (1938).

Once he reached New York in 1939, these experiments extended into a wide-ranging exploration of New World forms like calypso and blues. Sitting alone in the dive in 'September 1, 1939', he heard the music playing there as part of a Circean spell, but the second high point of the Britten–Auden collaboration, *Paul Bunyan* (1939–41), begun shortly afterwards, has a much less guarded relationship to popular song. By 1943 Auden was moving away from his early idea of

---

[12] Mendelson notes that the poem was probably based on a song in the repertory of Sophie Tucker (*Early Auden*, 80).

[13] In 1931–2, when Auden was struggling to exorcise the hermetic manner that had culminated in *The Orators*, he toyed with ideas that he only used in print some five years later. By then, as he wrote to E. R. Dodds (8 Dec. 1936, quoted in Carpenter, 207) he again felt it was 'time to gamble on something bigger.' In the autumn of 1932 he sent Arnold Snodgrass 'I have a handsome profile', describing it in an ALS as 'a little ditty to go to the tune of Frankie and Johnny' (Berg)—in 1937 he wrote another set of words for 'Frankie and Johnny', this time the early version of his ballad 'Victor'. And in *ca*. 1931–2 he wrote, though he never published, a poem with the refrain 'I'm having an affair'. (A holograph is in the 1930–2 notebook—listed as J5 in the *Bibliography*—now in the Harvard College Library.) In the spring of 1936 he picked up the line and used it as the refrain for an entirely different poem—see [7] below.

poetry as a tightly regimented dance of words. In a review of Eliot's anthology of Kipling's 'verse', he criticized Kipling for drumming language into the kind of unified formations that he had earlier praised in his 'Writing' essay: 'His virtuosity with language is not unlike that of one of his sergeants with an awkward squad . . . Under his will, the vulgarest words . . . execute complicated movements at the word of command, but they can hardly be said to learn to think for themselves.'[14] But Auden's experiments with popular lyric and light verse did not of course disappear overnight: he was still interested enough in the idiom to have Rosetta and Emble play pop songs on the Wallomatic in *The Age of Anxiety*. However, like the music in the dive on Fifty-Second Street, these songs are presented as vehicles of regressive wish-fulfillment. It was the end of this line in his work and he effectively severed his artistic connection to popular lyric when he and Kallman began writing the libretto of *The Rake's Progress* in 1948. As they did so, Auden abandoned an idiom which thrived on moods of romantic passivity and resignation and adopted one that insisted instead on what he called a 'passionate and wilful state of being'.[15]

III

The period of Auden's most sustained engagement with popular forms came between 1936 and 1940, that is, roughly between the appearance of *Look, Stranger!* and that of *Another Time*. In his introduction to *The Oxford Book of Light Verse* he listed the three kinds of poetry that he had included there as 'Poetry written for performance, to be spoken or sung before an audience . . . Poetry intended to be read, but having for its subject-matter the everyday social life of its period or the experiences of the poet as an ordinary human being . . . Such nonsense poetry as, through its properties and technique, has a general appeal.'[16]

These categories loosely describe the range of the pieces collected below, though in late 1939, when Auden was assembling the contents of *Another Time*, he hinted at the subtler, more ambiguous blending of seriousness and lightness that he was then aiming for in his own work by gathering the poems in the second section of the book under

---

[14] 'Poet of the Encirclement' (1943), repr. in *FA* 356.

[15] 'Some Reflections on Opera as a Medium', *Tempo*, 20 (Summer 1951), 8.

[16] (1938) repr. in *EA* 364. A draft of the introduction existed by mid-December 1937, but Auden probably only completed it in the summer of 1938.

the delicate, hybrid term 'lighter poems'—something more meaningful and explanatory than just 'light verse'.

The reasons for this change can be seen in the differences between two poems about victims of society which appeared in *Another Time*. In 'Victor' (1937), the lower-middle-class subject of the poem is trapped in a cage of rigid social detail and confining metre, sadistically viewed by his colleagues, and by the upper-middle-class poet, as a ready source of satiric potential. For all its knowing vigour, and its perhaps accurate account of the mood at a particular moment in history, there is an air of deadlock in the caricature. Two years later, though, the subject of 'The Unknown Citizen' (1939) is hidden by a veil of epistemological inscrutability and mystery. In the wake of his journey to China, Auden had managed to find ways of criticizing society without distorting the humanity of its victims. What is more, by speaking with the bureaucratic voice of the indifferent State reflecting on its dead citizen, Auden also managed to defuse, by emphasizing, some of the coercive power latent in the language of poetry. This greater complexity of viewpoint is reflected in the differing forms of 'Victor' and 'The Unknown Citizen'. Auden's later poem reconciles two differing accents, a prose and a verse rhythm, a comic and a tragic inflection, just as its masculine and feminine rhymes are sunk unobtrusively in the flow of the long, winding sentences, like cat's eyes in tarmac. It is one of several poems from the early months in America which embody the qualities of the Good Place that Auden hoped would be both 'integrated and free'.[17]

But this sense of balance, achieved just a few months before Auden put together his new collection, may have made many of the poems he had written earlier in England seem to belong to what the title ironically suggests was 'another time'. Certainly the extent of Auden's experiments with lighter poetry from 1936 to 1940 are not clear from the work printed in *Another Time*: many of the pieces that would have demonstrated these interests had been dropped or altered.

Some of these abandoned lyrics were probably only meant for the entertainment of children, Auden's pupils and others—a small task that Auden enjoyed and took seriously. (They may also have been connected with an anthology of children's verse that he was planning in 1937 and early 1938.[18]) Many other poems from these years,

---

[17] Introduction to *The Oxford Book of Light Verse*, EA 368.
[18] A memo of agreement between Auden and Faber & Faber, dated '8. 2. 38' (but not signed by Auden, who was in China), is in the files of his agents in Britain, Curtis

though, products of Auden's love of writing words for music, and specifically for Britten's music, were given a new, more conventionally literary context in the book. All three case-history ballads of 1937, for instance, had first been published in magazines with tunes specified for them and at least one, 'Miss Gee', was given to Britten to be set as a cabaret song for Hedli Anderson. The identification of the various tunes was omitted in *Another Time* and many other Auden songs were never collected at all.

By detailing his early ideas about poems that he later republished in a different context and by printing here as many as possible of his uncollected songs and lighter poems, as well as those that he published only in a drastically different or shortened form, this edition tries to uncover a previously buried part of Auden's creative history during his last years in England and his first years in America.

IV

It is difficult now to discern exactly how Auden first conceived of each of the poems. In mid-1937, for example, he sent a Miss Boyd (who appears to have been compiling an anthology of verse for children) the poem, 'Johnny', which he had also given to Britten, as one of their cabaret songs.[19] He also sent Miss Boyd the ballad 'James Honeyman'—not, so far as we know, ever given to Britten, though he did pass the composer a companion piece, 'Miss Gee', to set as a cabaret song. (Britten never composed any music for it.)

Although Auden independently pursued some of his experiments with popular forms, many of his best efforts were undertaken with Britten, perhaps because Britten's work demonstrably supplied Auden's poetry with a unity of sound and meaning, the voluptuous fullness of 'delight, cascading | The falls of the knee and the weirs of the spine',[20] which Auden was searching for. In the second half of the

Brown. It specifies a plan for an 'Anthology of Verse for Children'. Auden never finished the project, and there is no evidence that he even started it.

[19] ALS to Miss Boyd [no date, but probably spring or early summer 1937], written from Auden's home in Birmingham, and suggesting poems from his published works that might be suitable for children. He also sent her typescripts and a manuscript of the 'songs' 'Johnny', 'James Honeyman', and 'Nonsense Song' (see [14] below). The letter and poems were partially quoted in the entries for items 120–3 of the Sotheby's (London) catalogue (given the shorthand title 'Alfred' by the auctioneers) for a sale of English literary and historical books, letters, and manuscripts that took place on 16 June 1984. The present location of the letter and the poems is unknown, and I have not been able to find any record of an anthology of poetry edited by Miss Boyd.

[20] 'The Composer' (1938), repr. in *EA* 239.

decade Britten and Auden collaborated on a whole range of projects, including the song-cycles *Our Hunting Fathers* and *On this Island* and the radio play *Hadrian's Wall*. At the same time, Auden was also turning out a large number of songs in popular styles for Britten's music. Some were for performance (often in considerably pared-down versions) in *The Ascent of F6* and *On the Frontier*, and others were written for Hedli Anderson to use as cabaret songs. Two especially ardent periods of collaboration occurred during March–April 1936 and in April 1937. Many of the poems below were written during that first intense spell of work, when Auden also wrote a pair of love lyrics, 'Underneath the abject willow' and 'Night covers up the rigid land', that he later dedicated to Britten.

We do not know how many poems Auden wrote specifically for Britten to set as cabaret songs, nor how many of these were ever set, nor how they might have been grouped or ordered in performance. As happened in the case of 'Miss Gee', Britten did not write music for all the songs that Auden gave him, nor did Auden collect (or even publish) all the songs that Britten set—he never printed 'I'm a jam tart' (see [5] below), for instance. Plans were probably being hatched and discarded almost as quickly as composer and poet were producing the works themselves. Some of Auden's songs lay untouched for a while before Britten found time to compose music for them, and in at least one case ('Song (after Sappho)', see [19] below) a Britten tune had to wait for Auden words.[21]

However, the general working method seems to have been that Auden wrote his contribution first, providing Britten with more material than even this prolific composer could cope with. (This situation was to be repeated in more extreme terms with *For the Time Being* in 1942.) At times, Auden seems to have been scattering almost everything he wrote over Britten in the hope that some of it would take root: on 8 January 1937, for instance, just before Auden left for Spain, he wrote out 'Lay your sleeping head, my love' and 'It's farewell to the drawing-room's civilised cry' on scores that Britten

---

[21] Britten set at least seven of the poems as cabaret songs for Hedli Anderson—'Give up love', 'I'm a jam tart', 'Johnny', 'Funeral Blues', 'Tell me the truth about love', 'Calypso', and 'Song (after Sappho)'—but the music for only four of them—'Johnny', 'Funeral Blues', 'Tell me the truth about love', and 'Calypso'—has survived. Those settings were first published as *Four Cabaret Songs* (London, 1980). A recording, *Britten's Blues and Cabaret Songs* (London, 1993), with the soprano Jill Gomez, the pianist Martin Jones, and an instrumental ensemble, was issued by Unicorn-Kanchana Records (DKP (CD) 9138).

was carrying. Britten's diary indicates that he was far more excited by the second poem than he was by the first—'overwhelmingly tragic & moving' he called it.[22] Nothing ever happened with 'Lay your sleeping head, my love' but two years later Britten incorporated two stanzas from 'It's farewell' into his *Ballad of Heroes* (1939).

Along with all of Auden and Britten's other collaborations, the cabaret songs continued in dribbles and spurts well into 1939. Hedli Anderson commissioned more songs from Britten, which he intended to compose while he was in the States.[23] He took the text of at least one cabaret song, 'My Love Stolen Away', with him from England in 1939, and in the same year Auden wrote fresh, American-style songs, including 'Blues' and 'Calypso'.

V

A complete list of Auden's songs and 'lighter poems' from the period, in roughly chronological order follows (titles that were added by Auden later or are conjectural are given in square brackets):

MARCH 1936
'When I was only so high, I was amiable and gay'; 'I wonder if you've ever noticed'; 'The soldier loves his rifle'; 'Forget the dead, what you've read'.

APRIL 1936
['Funeral Blues'—*The Ascent of F6* version]: 'Stop all the clocks, cut off the telephone'; ['I'm a Jam Tart']: 'I'm a jam-tart, I'm a bargain basement'; 'From the moment that I saw you'; 'It's not easy to describe the state I'm in'.

EARLY 1937
'Blues (FOR HEDLI ANDERSON)'.

APRIL 1937
['Reds']: 'You would go raving mad if I told you all I know'; 'Johnny'; ['Give Up Love']: 'Cleopatra, Anthony'; ['Education']: 'Education's in its infancy as yet'; 'Miss Gee' (published in *New Writing* (Autumn 1937) with the note, 'Tune, St. James' Infirmary').

SUMMER 1937?
'The Ostnian Admirals'; 'Sue'; 'Nonsense Song'; ['Millions']: 'There are millions of things that we want to make'; ['Memories']: 'As I look in the fire I remember'; 'Little birds are playing'.

---

[22] *BBLFL* 461.   [23] See *BBLFL* 719–21.

JUNE 1937

'Victor' (published in *New Writing* (Autumn 1937) with the note, 'Tune, Frankie and Johnny' and a refrain at the end of each stanza—variously 'Have mercy, Lord, save our/your/their/his/her/my soul(s) from Hell').

AUGUST 1937

'James Honeyman' (published in a two-line stanza form in *Ploughshare* (Nov.–Dec. 1937) with the note, '(Air. Stagolee)').

OCTOBER 1937

'Roman Wall Blues'.

1937/1938?

'My Love Stolen Away'

JANUARY 1938

'Some say that love's a little boy' (which in the version set by Britten opens with an additional line, never reprinted in Auden's collections and probably not by him: 'Liebe—l'amour—amor—amoris').

1938?

'Listen, darling: I've got something I must tell you . . .'.

JANUARY 1939

'Epitaph on a Tyrant'.

MARCH 1939

['Blues']: 'Say this city has ten million souls'; 'The Unknown Citizen'.

MAY 1939

['Calypso']: 'Dríver drive fáster and máke a good rún' (dedicated in a TS in the HRC to Hedli Anderson); 'Song (after Sappho)'.

OCTOBER 1939

'Heavy Date'.[24]

'Sue' was probably written at around the same time as Auden's three published case-history ballads. An early, incomplete version is included here because he thought highly of the poem. In December

---

[24] Locations of songs not republished here (because they were collected by Auden) are as follows: 'Stop all the clocks, cut off the telephone'—*PDW* 350–1 (the original version performed in *The Ascent of F6*), *EA* 163, *CP91* 141 (the revised text that Britten set as a solo version for Hedli Anderson in June 1937); 'Johnny'—*EA* 213, *CP91* 142; 'Miss Gee'—*EA* 214–16, *CP91* 158–61; 'Victor'—*EA* 218–22, *CP91* 167–71; 'James Honeyman'—*EA* 223–7, *CP91* 162–6; 'Roman Wall Blues'—*EA* 289–90, *CP91* 143; 'Some say that Love's a little boy;—*EA* 230–1, *CP91* 143–5; 'Epitaph on a Tyrant'—*EA* 239, *CP91* 183; ('Blues') 'Say this city has ten million souls'—*CP91* 265–6; 'The Unknown Citizen'—*CP91* 252–3; ('Calypso') 'Dríver drive fáster and máke a good rún'—*CP91* 266–7; 'Heavy Date'—*CP91* 259–62.

1946, when he was discussing the ballads with Alan Ansen, Auden remarked: 'The best one I ever did was never published. It deals with a fashionable woman. The objects on her dressing table started talking to her. She committed suicide. I showed it to a lady who promptly tore it up. Not for any personal allusion, but because she felt it was an outrage on the sex.'[25]

There are two other songs in Auden's 1936–7 notebook in the Berg Collection.[26] The first, a pseudo-Gilbertian marching song, begins 'We're bulldog pluck in cartons'. The second, a more muted, topographical poem in quatrains, possibly called 'Night Starvation', begins 'There's moonlight on the pier at Wigan' and ends 'The little peers are all tucked up in Eton | But I'm alone and I've got no one to be sweet on'.[27] Both songs date from early or mid-1937, but they survive in fragmentary, only partially legible drafts and so are not printed here.

In cases where multiple texts of the same poem exist, I have printed what seems to be the latest version, giving brief descriptions of any earlier drafts or fair copies in the notes that follow each piece. A few of these poems were printed in magazines, but many have survived only in manuscript form. Usually, they have little punctuation. Auden's ways with punctuation were in any case inconsistent, or at least difficult to predict accurately. In the thirties, when he thought of poetry as 'memorable speech',[28] he does not seem to have been much concerned with the printed appearance of his work. In the forties his views evolved towards a more 'written' ideal, and he began to take a greater interest in the design of his books and the presentation of his poems. He often accepted suggestions from editors about punctuation, but he also sometimes rejected their ideas, saying that he believed punctuation in poetry could occasionally deviate from the norm. This means that there can be no certainty about how (if at all) Auden

[25] Ansen, 14. These rather coldly cynical poems have always inspired strong reactions in people who connect themselves with the subject-matter. Isherwood explained that in August or September 1937 he refused to give Auden permission to write one about his separation from his boyfriend Heinz. Later, feeling less sensitive, he regretted it. (See *C&HK* (US) 288.)

[26] Referred to hereafter as the 'Berg *F6* notebook', it contains drafts and fair copies of poems, songs, and parts of *The Ascent of F6*.

[27] The title comes from a list of poems and songs in another notebook used during 1937, which contains drafts and fair copies of poems, songs, and drafts of what is apparently the first version of *On the Frontier* (see *PDW* 654–60). The notebook is referred to hereafter as the '*OTF* notebook'.

[28] Introduction to *The Poet's Tongue* (1935), repr. in *EA* 327.

would have wanted these fugitive pieces from the thirties to appear in the pages of a book. I have therefore tried to leave things as they are and to alter the poems as little as possible during their transition from script to print. (This conforms with Edward Mendelson's practice in his edition of the *Complete Works of W. H. Auden*.) Auden's orthography has been corrected and regularized ('dont' silently emended to 'don't', for instance), because this could not distort the sound or rhythm of a poem, but aside from closing a quote here and there I have not changed, or supplied, any punctuation which might have altered the meaning of the lines or which might have made these sometimes fragile skeins of language seem solider and more 'finished' than they actually are.

'For Hedli': Britten and Auden's Cabaret Songs

DONALD MITCHELL AND PHILIP REED

It was for the remarkably versatile singer and actress Hedli Anderson (1907–89) that Benjamin Britten and W. H. Auden collaborated to produce their so-called 'cabaret songs', sophisticated examples of vernacular music which amply demonstrated both the composer's and the poet's sharp wit and youthful high spirits. But in every sense the songs—there were at least seven composed—were inspired by, and in performance relied on, her outstanding gifts.

Even before Auden first met her during the Group Theatre's production of his play *The Dance of Death* in February 1934, Hedli Anderson had already become an accomplished artist. She began her musical training in London at the age of 17 with Victor Beigel, a coach well known to Elisabeth Schumann and Lotte Lehmann, but as Hedli recalled in 1980, 'quite, quite wrong for any little person who came to him to start singing'.[1] In spite of this unpromising start, Hedli followed Beigel to Bayreuth and later to Hamburg, where she took lessons at the conservatoire. She also worked hard at her piano playing at this time—'they thought I'd be better as a pianist than as a singer'—and subsequently travelled to Berlin where she studied the type of stage-craft appropriate for a potential opera singer.

It was in Berlin that she first began to realize that she was never going to possess the vocal equipment for a career in the opera house. But her vivacious personality and individual vocal style, coupled with a new-found enthusiasm for the work of Bertolt Brecht and his disciples, brought about an important change of direction in her career. Modelling herself to some extent on Yvette Guilbert—always one of her favourite artists—Hedli embraced the sophisticated European tradition of cabaret. Thereafter she enjoyed a career which encompassed theatre, opera, broadcasting, revue, and cabaret.

In a French dictionary of music (Bordas), Guilbert is described succinctly as 'chanteuse et comédienne', a description which certainly accounts for two of Hedli's principal capabilities; and for yet another,

---

[1] Interview with John Evans (Paris, Oct. 1980). A transcript of the interview is available at the Britten–Pears Library, Aldeburgh. All subsequent unattributed memories of Hedli Anderson's are taken from this source.

we have to rely on a further French term, for a special talent and a special genre—'diseuse': 'A female artiste who entertains with monologue' (*OED*). The accompanied monologue, with its implication of theatrical possibilities, was a stage 'turn' that perfectly suited Hedli's gifts. It is no surprise, perhaps, that during the war she showed herself to be an accomplished reciter in Schoenberg's *Pierrot lunaire* and Walton's *Façade*.

The rise of fascism forced her to return to London in the early 1930s, where her twin skills as a musician and an actress made her an inevitable choice for Rupert Doone's Group Theatre. She accepted the role of the Cabaret Singer in Auden's *The Dance of Death*, a play whose political stance was entirely in tune with her own convictions, born out of her grim experiences in Europe.[2] Doone's company gave Hedli the opportunity to establish herself in the English theatre and she did much to bring professional standards to an organization she once described as 'a sort of vicar's tea-party'. It was not a description that the temperamental Doone would have recognized. Hedli had only one recollection of Auden in 1934: 'I must have met Wystan at the Group Theatre, because I can't remember [anything] except for seeing him on the stage writing out a piece of dialogue, changing a piece of dialogue Rupert wanted changing . . . and thinking it was a proper way to be working.' Following *The Dance of Death*, Hedli performed 'old and new songs of satire' in the Group Theatre's *Midnight Cabaret* during October 1934, and a year later she took part in the revival of *The Dance of Death* at the Westminster Theatre. At the same theatre, in January 1936, she created several roles in the first of Auden and Isherwood's collaborations, *The Dog Beneath the Skin*, including the role of Madame Bubbi of the Hotel Nineveh, a part specially written for her. It was, however, her involvement in the second Auden–Isherwood venture, *The Ascent of F6*, with magnificent incidental music composed by the 22-year-old Benjamin Britten, that brought her much personal and public acclaim.

It was in connection with rehearsals for *F6* that Hedli makes her first appearance in Britten's diaries from this period, on 19 February 1937: 'Go at 10.30 for F6 rehearsal & stay till 4.30—do quite a lot of

---

[2] Michael Sidnell in *Dances of Death: The Group Theatre of London in the Thirties* (London, 1984), 319, notes that at Hedli's lodgings in Germany, 'the son of the family committed suicide and the daughter sold herself to a business man'. To John Evans she recollected, 'the circumstances were so awful, young people couldn't make up their minds whether to be Communists or Nazis and two or three of the ones I knew committed suicide, and people began to disappear, and there was this Jewish thing . . .'

useful stuff—tho the play's still in a very unboiled state. Lunch with Rupert Doone, the Easdales,[3] Hedli Anderson (who will sing splendidly) & Christopher Isherwood.' But while *F6* may have given Hedli an opportunity to impress the youthful Britten, in 1980 she gave a different account of her first encounter with the composer, apparently pre-dating the *F6* rehearsals: 'As far as I can remember, I think it was to do with a film, Auden, GPO, I think . . . and I was asked to sing a song that Benjamin had written for them and that's how I met him . . . It was something very small I had to do and films . . . were very strange to me.'

No direct evidence can be found to link Hedli's vague memory—she could not, for instance, recall the film's title—with a tiny, unpublished, and unattributed cabaret-style song by Britten, 'When you're feeling like expressing your affection', that has come to light at the Britten–Pears Library in recent years. But it seems possible that this is the song that Hedli recollected. Edward Mendelson thinks Auden a likely author of the song's witty text,[4] and the chronology of Hedli's memory coincides with Auden's six-months' residency at John Grierson's GPO Film Unit and Britten's employment there. The catchy character of the song, marked 'Vivace', in F, with harmony coloured by an unstable major/minor third, is not unlike the later specifically designated cabaret songs known to be from the Auden–Britten stable, even if 'When you're feeling' is much less sophisticated or pungent than, say, 'O tell me the truth about love' or 'Funeral Blues'. The song amusingly extols the virtues of the public telephone service and would probably have been intended for one of Grierson's many publicity films.[5] If the text is indeed by Auden and Hedli's memory was accurate—but note that she does not mention the poet's name in this context—there is a good case for considering

---

[3] Brian and Frida Easdale. Brian Easdale was the musical director for *F6*. See also Kevin Macdonald's interview with Brian Easdale, 'The Composer Who Scored', *Guardian* (20 Mar. 1992).

[4] For the text, see *PDW* 673.

[5] Professor Mendelson is surely correct in suggesting that the song might have belonged to a sketch for a film 'not unlike the brief GPO publicity film, *The Fairy of the Phone*'. The latter, directed in 1936 by William Coldstream with music by Walter Leigh, included a dozen female telephone operators singing at their switchboards: 'Just telephone, and we will put you through.' The film also featured the composer Walter Leigh's sister, Charlotte (like Hedli, a noted singing-actress) who played the role of the fairy. See also Rachael Low, *Documentary and Educational Films of the 1930s* (London, 1979), 114.

'When you're feeling' to be a precursor of the subsequent Auden–Britten songs written for her.

The quality of her performance in *F6* undoubtedly impressed Britten and Auden, who set about creating a dedicated repertory of cabaret material specifically for her. According to Hedli, it was Rupert Doone who suggested to Auden and Britten the possibility of creating a small repertoire of 'cabaret songs' for her, very much in the German and French tradition. She recalled, 'Doone probably also had the same idea as I had about myself and said to Auden and Benjamin, "You must make songs for this woman. This is very important to her and will be a very good thing for the Group Theatre . . . it's part of the Group Theatre and you must do this."'

The poet John Berryman, writing to his mother in January 1939, described attending 'a ball in town where a gorgeous creature sang two of Auden's new songs',[6] and a friend of Britten's recently recalled that Hedli 'looked absolutely stunning, indeed ravishing. What marked her out from all the others was above all the effect produced by her voice.' While almost a dozen cabaret songs were planned by Britten and Auden, only four complete examples have survived: 'Funeral Blues'; 'Johnny'; 'Tell me the truth about love'; and 'Calypso'. The surviving songs were first published by Faber Music in 1980, and broadcasts and a commercial recording two years later firmly established the songs in the repertoire.[7]

Hedli Anderson first met the poet Louis MacNeice (1907–63) during the pre-war period at the Group Theatre (she took part in performances of his translation of Aeschylus's *Agamemnon* (1936) and *Out of the Picture* (1937)), and they married in 1942. MacNeice's close association with the Features Department of the BBC ensured her involvement in a number of his most significant programmes, including *Christopher Columbus* (1943) and *The Dark Tower* (1946). In the latter her association was continued with Britten, who provided one of his most perfectly tailored radio scores for the occasion. In 1943 Hedli also took the role of Athene in one of the most memorable and ambitious radio melodramas from these years, Edward Sackville-West's *The Rescue*, based on *The Odyssey*, also with music by Britten. It has gone unnoticed that George Bernard Shaw was much impressed by the broadcast of *The Rescue*. He wrote to Gabriel Pascal

[6] Richard J. Kelly, ed., *We Dream of Honour: John Berryman's Letters to His Mother* (New York, 1988), 115.
[7] See 'A Cabaret Song Chronology', below, pp. 66–8.

in November 1944: 'I was very much struck by a broadcast of a classical play (Greek) with music by Benjamin Britten. It had style and
great refinement . . . It had the forgotten quality of elegance.'

MacNeice dedicated many of his poems from the war years to his
wife, and in the post-war period she and her husband gave occasional
joint recitals of music and poetry. He was to write in a poem that he
loved her

> because Rejoice
> Is etched upon your eyes, because the chaff
>
> Of dead wit flies before you and the froth
> Of false convention with it, because you are half
> Night and half day, both woven in one cloth,
>
> Because your colours are onyx and cantaloupe,
> Wet seaweed, lizard, lilac, tiger-moth
> And olive groves and beech-woods, because you scoop
>
> The sun up in your hands.[8]

However, their marriage came to an end in September 1960, three
years before MacNeice's untimely death. Their daughter Corinna, an
artist, survives them.

It is hard to think of a comprehensive epitaph for this extraordinar-
ily talented artist of such varied vocal and theatrical gifts. Perhaps one
can catch a flavour of her pungent personality—and a flavour of the
period when she was at the height of her powers—from a verse of
one of the unforgettable cabaret songs that Britten and Auden devised
for her. The music, alas, is lost, but the words bring Hedli vividly,
brilliantly, laughingly to life:

> I'm a jam tart, I'm a bargain-basement,
> I'm a work of art, I'm a magic casement,
> A coal cellar, an umbrella, a sewing machine,
> A radio, a hymn book, an old French bean,
> The Royal Scot, a fairy grot, a storm at sea, a tram—
>   I don't know what I am,
>   You've cast a spell on me.

Hedli Anderson—a work of art in her own right—cast her spell on a
whole generation.

---

[8] From 'Flowers in the Interval', *Collected Poems*, ed. E. R. Dodds (London, 1966),
324.

A Cabaret Song Chronology

1937   *20 April, BB's diary*: '. . . coffee here after dinner with Hedli
Anderson & Wystan Auden (here to discuss future songs &
plans)'; *5 May, BB's diary*: 'In the morning I set a serious
poem of Wystan's (from Dog-Skin)—Nocturne, & in the
afternoon a light one for Hedli Anderson—Johnny'; *6–8 May*:
BB composes three further cabaret songs for HA, including
'Jam Tart' and 'Give up love'. The unidentified third song
may have been a setting of either 'Miss Gee' or 'Blues (for
Hedli)', both of which WHA sent to BB around this time (see
BBLFL, 545); *10 May, BB's diary*: 'Hedli comes with her
accompanist in the morning & we go thro' the songs—now
completed by me—they are going to be hits I feel!'; *15–18
June*: BB, HA, and the artist William Coldstream visit
Colwall, where WHA is teaching at the Downs School; *16
June, BB's diary*: 'Spend day making alterations in the cabaret
songs'; *17 June, BB's diary*: 'A tremendous amount of work—
rewriting things—doing a new version of F6. blues' [a solo
voice version of the highly successful choral blues number
from BB's incidental music to WHA's and Christopher
Isherwood's *The Ascent of F6*, in which HA had taken part];
18 June, BB's diary: 'Hedli is a dear & I'm very fond of her';
9 November: 'Jam Tart', 'Johnny', and 'Funeral Blues' sung
by HA to a BBC Audition Panel at Broadcasting House.

Also probably belonging to 1937 is the text for another
song, 'I sit in my flat in my newest frock', which BB took
with him to North America in 1939 (see *BBLFL*, 548); the
text was apparently not set by BB.

1938   *18 January*: At the Group Theatre's farewell party for WHA
and Christopher Isherwood (about to leave for China), HA
and BB perform cabaret songs, including 'Jam Tart' and
'Tell me the truth about love' (composed January 1938); *19
January*: HA sings 'Johnny', 'Jam Tart', and 'Funeral Blues'
to Britten's publisher (it seems likely that 'Tell me the
truth' was also sung); *14 July*: HA and BB record for the
Columbia label (producer: Walter Legge) 'Funeral Blues',
'Give up love', 'Jam Tart', and 'Johnny', but the discs were
never commercially issued and the masters were subsequently destroyed.

Also probably dating from the autumn of 1938, because of its topical references, is a quasi-dramatic monologue which includes a three stanza song, 'When the postman knocks'.

1939 *18 January*: HA and BB record 'Johnny' and 'Tell me the truth about love' for Columbia, but the recording suffered the same fate as the earlier discs;[9] *January/May*: WHA, now in the US, sends BB 'a blues for Hedli' ('Say this city has ten million souls') which BB apparently never sets; *May*: WHA sends BB, also now in North America, the texts for two further cabaret songs—'Song (after Sappho)' and 'Calypso' (*BBLFL*, 657–9); *5 June*: BB (now in Canada) thanks WHA for the pair of texts; 'Calypso' is set by BB at this time but no music for 'Song (after Sappho)' has been discovered; *October*: HA evidently anxious about the commissioning of further cabaret songs from BB which had failed to appear—BB writes, 'But, Hedli, I promise you— you will get your songs one or two or possibly three (God help me!) by air-mail either at the end of this or most probably next week'; none of these new songs (presumably to the texts supplied by WHA earlier in the year) has come to light; *December*: proposal made for a new recording of the cabaret songs (unspecified) by HA and Arthur Young.

1940 *January/February*: HA proposes to perform 'Tell me the truth' in one of a series of films she was making for British Films Ltd, entitled *Let's Be Famous*; the film has not been traced.

1941 *14 December*: Peter Pears and BB perform 'Funeral Blues' and 'Calypso' as the concluding items in a recital programme given at the Southold High School Auditorium, Long Island.

Pears and BB rarely included the songs in their joint recitals after this time, although an archive recording exists of a hastily improvised performance of 'Tell me the truth'. HA continued to use the material in her programmes until her retirement in the 1960s.

---

[9] The Britten–Pears Library, Aldeburgh, possesses a copy of an archive recording of the four cabaret songs that have since been published, sung by HA with an unidentified accompanist (source: Corinna MacNeice).

1980   First publication of the extant cabaret songs—'Tell me the truth about love', 'Johnny', 'Funeral Blues', and 'Calypso'—by Faber Music, Britten's publishers since 1964.

1982   *14 March*: first broadcast performance of the cabaret songs on BBC Radio 3, given by Margaret Field and Douglas Young; *23 March*: a subsequent broadcast given by Norma Winstone and Courtney Kenny, introduced by Donald Mitchell.

Later in 1982, Meridian Records release the first commercial recording of the cabaret songs, in a performance recorded live at Dartington Hall, Devon, by Sarah Walker and Roger Vignoles (E77056).

Songs and Poems

W. H. AUDEN

Edited by Nicholas Jenkins

[1]

When I was only so high, I was amiable and gay
But mother left the larder door ajar one summer day
And that night before he smacked me I heard dear father say
  'He's nice but he's weak'.

At school I was in trouble and as teacher took the cane
He said 'you mustn't do it for you know it gives me pain'
And I promised him I wouldn't but I gave him pain again
  I'm nice but I'm weak.

In the office I'm a ray of sunshine, everyone agrees
I emptied out the till one day and put it on the gees
The boss said 'Damned dishonest' but I said 'No language please'
  I'm nice but I'm weak.

If there's one thing more than all the rest I simply can't abide
It's drunkenness, I think it such an insult to man's pride
But when I pass a public house I find myself inside
  I'm nice but I'm weak.

And as for petting, well, I don't approve of it at all
And I don't know how it is that when I hear the sirens call
Though I know it's not being quite nice yet it feels so nice to fall
  I'm nice but I'm weak.

So why think about the future, dear, or why drag up the past
I'm really not unscrupulous or faithless or too fast
I know you're not the first I've kissed, and you will not be the last
  I'm nice but I'm weak.

[March 1936. Possibly intended for *The Ascent of F6*? Auden holograph in the
Berg *F6* notebook.]

[2]

I wonder if you've ever noticed
   Walking round in Spring
That there's a most peculiar power
   Affecting everything
Birds leave the early worm alone
And dogs forget to gnaw the bone
   And the sheep and the hen
   And the cow and the dove
   And the fishes and the men
   Have got a date with Love.

For solemn doctors
   Leave patients in the middle of a major op
And Oxford Proctors
   See bonfires in St. Giles but let the matter drop
The burly sailor
   Jumps his ship and swims a thousand miles to shore
The High class tailor
   Throws the trousers he is mending on a very dirty floor
They've got a date with Love.

The chimney sweepers
   Wash their faces and forget to wash the neck
The lighthouse keepers
   Let their lamps go out and leave the ships to wreck
Deep sea divers
   Cut their boots off and come bubbling to the top
And engine drivers
   In the middle of the tunnels bring expresses to a stop
They've got a date with Love.

The band conductor
   Thrusts his baton through the drum and leaves it there
The gym instructor
   Leaves his class standing with one leg in the air
The prosperous baker
   Leaves his rolls in hundreds in the ovens to burn
The undertaker

Pins a small note on the coffin saying 'Wait till I return
I've got a date with Love'.

Judges like most men
  Forget what's what, who's who, or which is which
And country postmen
  Throw the postcards they are reading in the ditch
The village rector
  Dashes down the side aisle halfway through a psalm
The sanitary inspector
  Runs off with the cover of the cesspool on his arm
To keep a date with Love.

So that is why dear
  When the sudden urgent message comes to kiss
That you and I dear
  Give whatever we were going to do a miss,
For there are dangers
  In postponement and we've such a lot to do
So tell these strangers
  'We've a pressing engagement and we're not at home to you,
We've got a date with Love.'

[March 1936? Auden holograph in Berg *F6* notebook. When Auden wrote out
the fair copy there, he gave the first stanza a markedly different shape from
those in the rest of the song. I have taken the layout of the first stanza from
the *F6* notebook and slightly regularized the form of the remaining five stanzas, using as a model the shorter version of the song that Auden printed in
The Ascent of F6: see *PDW* 306–7. In the spring of 1936 Auden also gave this
poem to R. D. Smith, a Birmingham University acquaintance, for possible
use in an undergraduate review, see *PDW* 599.]

[3] Foxtrot from a Play

Man.   The soldier loves his rifle
        The scholar loves his books
    The farmer loves his horses
        The film star loves her looks
    There's love the whole world over
        Wherever you may be
    Some lose their rest for gay Mae West
        But you're my cup of tea

Woman.   Some talk of Alexander
        And some of Fred Astaire
    Some like their heroes hairy
        Some like them debonair
    Some prefer a curate
        And some an A. D. C.
    Some like a tough to treat 'em rough
        But you're my cup of tea

Man.   Some are mad on Airedales
        And some on Pekinese
    On tabby cats or parrots
        Or guinea pigs or geese
    There are patients in asylums
        Who think that they're a tree
    I had an aunt who loved a plant
        But you're my cup of tea

Woman.   Some have sagging waist lines
        And some a bulbous nose
    And some a floating kidney
        And some have hammer toes
    Some have tennis elbow
        And some have housemaid's knee
    And some I know have got B. O.
        But you're my cup of tea

Together.   The blackbird loves the earthworm
           The adder loves the sun
           The polar bear an iceberg
           The elephant a bun
           The trout enjoys the river
           The whale enjoys the sea
           And dogs love most an old lamp-post
           But you're my cup of tea

[March 1936. Auden holograph in the Berg *F6* notebook and in the Lockwood Memorial Library, State University of New York at Buffalo. Published as 'Foxtrot from a Play' in *New Verse* (Apr.–May 1936). The Buffalo MS was the basis of the *New Verse* text, see *EA* 159–60. A shorter version of the song was used in *The Ascent of F6*, see *PDW* 341.]

[4]

Forget the dead, what you've read
All the errors and the terrors of the bed
Slake the ache in your head at what the cruel neighbours said
    Dance John Dance
Forget the gloom in the room
The encroaching and approaching of the tomb
And the shadows that loom and the distant mutterings of doom.
    Dance John Dance
      Chin up
      Kiss me
      Atta Boy
  Dance till dawn among the ruins
    Of a burning Troy.

Forget the boss when he's cross
All the bills and ills that make you toss
Forget if it's poss, your feelings of eternal loss
    Dance John Dance
Though you weep in your sleep
Though your fears and your despairs go very deep
Keep in time for time's cheap, and there's nothing else to keep
    Dance John Dance
      Chin up
      Kiss me
      Atta boy
  Dance till dawn among the ruins
    Of a burning Troy.

Ignore the law, it's a bore
Don't enumer all the rumours of a war
Fly the cry of the poor, as you go gliding round the floor
    Dance John Dance
Men miss their goal, lose their soul
Men grow hopeless and grow jokeless on the dole
Sudden death takes its toll, some die like rats inside a hole

Dance John Dance
   Chin up
   Kiss me
   Atta boy
Dance till dawn among the ruins
   Of a burning Troy.

Some get disease, others freeze
Some have learned the way to turn themselves to trees
Some go down on their knees, but let us do just what we please
   Dance John Dance
Some start to sigh, others cry
Some tap their forehead, say it's horrid and then die
Friendship ends by and by, but that's the very reason why
   Dance John Dance
      Chin up
      Kiss me
      Atta boy
Dance till dawn among the ruins
   Of a burning Troy.

[March 1936? Auden holograph in Berg *F6* notebook. A shorter version was used in *The Ascent of F6*, see *PDW* 343–4.]

[5] [I'm a Jam Tart]

I'm a jam-tart, I'm a bargain-basement,
I'm a work of art, I'm a magic casement,
A coal cellar, an umbrella, a sewing machine,
A radio, a hymn book, an old French bean,
The Royal Scot, a fairy grot, a storm at sea, a tram—
  I don't know what I am,
  You've cast a spell on me.

I'm a dog's nose, I'm Sir Humphrey Davy,
I'm a Christmas rose, I'm the British Navy,
A motor, a bloater, a charcoal grill,
An octopus, a towpath, Hindenburg's will,
A village fair, a maiden's prayer, the B. B. C., a pram—
  I don't know what I am,
  You've cast a spell on me.

I'm a salmon, I'm a starting-pistol,
I'm backgammon, I'm the Port of Bristol,
A Times leader, a child's feeder, an aspirin,
The Ritz hotel, a boy scout, the wages of sin,
A shaving brush, a schoolgirl's crush, the letter B, a ham—
  I don't know what I am,
  You've cast a spell on me.

I'm an off-break, I'm a clump of beeches,
I'm a tummy ache, I'm Mussolini's speeches,
I'm Balmoral, I'm a sorrel mare, I'm a tug,
A cigarette, an organ, a big bed-bug,
A traffic sign, a rubber mine, a coffee tree, O damn—
  I don't know what I am,
  You've cast a spell on me.

[Late March 1936? Text from a Boosey & Hawkes TS, not made by Auden,
now in the Britten–Pears Library, Aldeburgh. There are earlier MS versions
by Auden in the Berg *F6* notebook and in the Cambridge University Library.
1936 was the high point of Auden's sceptical interest in Surrealism and the
first stanza of this poem alludes to the famous collocation in the sixth book of
the Surrealists' bible, *Chants de Maldoror* (1868) by the Comte de

Lautréamont (Isidore Ducasse)—'beau . . . comme la rencontre fortuite sur une table de dissection d'une machine à coudre et d'un parapluie' ('handsome . . . as the chance juxtaposition of a sewing machine and an umbrella on a dissecting table', *Maldoror and Poems*, tr. Paul Knight (Harmondsworth, 1978), 217).]

[6]

From the moment that I saw you
I've been feeling very queer
The truth is that I just adore you
Yes, I'm mad about you, dear.

Till I don't know if I'm standing
On my head or on my heels
In the street or on the landing
Let me tell you how it feels.

[April 1936? Auden holograph in Berg *F6* notebook. Probably intended as a lead-in to the following song.]

[7]

It's not easy to begin to describe the state I'm in
For I feel almost light headed I'm just walking on air
I'm the shame of all my friends, they're going to cut me till it ends
But that's how I'm affected when I'm having an affair.
  Sixpence on the Income tax
    I don't care
  England beaten by the All Blacks
    I don't care
  Grave disturbances in France
  High death rate among maiden aunts
  Girl bites bishop at a dance
    But what do I care
    I'm having an affair.

It's costing me a lot of cash I haven't got
When I go to see my banker he's just like a blank brick wall
I can't even raise a loan upon note of hand alone
The bats are in the belfrey and the bailiffs in the hall.
  Boy shoots mother for a joke
    I don't care
  Quadruplets in Basingstoke
    I don't care
  Traffic stopped by storm of hissing
  Surrealist reported missing
  Professor says there's too much kissing
    But what do I care
    I'm having an affair.

I'd got a job to do with a pretty tidy screw
The boss was an old friend of mine but sent for me to-day
He gave a little cough, said 'Your work's been falling off'
I made a rather rude noise and then I went away.
  They're burning coffee in Brazil
    I don't care
  German marks are frozen still
    I don't care

Bankers wear an ugly frown
Rubber shares are falling down
There's not a decent show in town
But what do I care
I'm having an affair.

I'd a happy married life with a most devoted wife
We never had an angry word, she was all that I could wish
I'd a girl and boy as well who think their daddy swell
But the thought of them this evening's like a cold wet fish.
Mussolini's lost his hair
I don't care
Hitler baits the Russian Bear
I don't care
The pleasure never seems to pall
Of shooting men against a wall
Europe's tottering to her fall
But what do I care
I'm having an affair.

[April 1936? Auden holograph in Berg *F6* notebook.]

[8] Blues
(for Hedli Anderson)

Ladies and gentlemen, sitting here,
Eating and drinking and warming a chair,
Feeling and thinking and drawing your breath,
Who's sitting next to you? It may be Death.

As a high-stepping blondie with eyes of blue
In the subway, on beaches, Death looks at you;
And married or single or young or old,
You'll become a sugar daddy and do as you're told.

Death is a G-man. You may think yourself smart,
But he'll send you to the hot-seat or plug you through the heart;
He may be a slow worker, but in the end
He'll get you for the crime of being born, my friend.

Death as a doctor has first-class degrees;
The world is on his panel; he charges no fees;
He listens to your chest, says—'You're breathing. That's bad.
But don't worry; we'll soon see to that, my lad.'

Death knocks at your door selling real estate,
The value of which will not depreciate;
It's easy, it's convenient, it's old world. You'll sign,
Whatever your income, on the dotted line.

Death as a teacher is simply grand;
The dumbest pupil can understand.
He has only one subject and that is the Tomb;
But no one ever yawns or asks to leave the room.

So whether you're standing broke in the rain,
Or playing poker or drinking champagne,
Death's looking for you, he's already on the way,
So look out for him to-morrow or perhaps to-day.

[Spring 1937? Auden holograph in the Lockwood Memorial Library, State University of New York at Buffalo, is the basis of the text first published in *New Verse* (May 1937). See *EA* 209–10.]

[9] [Reds]

You would go raving mad if I told you all I know
They put all old women out in the snow
If you sneeze you are thrashed with a bakelite truncheon
Babies are pickled and eaten for luncheon.

Reds Reds
On the stairs and under chairs and in the beds
Tiptoeing over floors, trying handles of the doors
In the drive with a knife for your life or a gun
Run Run
Look round, watch the ground, as you walk and you talk
Take care Take care
When you give a pearl to a girl
Beware
Look out
Where
Over there
Ssh it's the
Reds.

They've nationalised women and children for fun
Opium is sold in the streets by the ton
To wear silk pyjamas means death or hard labour
Collectors of stamps are slashed with a sabre.

Reds Reds
Creeping softly in the loft and on the leads
Watching as you pass through a powerful opera glass
To take by stealth all your wealth and your health and your fun
Run Run
Look for signs when you dine, be alone when you phone
Take care Take care
When you get a letter then you'd better
Beware etc.

They've invented a drug to make people say
That pigeons are blackbirds and December is May

And a surgical technique, a patent new suture
So that faces shall look all the same in the future.

Reds Reds
If you flu or get the blues or sudden dreads
If you're feeling cold if you think I'm old
If you quiver by the river if you shiver in the sun
Run Run
If your wit and your it and your food are no good
Take care Take care
If you wake from a dream with a scream
Beware etc.

[April 1937? Auden holograph in Berg *F6* notebook. The refrain perhaps echoes the cries of 'Rats! Rats!' in the 'Rats away!' song in Britten's *Our Hunting Fathers* song cycle. It is picked up again in the 1st Old Tree's cries of 'Reds' in the Prologue to *Paul Bunyan, Libretti* 6.]

[10] [Give Up Love]

Cleopatra, Anthony
Were introspective you'll agree
Got in a morbid state because
They lounged about too much indoors
If they'd gone in for Eton Fives
They wouldn't have gone and lost their lives

For if you love sport then you won't give a thought
    To all that goes on in the park
Learning to bowl will keep your heart whole
    You won't want to go out after dark
Love is unenglish and sloppy and soft
    So be English and stringy and tough
If you keep yourself fit you will never want It
      So give up Love.

Abelard and Heloise
Were a pair of sentimental geese
They ought to have taken exercise
Not spent their time in sighs and cries
Gone in for netball or sailing boats
Instead of writing sloppy notes.

For if you can jump then you won't want to bump
    By mistake into girls in the park
If you can dive you won't yearn for High Life
    You won't want to go out after dark
Love is unenglish and sloppy and soft
    So be English and stringy and tough
If you hole in in one, then love seems poor fun
      So give up Love.

Dante wrote a lot of slush
Because he got an unhealthy crush
On Beatrice who was dead to him
He ought to have kept himself in trim

Upon the horizontal bars
Not written tripe about the stars.

For if you keep a straight bat then love will seem flat
    It won't tempt you to spoon in the park
If your back hand's like this, then you won't want to kiss
    You won't want to go out after dark
Love is unenglish and sloppy and soft
    So be English and stringy and tough
You won't feel the loss if you're good at lacrosse
        So give up Love.

Don Juan was another one
For whom something should have been done
Compulsory games would have been his cure
For his nasty Spanish habits I'm sure
Had someone seen that he played cricket
He would not have been so wicked.

For if you play games you will never write names
    On seats in the public park
Riding to hounds puts love out of bounds
    You won't want to go out after dark
Love is unenglish and sloppy and soft
    So be English and stringy and tough
Love makes you laugh if you play centre half
        So give up Love.

[April 1937? Auden holograph in Berg *F6* notebook.]

[11] [Education]

Education's in its infancy as yet
It's a crying scandal we must not forget
   That ever since the schools began
   They have only dealt with man
And the needs of nature have been barely met

For the cuckoo needs his corners rubbing off
And the robin won't cooperate enough
   And the language of the owl
   I suspect is rather foul
And the nightingale thinks far too much of love

And the stork is always showing too much leg
And the hen swanks all the time about her egg
   And the cock should be corrected
   For he's getting so affected
And the Eider duck needs taking down a peg

And the butterfly's a passenger I'm sure
And the squirrel's sense of loyalty is poor
   And the lobster and the louse
   Take no interest in the house
And the cat is lacking in esprit de corps

For example who has ever really known?
What goes on among the beasts beneath a stone
   Or what takes place at dawn
   Among the worms upon the lawn
Or what the fish are up to when alone

We must plan the summer afternoons somehow
Of the swallow and the slow-worm and the sow
   We must find some exercise
   In the winter for the flies
We must organise the free time of the cow

We must keep a careful eye upon the ox
We must cut down the meat diet of the fox
  And the lion and the lark
  We must keep up to the mark
We must see the elephant pulls up his socks

We must see that even tiger dries his tail
We must teach the shag to do things on the nail
  We must see the polar bears
  Don't forget to wash their ears
We must supervise the hygiene of the whale

We must use our patience and all our resources
To teach better table manners to the horses
  We must teach the little seals
  To say grace before their meals
And not to fidget in between the courses

We must never let the herring and the hawk
Get out alone together for a walk
  We must find the right correction
  When the cod gets introspection
When the raven looks pale we must have a talk

Even then we have only just begun
There's the world of vegetables to be done
  For the pansies in the borders
  Haven't learnt to obey orders
And the tulip only thinks of No. 1

In the water too we should be interested
For the algae should be quarantined and tested
  And every drop of rain
  Should be packed in cellophane
And moonlight saved and carefully reinvested

I am worried by the conduct of the stars
I don't suggest that you should lock them behind bars
  No Orion and his Pole
  You might try out on parole
But you must be firm with Venus and with Mars

And the universe I'm given to understand
Has been permitted to contract and to expand
   So I see I must begin
   To instil some discipline
And take the slapdash universe in hand

[April 1937? Auden holograph in Berg *F6* notebook.]

[12]

The Ostnian Admirals
Are always tight
The generals of Westland
Take drugs to sleep at night
Now what do you know about that?
The Chancellor when he's alone
Speaks baby talk to his dictaphone
The Minister for war was seen
On the cliff sending signals to a submarine
And someone left a time bomb on the King's doormat
  But ssh
Keep this under your hat.

The Queen is hiding
Tiaras in the ponds
The State bank President
Is buying bearer bonds
Now what do you know about that?
The Secretary of Mines appeared
At the Opera in a huge false beard
And people say who [are] in the know
They're opening all the letters at the G.P.O.
And the sausages the butchers sell as Pork are cat
  But ssh
Keep this under your hat

The Ostnia Crown Prince
Has petit-mal attacks
The sons of the Leader
Are Haemophiliacs
Now what do you say about that?
The High Court Judge is said to be
Taking up astrology

There's a [*illegible*] in the Board of Trade
The Colonel of the cavalry wears corsets on parade
And the cardinal keeps a girl friend in a cosy flat
  But ssh
Keep this under your hat

[Summer 1937? Auden holograph in *OTF* notebook. The song was evidently
intended for *On the Frontier*.]

[13] Sue

Once upon a time there was a girl called Sue.
She lived in Half Moon Street and had nothing to do.
She'd a handsome income from alimony
But she wasn't very happy as you soon shall see.

She bought a new frock every week
And hoped that it would pay her dividends in chic.
She'd a shell-shaped pleated organza hat.
Her pockets were amusing, too. She saw to that.

The stockings she wore were six-and-eleven per pair
But O they were frankly class-conscious and sheer.
Her shoes were of glacé with a fringed suede tongue.
Bangles [on each arm, as she liked] to look young.

Her lounging pyjamas were a casual brown.
She carried a watch set in a tiny gold crown.
Her holiday bag was shaped like a fish,
As bright and irresponsible as she could wish.

One morning at eleven she went to her coiffeur.
He looked at her hair and said to her:
'Soft plastic curls in front, Modom, I see,
Are just the thing to suit your personality.'

She dropped in on [a friend] at half-past four.
A white [jade] satin teagown she wore.
She went about in a phantasie of tulle
Or a [frilly] Watteau skirt if she was feeling dull.

Her car was a Terrapin, long and low,
With a cigarette-lighter and a radio.
Dove grey in colour, on the seats
Were five half-empty boxes of expensive sweets.

There are twenty-four hours in every day.
She managed to get by all in her own way.

365 days in a year:
She'd [look at the clock and time would] disappear.

She went to Monte Carlo with a few of her set,
Lost two thousand playing roulette.
She went to Honolulu for a change of air,
To Paris then to see a man about her hair.

She had a lover for every mood:
John danced so daringly, Phil knew about food,
Tom was so amusing, Tony was so rich,
Bob brought the art of [kissing?] to its highest pitch.

William wasn't handsome but was her ideal.
He was an artist. She thought him 'real'.
She sent him telegrams six times a day
And O the scenes whenever he said 'I can't stay'!

At William's suggestion she took up reading books,
But found that concentration didn't suit her looks.
She went on a diet of Doctor Hay's
But lost the directions after two or three days.

But in spite of all the clothes and lovers she had
You may not believe [it], but Sue felt bad.
She woke up every morning and wondered what for.
She felt as sober and stuffy as a Woolworth store.

She went to church one Sunday in a [check] tweed skirt,
She tried to catch religion but it didn't work.
She gave ten shillings to a beggar in the street.
She saw a [raggamuffin] and offered it a sweet.

She went to Dr. Coughdrop, a psychoanalyst,
Said, 'I'm so unhappy, can you assist?'
He looked at her gravely, said, 'Of course, my dear.'
She went to him an hour a day for quite a year.

She told him her dreams, she confessed every crime.
He listened and charged her two guineas each time.

In the end he said, 'The trouble is you
Believe in nothing and [have] nothing much to do.'

She came [back] one evening as the clock struck twelve,
Went up to her bedroom and [sighed to] herself.
She went to the mirror and started to cry.
The mirror whispered suddenly, 'You're [ugly,] die.'

A jar of skin food asked in scorn,
'Tell me, why was this woman born?'
A bottle of toning lotion replied,
'Why indeed? It's high time that the woman died.'

Then some eyebrow tweezers began to scold,
'Why should I look after anything so cold?'
And a bottle of 4711
Said, 'I like a girl with character and she has none.'

'No one will mourn her when she is dead,'
A [fluted? robe] severely said.
A pair of directoire knickers agreed,
'I think that she's a most unpleasant girl indeed.'

Then a poult-de-soie dress with a taffeta cloque,
Shut in the wardrobe, stirred and spoke,
'I disliked [her] from the moment I saw her in the shop.
I shan't be sorry when I see her drop.'

A bottle of sleeping-tablets in the [drawer then]
Said, 'I suppose I must do it again.
I have rescued the brave from dishonour and grief,
So I shall have to offer even her relief.'

She went to lie down, at last she knew
The only thing left for her to do,
Poured out all the tablets upon her palm,
Swallowed them and sank into a permanent calm.

[Summer 1937? In the spring of 1977 Christopher Isherwood, John Fuller,
and Edward Mendelson made a transcription of 'Sue' from Auden's draft in a

notebook that belonged to Isherwood. Their version, containing 'a number of guesses and reconstructed phrases', was published as *Sue*, Sycamore Broadsheet 23 (Oxford, 1977). In the version printed here I have put square brackets around their reconstructed phrases and around one or two of my own conjectures; any especially doubtful readings are followed by a question mark. The order and punctuation of the stanzas are also largely the work of Isherwood, Fuller, and Mendelson. This case-history of alienation is a sardonic re-writing of 'The Rape of the Lock', crossed with the dour influence of James (B. V.) Thomson's 'In the Room', in which the furniture and fixtures discuss the corpse of their recently deceased owner.]

[14] Nonsense Song

My love is like a red red rose
Or concerts for the blind,
She's like a mutton-chop before
And a rifle-range behind.

Her hair is like a looking-glass,
Her brow is like a bog,
Her eyes are like a flock of sheep
Seen through a London fog.

Her nose is like an Irish jig,
Her mouth is like a 'bus,
Her chin is like a bowl of soup
Shared between all of us.

Her form divine is like a map
Of the United States,
Her foot is like a motor-car
Without its number-plates.

No steeple-jack shall part us now
Nor fireman in a frock;
True love could sink a Channel boat
Or knit a baby's sock.

[Summer 1937? The TS of this song, with the title added in Auden's hand, is listed as item 123 in the Sotheby's (London) catalogue (given the short-hand title 'Alfred' by the auctioneers) for the sale on 16 July 1984. There is also a draft in Auden's hand in the *OTF* notebook. The poem was sent in mid-1937 to a Miss Boyd along with 'James Honeyman', 'Stop all the clocks, cut off the telephone', and 'Johnny' (see Introduction, p. 54).]

[15] [Millions]

There are millions of things that we want to make
Money and music and history and cake
   There's so much to do
There are millions of places we want to go
There are millions of facts that we want to know
Some we may still, and some we never will
   But I've got to know you

There are millions of stars up above us in the sky
That will go on burning till the day that I die
   But one is enough
There are millions of fish in the sea it's true
That may be just as beautiful as you
Millions are sweet whom I shall never meet
   But it's you I love

There've been millions of people since Adam and Eve
Have said to themselves I'm in love I believe
   I'm in love. And now
My arms are open. O enter them and kiss
There is no joy in all the world like this
Love cannot wait; too soon it is too late
   But it's my turn now.

[Summer 1937? Auden holograph in *OTF* notebook.]

[16] [Memories]

As I look in the fire I remember
  The wonderful summer that's past
The wonderful days when he loved me
  But the wonderful love didn't last
The leaves spin down; it will soon be winter now.

When I woke there was always a letter
  Posted the evening before
He never came without flowers
  He never let me open a door

We used to ride every morning
  We used to ride in the Row
His picture was in the papers
  There was no one he didn't know.

We used to have tea in his apartment
  There were etchings on the walls
He always said to the servants
  'Say I'm out if anyone calls'

We used to dine at the Beckley
  We dined there again and again
The manager himself took the order
  For lobsters and cold champagne

O when he put his arms round me
  O when he gave me a kiss
It was like having gas at the dentist
  O I floated away in bliss.
But the leaves spin down, it will soon be winter now.

[Summer 1937? Auden holograph in *OTF* notebook.]

[17] My Love Stolen Away

I sit in my flat in my newest frock
   But he never comes near my door
I listen in vain for the postman's knock
   And the telephone rings no more.
How could he be so bamboozled
   By the crudest kind of charm
In another place with a grin on his face
   He nuzzles her silly arm.

It's not as though she were really his tea
   It's simply the summer heat
And he's young of course and it's easy to see
   How she flatters his boyish conceit
It can't take more than a fortnight
   Before he awakes from his dream
By then I am sure he will find her a bore
   But I want to hear her scream.

I want to see her crawl on her knees
   With blubbering swollen eyes
Her face all covered with skin disease
   Like a horrible sort of disguise
O let her lose all her money
   And all her pretty hair
I must be brave; when they dig her grave
   I shall be dancing there.

Let the fishes float poisoned on top of the sea
   And the bird drop dead from the sky
Let ivy strangle the apple tree
   And the little children die
Punish the earth with thunder
   And tear in half the day
Destroy all trace of the human race
   It has stolen my love away.

[1937/8? (Paper is watermarked 'STANFORD & MANN L^{td} | INCOMPARABLE | BIRMINGHAM'.) An unsigned TS, probably by Auden, amongst the Britten papers in the Berg and with the title added in pencil in Auden's hand.]

[18]

Listen, darling: I've got something I must tell you. I've been meaning to all this week. It's not very pleasant news, I'm afraid. I don't know how to begin. But I've never told you lies, have I. You see, darling, the fact is . . .

> When the postman knocks
> My pulse no longer thunders like a drum
> But I amble slowly to the box
> And I read my morning letters in the order that they come
> And if I see you coming down the street
> My heart no longer misses a beat
> And waiting for an evening rendez-vous
> Or waiting for a bus are much the same
> I suppose I should be mildly worried if you never came
> I've fallen out of love with you.

No, there isn't anyone else. I promise you there isn't. And I haven't been talking to mother or anybody. No, of *course* it isn't your fault, darling. You've never been anything but perfectly sweet to me. I feel an awful beast, but I can't help it. It just happened. Like that.

> On a country walk
> I look at trees, then realise with a jerk
> That you're with me and you want to talk,
> So I take your hand as usual, but I think about my work
> And if I've an engagement, it's a shock
> To find how much I look at the clock
> And at the restaurant-table set for two
> It's the wine I mean when I say 'You're sweet'.
> And what makes me look so happy are the things we're going
>   to eat
> I've fallen out of love with you.

When did it happen?   I dunno. It just did.
The band was playing a fox-trot   (do do da dy o do)
Someone made a joke at the next table   (whoo ha ha Whoo ha ha)
The Dictators were making speeches   (Grrrrrrrr——)

Mr. Chamberlain was appeasing someone	(cluck cluck cluck cluck cluck)
Several records were broken on land, water and air	(Hip Hip Hip Hurrah. Hip Hip Hip Hurrah)
Ten people wrote letters to the Times	(I am dear sir, your obedient servant)
Several thousand people were born	(sound of crying)
Several thousand people got married	(Wedding March)
Several thousand people died	(Dead March)

In fact the world was its usual self
When suddenly—click—there we were.
   Fini—schluss—over

   O forgive me, dear
   I never dreamt that I could alter so
   I never meant to lie last year
   When I said I'd never leave you, darling; how was I to know
   That eyes which were enchanted lakes to me
   Would become just normal so suddenly
   Those lips to which I promised to be true
   Just human features not unlike my own
   And that, like Greta Garbo, I'd prefer to be alone
   I've fallen out of love with you.

[1938? MS by Auden, now in the Britten–Pears Library, Aldeburgh.]

[19] Song (after Sappho)

O What's the loveliest thing the eye (the eye)
Can see on the black earth before we die?

To some it's horses, to some the Rhine   (the Rhine)
To others it's battleships steaming in line

Men say this, and Men say that
Say that and this,
But I say it is
The one I love
The one I love.

> (for *one* read boy, man, girl
> or goat to taste)

[May 1939? Auden holograph in the Britten–Pears Library. Auden told Britten that he thought of this as just an 'encore 30 second song' (quoted in *BBLFL*, 658). The paper is watermarked 'SAWACO BON BAG CONTENT USA'.]

Gerhart Meyer and the Vision of Eros: A Note on Auden's 1929 Journal

DAVID LUKE

Absence of fear in Gerhart Meyer
From the sea, the truly strong man.[1]

AUDEN'S sometimes quoted but not yet published Berlin journal of 1929 is a manuscript in which I have a certain personal interest, since it was in his lately tenanted sixteenth-century brewhouse cottage in Christ Church, where he had lived during his last six months in Oxford, that I found this document a day or two after his death in Vienna in September 1973. It is a bound quarto notebook containing upwards of a hundred pages of handwritten material, often more or less illegible; a label on the front cover bears the words 'Journal. April 1929—'. Much of it is intimately autobiographical, especially the dated entries on the first forty pages or so, covering the period 23 March to 26 April; the remainder would be better described as a notebook or repository of miscellaneous psychological and literary reflections, some of them excerpted from Auden's reading at the time. The manuscript has been placed in the Berg collection, and a complete critical edition of it is expected to appear in a later volume of *Auden Studies*. As is well known, Auden sought to debar, in effect, future biographers from using material such as this journal, or intimate personal letters which he accordingly asked the recipients to destroy. On the other hand, a certain unofficial ambivalence in this embargo has been widely perceived; Wystan loved to scandalize, and what could be more fun than posthumous scandalization? As to the journal, it also seems significant that he kept this manuscript all his life and neither burnt it nor locked it away in his Christ Church cottage, but in the end left it conspicuously lying on the sitting-room floor. The purpose of the present article is to highlight a particular passage in the Berlin journal which seems both to express the 22-year-old Auden's conception of the nature of sexual love, and to

---

[1] From 'It was Easter as I walked in the public gardens', *P30*; *EA* 37.

reveal a link between his youthful thoughts on this subject and those of his later period.

The background to the passage I have in mind is the journal's narrative of Auden's brief association with Gerhart Meyer, one of the boys he picked up in various bars and cafés for homosexuals during his year in Berlin between the autumn of 1928 and the summer of 1929. This background has already been sketched in Humphrey Carpenter's biography, with some quotations from the journal, such as the list (reminiscent of Don Giovanni's catalogue of women, though briefer) of 'Boys had, Germany 1928–9: Pieps, Culley, Gerhart, Herbert . . .' etc. Carpenter rightly points out that it would be a mistake to reduce these experiences to nothing more than (in Auden's own phrase) 'brothel-crawling'; he quotes in this connection the important entry of 13 April in which Auden refers to the unsatisfactoriness of mere promiscuity.[2] His Berlin affairs certainly, of course, involved financial inducements and gifts in kind. If money be the food of love, pay on; or as he himself put it in a late epigram:

> Money cannot buy
> The fuel of Love:
> But is excellent kindling.[3]

It is equally clear, however, that the affair with Gerhart was more emotionally involving than any of the others. The narrative covering it, though interwoven with other themes, dominates nearly twenty pages of the entries, from 31 March to 16 April. There is, I think, also some internal evidence that Auden was prompted to keep a written record less by Isherwood's visit to Berlin in late March, as the journal's opening words might seem to indicate ('Christopher's visit will serve as well as anything else as the introduction to this journal'[4]), than by his first meeting with Gerhart on Easter Sunday, 31 March, and their first assignation in Auden's lodgings on 1 April. It may not be accidental that the whole journal is labelled '*April 1929*—'; and the two passing proleptic references to Gerhart on 23 and 28 March[5] even suggest that the material for this first 'introduc-

---

[2] See Carpenter, 97 ff.

[3] From 'Postscript' to 'The Cave of Nakedness' in 'Thanksgiving for a Habitat' (1965); *CP91* 713.

[4] 23 Mar.; cf. Carpenter, 96.

[5] '. . . the temporary revival [I deal with later *deleted*] over Gerhart' (23 March), and 'I thought [Franz] attractive then [i.e. before meeting Gerhart]. How could I?' (28 March).

tory' week may have been written up retrospectively, after the new affair began.

Gerhart Meyer was apparently a sailor from Hamburg, and at the time of their meeting must have been only slightly younger than Auden, perhaps even slightly older.[6] He spoke English with reasonable fluency, which may partly account for Auden's spending so much time with him (though on the evidence of the journal, which records many conversations, Auden also talked German much of the time). I can discover nothing further about his origins or subsequent history, though Stephen Spender has told me in conversation that many years later, learning that Auden was in Berlin, Meyer called on him, and (as Auden reported) 'in walked the fattest man I have ever seen'. From the journal he comes across as physically very attractive but fairly primitive and unscrupulous. Auden records their dealings without sentimentality and with a proper ingredient of irony at his own expense, but the degree of passionate feeling that developed on his side of the relationship is nevertheless unmistakable. Over and above the mere money–sex transaction he can be said to have been, for about a fortnight, in love with Gerhart, even 'romantically' so, for what that is worth. The entries of the first few days (covered by the words 'Meeting Gerhart' in an underlined heading) record the details of their first encounter, Auden's impatience at having to wait twenty minutes for him at their first date, and his excitement when the boy proposes a trip to Hamburg at a few hours' notice. He rushes home, invents excuses for his friends, and borrows money from his landlady for the train fare. 'Few things are better than a hurried meal when one is packing to go off to a lover. I wondered what books one takes on these occasions. I took Donne, the Sonnets, and Lear . . .' The choice of the Shakespeare sonnets is noteworthy, as we shall see. In the tube on the way to meet Gerhart at the Lehrter Bahnhof he stares defiantly at a female whore, feeling like 'the king of Berlin'. Waiting for him, he thinks of the misery of John Layard[7] as a background enhancing his own happiness. In the train Gerhart

gets off at once with a girl. He has the most extraordinary power I have met in anyone. He laid his hand on my knee and switched on the current, an

[6] In one entry (4 April) Auden writes 'I want him to be an elder brother' (which does not, of course, prove that he was older in reality).

[7] The psychologist John Layard, a pupil of Homer Lane whose ideas interested Auden, was then 38 and living in Berlin. The story of his dealings with Auden at that time, his involvement at first in the Gerhart affair, and his attempted suicide has been well covered by Carpenter (85–90, 98–101) and need not be repeated here.

amazing sensation. What is odd is that when he could have any woman he liked from the Queen of England upwards, he chooses whores and not the prettiest ones either. I am so jealous with him that I am frightened when he goes to the lavatory that he won't come back.

Reflections on the psychology of jealousy follow, concluding 'He seems to belong to another world and might go up in smoke any moment.'

At the hotel in Hamburg (5 April) the boy has gone off to meet another lover or client, and Auden waits up most of the night in a frenzy:

First I posture before the glass, trying to persuade myself, but in vain, that I am up to his physical level. Then I read the Sonnets to prove my superiority in sensibility. Every time I hear a taxi I go to the window but it's only a whore returning. At three the porter comes and takes away my key locking the door. By five I am convinced that Gerhart has run off with my money.

Next day they wander about visiting various *Lokale* and meeting various 'whores'; to one of these Gerhart behaves with what Auden takes to be tenderness, describing it as 'one of the most beautiful things I have ever seen.' Later he makes a scene with the boy, expostulating that he is not getting good value for the 170 marks he has spent. Gerhart flounces off with a girl and they return to Berlin separately. A day or two later Gerhart installs himself in Auden's lodgings in Hallesches Tor; on 10 April Auden writes 'Having breakfast the morning after is the best sensation in the cycle of love'. The distress of another friend, Pieps, whom Gerhart has replaced, prompts reflections on infidelity, the instability of affection, its emotional evolution, and the need for attachments and relationships. Meanwhile his feelings about Gerhart are also changing: he remarks 'He is not the Prince of Wales he was in Hamburg', and goes on to reflect on the masochistic attractiveness of one-sided homosexual involvements, by comparison with which reciprocated heterosexual love seems so tame and easy (13 April).

Gerhart now demands further presents—shoes, a cap, underwear—and sulks when he is told 'If you have those shoes, then you don't get the cap'. With Auden, disillusionment is rapidly setting in: 'I wish I could make up my mind about him. Reason says "A strumpet", sex "Look at his eyes."' And on 15 April:

I have only realized this afternoon how the following conversation affected me. 'I should like to take you to the mountains with me'. 'I don't like mountains. I only like towns where there are shops' . . . This is the revolt of the symbol. The disobedience of the day-dream. From that moment I love him less . . . As a character compared with Pieps Gerhart is a cypher. His conversation bores me. But this is a nonsense. I mustn't forget him with that little weeping whore in Hamburg.

On 16 April they have another row about money, and Gerhart gets up in the middle of the night and goes back to Hamburg, leaving a scribbled address and taking Auden's dressing-gown and John Layard's revolver[8] with him. Reflecting on 'this little history', Auden feels that to dismiss the boy as a scoundrel he is well rid of would be to oversimplify; he himself is partly to blame. He thinks of writing him a haughty letter, then an affectionate letter, but does neither, resigning himself to Gerhart's total incomprehension of his feelings. It is in this context (16 April) that the important passage about love occurs, an account of the phenomenon of falling out of love which stands out suddenly from the rest of the narrative:

When someone begins to lose the glamour they had for us on our first meeting them, we tell ourselves that we have been deceived, that our phantasy cast a halo over them which they are unworthy to bear. It is always possible however that the reverse is the case; that our disappointment is due to a failure of our own sensibility which lacks the strength to maintain itself at the acuteness with which it began. People may really be what we first thought them, and what we subsequently think of as the disappointing reality, the person obscured by the staleness of our senses.[9]

In the remainder of the journal (about eighty-five pages) Gerhart Meyer is mentioned again only twice, as a figure now consigned to the past. In Auden's other and subsequent writings he is, so far as I know, referred to overtly only once: in the lines I have quoted as an epigraph, which were possibly written in April 1929.[10] There is no evident connection between him and the sequence of five sonnets in bad German which were first published only recently[11] and which

[8] See n. 7 above. Auden had taken charge of the revolver.

[9] The last two lines of the entry are barely legible and the syntax is not quite clear; the sense appears to be 'and what we subsequently think of as the disappointing reality [may be] the person obscured by . . .'

[10] The poem is divided into four parts, dated in Auden's MS Apr., May, Aug., and Oct. 1929 to indicate when each was written; at least some passages seem to have been written in Germany. The lines invoking Gerhart Meyer occur in the first (April) section, which begins with a reference to Easter (it may or may not be significant that Auden met Gerhart on Easter Sunday). In later editions Auden gave the whole poem the title '1929'.

[11] 'The German Auden: Six Early Poems', tr. David Constantine, *AS1* 1–15.

appear, as David Constantine points out, to have been written after
Auden had taken up a teaching post in Scotland in September 1930.
It is interesting, nevertheless, that these sonnets imitate the metre and
rhyme-scheme of Shakespeare's, which Auden took with him on his
trip to Hamburg with Gerhart, and which he read to himself as he
watched the clock for the boy during the world-without-end hours of
his absence. Nearly thirty-five years later, he would write an important essay on Shakespeare's sonnets,[12] which he must have recognized
as the greatest expression of the *emotion* of love in English poetry.
The profound link between the Berlin journal and this Shakespeare
essay published in 1964 is evident if we consider the above-quoted
passage about the lover's disillusionment.

The theory of love here proposed in passing by the 22-year-old
Auden, a theory which remained with him during those thirty-five
years and indeed for the rest of his life, rests on an essentialist view
of the human person, deriving ultimately from Plato, which is now
out of fashion. The lover, it suggests, perceives the beloved as he or
she 'really' is; the eyes of love are not blind but visionary, they
behold a deeper, 'more real' reality, but only while the passion of love
is sustained. When that fades, the vision fades with it into the lesser
light of common day. As Auden implies, reductive psychology or
common sense gives the exact contrary of this account. The lover, it
says, begins by being 'infatuated', that is to say he compulsively idealizes the loved person, failing under the influence of sexual emotion to
appreciate what would ordinarily be called that person's 'real' qualities and defects. He is enchanted, glamoured, besotted. Then, as his
emotion subsides and 'the daydream disobeys', the world of what we
ordinarily call 'reality' returns. Auden suggests a possible reversal of
this view of the process, though he would no doubt have conceded
that the same kind of reductive analysis could also be applied to his
alternative, the theory of the 'vision'. The narcissistic wound, it
would say, of discovering the unworthiness of what one valued so
highly is so painful, more painful even than the loss of the loved
object, that we persuade ourselves in hindsight that the failure, the
defect, was in ourselves and not in the beloved. Love granted us a
vision which by 'the staleness of our senses' we lost; but the beloved
himself is not lost, our masochistic self-blame preserves him eternally

---

[12] 'Shakespeare's Sonnets', first pub. in *The Listener*, 2 and 9 July 1964; then as
introd. to William Burto's Signet Classics edn. of the sonnets (New York, 1964). Repr.
in *FA* 88–108.

in the visionary world. Recourse to such a belief compensates, as do all religious beliefs perhaps, for a sense of unbearable loss.

In the 1929 passage Auden does not commit himself to any clearly metaphysical or religious conception of the 'real' content of the lover's vision. The word 'vision' is not used; what the lover sees until he has fallen out of love is merely said to be a measure of the strength and 'acuteness' of his sensibility, and his loss of it is due to 'the staleness of our senses'. The words 'really' and 'reality' are the only clue: a Platonic conception of different ontological levels seems to be implied. The world of the vision is 'more' real than that of the sober perceptions. This is essentialism, at the least; the question of whether there was a source for it in the young Auden's reading must be left to the experts. Today's sceptic would say that there is no such thing as the essential, 'objective' reality of a person: it is an intersubjective construction, something generated by the dynamics of a relationship between two persons and, so to speak, existing only 'between' them. Auden, I suppose, was a modernist but not an existentialist. In the *Sonnets* essay, and in an unpublished letter written to me at about the same time and expounding the same train of thought, he spells out quite clearly a religious and indeed specifically Christian development of the concept.

In the essay he writes: 'I think the *primary* experience—complicated as it became later—out of which the sonnets to the friend spring was a mystical one.' One of the defining general characteristics of mystical experiences is that

whatever the contents of the experience, the subject is absolutely convinced that it is a revelation of reality. When it is over, he does not say, as one says when one awakes from a dream: 'Now I am awake and conscious again of the real world.' He says, rather: 'For a while the veil was lifted and a reality revealed which in my "normal" state is hidden from me.'

Auden calls this form of natural (secular) mystical experience 'the Vision of Eros'.[13] Similarly, in the letter to me he states that the 'vision of Eros', though channelled through sex,

is in my opinion a religious vision, i.e. an indirect manifestation of the glory of the personal Creator through a personal creature. My chief reason for thinking that sex is its channel not its cause is that *all* the authorities agree that the vision cannot survive any prolonged sexual relations. This does not mean, of course, that it forbids them; it does, however, enormously increase

[13] *FA* 100.

the personal risk . . . When the vision fades, . . . the contrast between the glory of the vision and the sober world (I do *not* say reality) is too great to forgive.[14]

Auden would certainly have disclaimed as pretentious any suggestion that there had been a visionary or mystical element in the feelings briefly evoked in him by Gerhart Meyer; he would probably have reverted to the overworked distinction between love and lust, and left it at that. The differences between this Berlin attachment and the visionary passion which Auden perceives in Shakespeare's sonnets to his friend (or, as he says, in Plato or in Dante's *Vita Nuova*) are indeed all too obvious. For instance (to quote the Shakespeare essay again): 'Class feelings also seem to play a role; no one, apparently, can have such a vision about an individual who belongs to a social group which he has been brought up to regard as inferior to his own, so that its members are not, for him, fully persons.' And nevertheless:

The story of the sonnets seems to me to be the story of an agonized struggle by Shakespeare to preserve the glory of the vision he had been granted in a relationship, lasting at least three years, with a person who seemed intent by his actions upon covering the vision with dirt.

As outsiders, the impression we get of his friend is one of a young man who was not really very nice, very conscious of his good looks, able to switch on the charm at any moment, but essentially frivolous, cold-hearted, and self-centred, aware, probably, that he had some power over Shakespeare—if he thought about it at all, no doubt he gave it a cynical explanation—but with no conception of the intensity of the feelings he had, unwittingly, aroused.[15]

If we discount the time-scale ('three years') and perhaps the words 'agonized struggle' and 'glory', this description applies quite closely to the Gerhart Meyer episode.

Two conclusions seem to follow from this interpretation of that almost forgotten Berlin story. One is that the commonly expressed view that Auden did not 'become religious' until ten or eleven years after his Berlin period may need rethinking. The other is that there was a stronger streak of 'romanticism', or of what might be called romantic emotional masochism, in the young Auden than is usually recognized. Isherwood perceived this trait, seeing it as an aspect of

---

[14] ALS, June 1963, in my possession. This letter incidentally also contains confirmation that Auden was (as one would expect), familiar with Plato's thought: 'Nothing is drearier to my mind than silly old Plato's ladder—from fair forms to fair conduct to fair principles—etc. Has a Principle a Prick? *Bah*!'

[15] *FA* 101, 103.

the contrast between the young Auden's temperament and his own.[16] The tendency was something against which Auden took a severe reactive stance in later life, as is well known; this even went so far as his deciding to exclude his most famous love-lyric 'Lay your sleeping head' ('that old war-horse', as I recall him saying) from his collected works, which Chester Kallman quickly persuaded him not to do. He would no doubt have dismissed my tentative use of the word 'romantic' in the context of the Gerhart Meyer affair as 'absolute crap'. It is always possible, however, 'that the reverse is the case'.

---

[16] *C&HK* (UK) 226 ff. Cf. Auden's remark 'How one likes to suffer' in the journal entry of 13 April. Layard, in his memoirs, also claimed to have observed an element of physical masochism in Auden's dealings with his Berlin lovers ('Wystan liked being beaten up a bit'; quoted by Carpenter, 90).

'Whatever You Do Don't Go to the Wood': Joking, Rhetoric, and Homosexuality in *The Orators*

RICHARD BOZORTH

I

PROBABLY no work of Auden's has so consistently fascinated and troubled its readers as *The Orators*. For while it is easy to identify this book's major themes—social crisis and revolution, fascism, leadership, group movements—deciding what Auden is saying about such issues is another matter. Does he really mean it when he says, 'All of the women and most of the men | Shall work with their hands and not think again'?[1] Or is he satirizing this Lawrentian ideal? Auden's comments about *The Orators* clarify little. In a 1932 letter he called it 'a stage in my conversion to communism', but in 1966 he remarked: 'My name on the title-page seems a pseudonym for someone else, someone talented but near the border of sanity, who might well, in a year or two, become a Nazi.' Like another from the same essay, such comments are as coy as they are suggestive: 'My guess to-day is that my unconscious motive in writing it was therapeutic, to exorcise certain tendencies in myself by allowing them to run riot in phantasy.'[2] Thus, the issue of the political valence of *The Orators*—which has been seen as fascist, anti-fascist, and simply confused[3]—is also the issue of Auden's 'seriousness'. F. R. Leavis was responding to this quality of *The Orators* when he said that Auden 'does not know just how serious he is'.[4]

In fact, these uncertainties—Auden's seriousness (or lack of it), his

For their help with this essay I would like to thank Kevin L. Gustafson, Jerome J. McGann, and R. Jahan Ramazani.

[1] *EA* 105. All quotations are from the text of *The Orators* in *EA*.

[2] *O*³ vii. The 1932 letter to Henry Bamford Parkes is quoted in Haffenden, 122.

[3] e.g. Graham Greene: 'The subject of this book is political, though it is hard to tell whether the author's sympathies are Communist or Fascist' ('Three Poets', *Oxford Magazine*, 51 (10 Nov. 1932), repr. in Haffenden, 115). For an indictment of *The Orators* as fascist, see A. T. Tolley, *The Poetry of the Thirties* (London, 1975), 99–101.

[4] Untitled review, *The Listener* (22 June 1932), repr. in Haffenden, 101.

ambiguous politics, the question of the book's coherence—recall moments within *The Orators* itself. The anxiety about whether or not Auden is promoting fascism, for instance, recalls the Airman's concern over complicity with the enemy. Moreover, the weird, messianic 'He' of 'The Initiates' has a 'fondness for verbal puzzles,'[5] and the Airman of Book II fights the enemy with practical jokes. We might do well to hesitate before invoking criteria of aesthetic seriousness and ideological coherence in judging *The Orators*, because Auden is apparently flouting these readerly values. But if so, then what are the aesthetic and political rationales behind this book?

In this essay I shall argue that we can understand how and why *The Orators* troubles the standards by which it has been assessed only by exploring its treatment of homosexuality. Some studies of *The Orators* do refer to this subject—noting, for example, that the Airman is apparently homosexual[6]—but same-sex desire has far more to do with why *The Orators* is a difficult, contradictory work than critics have realized. For the political implications of homosexuality in *The Orators* are themselves contradictory. Same-sex desire at once preserves the political order and makes the homosexual a criminal according to that order, and this is the governing contradiction of Auden's 'English Study'.

Starting with the title, Auden represents social control in this work as rhetoric—public linguistic power used to subdue dissent and enforce group unity—and rhetoric often masquerades here as disinterested analysis. As a homosexual, Auden may have been peculiarly well situated to perceive this reality. But if the rhetoric of analysis is a form of social control, how is it possible to expose it as such and resist it except in a critique that has its own, equally questionable, rhetorical aims? And if the ruling class is constructed through bonds of sublimated male desire, can a conscious homosexual 'identity' be a difference that enables cultural critique? For homosexuality may be less a transgression than an emulation—crassly literal, to be sure—of 'normal' social bonds. Auden's problem of political opposition thus implies an epistemological one, arising because there is no position of true detachment from which to render political critique and to promote change: political complicity with an enemy has its analogue in

[5] *EA* 68.
[6] See, for example, *Early Auden*, 110–11; Peter Firchow, 'Private Faces in Public Places: Auden's *The Orators*', *PMLA* 92.2 (Mar. 1977), 267–9; Spears, 51.

the impossibility of isolating subject from object, observer from observed.

The Orators, I shall argue, is both an exploration of this crux and an oppositional exercise that exploits the culturally contradictory position of the homosexual, who is both criminal and complicit with the powers that be. Against rhetorics that enforce cognitive order and social uniformity, Auden deploys a poetic of joking that exploits cognitive contradiction and social difference.[7] *The Orators* notoriously frustrates analyses that employ mutually exclusive binary terms— coherence/incoherence, seriousness/frivolity, fascism/anti-fascism. Formally and stylistically it is an overt hybrid, and at its centre is the hybrid of the homosexual[8]—the 'Airman', waging his war against the 'enemy' in Book II. Stan Smith has argued that the enemy's governing trait is 'single-mindedness' (in the Airman's words, 'He means what *he* says'[9]), and that the enemy's discursive modes are 'oral public forms that posit an audience of participating equals'.[10] The Airman combats this ideology with public practical jokes that highlight human differences, so as to expose the enemy's rhetorical lie of political uniformity and equality. At the same time, the Airman fights the parallel lies that the individual is free of contradiction and able to speak univocally.

In short, the Airman is Auden's model for the homosexual poet. His 'Journal' implies an oppositional homosexual poetic based on joking, but this poetic also operates throughout the whole book. Political opposition in *The Orators* takes the form of a resistance to readings that, like public rhetoric, would erase social and sexual differences in order to seek impersonal meaning. If readers—including Auden in 1966—have found it hard to discover in *The Orators* any clear, coherent authorial intention, that is because it is resisting as dangerous the orator's desire for uniformity. Auden's poetic of joking, duplicity, and camp both celebrates and criticizes homoerotic group bonds, the appeal of a leader, and the power in deviance for the homosexual poet.

---

[7] Cf. 'Preliminary Statement' on psychology and drama (1929), where Auden writes, 'The joke includes its own contradiction. It is therefore the only form of absolute statement' (*PDW* 461).

[8] I borrow here from Harold Beaver, who argues that the homosexual contradicts the binary logic of Judeo-Christian moral systems: see 'Homosexual Signs: In Memory of Roland Barthes', *Critical Inquiry*, 8.1 (Autumn 1980), 111.

[9] *EA* 78.

[10] Smith, 62. I am much indebted to Smith's analysis of *The Orators*, particularly of the Airman.

II

If, as Auden once suggested, *The Orators* is about a failed 'revolution-ary hero,'[11] why does Book I, 'The Initiates', begin with a speech to schoolboys about love? The answer to this question is connected with the contradictory political valences of same-sex desire in Book I. The 'revolution' it describes is rooted in the homoerotic group identifica-tion encouraged by public school life. But it fails because, like the dominant power structure which has engendered it, its group ethos cannot tolerate individuality. Ultimately, 'The Initiates' is about the leftist political pretensions of Auden and his contemporaries as prod-ucts of public schools, and about how homosexuality renders them both victimized by and complicit with the powers that be.

The intolerance of this power structure is set out in the opening of Book I, 'Address for a Prize-Day'. What starts as typical school rhetoric on the value of the past modulates into a peculiar analysis of 'England, this country of ours where nobody is well'.[12] The speaker diagnoses the ills of the polity by dividing the boys into the three kinds of improper lovers in Dante's *Purgatorio*—excessive, defective, and perverted lovers. While the first two can be saved, the perverted lovers are 'struggling in towards a protracted deathbed, attended by every circumstance of horror'.[13] These incurables must 'die without issue', he says, rousing the other boys to thrust them into the 'Black Hole' under the hall. As he ends his speech, the purge begins: 'Quick, guard that door. Stop that man. Good. Now boys hustle them, ready, steady—go.'[14]

As some have noted, 'Address for a Prize-Day' conveys ideas Auden expressed less obliquely in 'The Liberal Fascist' (1934). Describing the honour system at Gresham's School, Auden remarked, 'The best reason I have for opposing Fascism is that at school I lived in a Fascist state.' The honour system (which banned swearing, smoking, and 'indecency', and required boys to report violators) relied on 'the only emotion that is fully developed in a boy of fourteen . . . the emotion of loyalty and honour'.[15] In parodying a lecture on inde-cency, 'Address' offers a critique of 'honour' in school life. But the

---

[11] See *Early Auden*, 96.

[12] *EA* 62. The speech parodies the style of the headmaster at St Edmund's School. See *Early Auden*, 98.

[13] *EA* 63.   [14] Ibid. 64.

[15] First printed as 'Honour' in *The Old School*, ed. Graham Greene (London, 1934), repr. *EA* 325.

speaker's move from lecture to fascistic pogrom suggests not only that schools exploit authoritarian fear, but that seeds of fascism lie in the ethos of group loyalty inculcated in the public schools. What is so dangerous, after all, about the perverted lovers that they need extermination? The speaker specifies nothing, but his prognosis of 'the hard death of those who never have and never could be loved'[16] implies that their disease has short-circuited 'love', i.e. group unity, public attachments. Their crime is individuality, which cannot be made to fit. The Prize-Day speaker is mistaken, of course—Dante does not depict the perverted lovers in purgatory as irremediably damned. But his error implies a link between moral order and rhetorical power, and thus exposes the social, and ideological aims of applied morality. His pretence of disinterested analysis is a rhetoric to 'straighten out' those who violate social order.

The speaker proceeds diagnostically, listing the symptoms of each case and the cure. The symptoms of the curable ones are odd but explicable. 'Excessive lovers' are Wordsworthian nature-lovers, prone to long walks and bird-watching, while 'defective lovers' collect the industrial detritus that indicates social decay. But the symptoms of the perverted lovers are literally inexplicable: 'A slight proneness to influenza, perhaps, a fear of cows, traits easily misunderstood or dismissed,' 'extreme alarm' at 'a simple geometrical figure', but otherwise they just look sick.[17] Their symptoms, that is, fit into no cognitive order, just as they refuse to fit into the social order.

Yet as always in *The Orators*, things are not so simple, and here we arrive at one of its many contradictions. While 'Address' ends in an anti-homosexual pogrom, the punishment is suggestively homoerotic. What happens in the 'Black Hole' has been called 'a fatal parody of initiation', and 'The Initiates' is, of course, the title of Book I.[18] It has been shown that the Airman reflects John Layard's work on the Bwili, the New Guinea sorcerers whose initiation rites supposedly involved death, resurrection, and anal insemination by 'ghosts'. Something similar is implied here, for just after 'Address', 'Argument' opens with images of death and rebirth: 'Lo, I a skull show you, exuded from dyke when no pick was by pressure of bulbs: at Dalehead a light moving, lanterns for lambing. Before the forenoon

---

[16] *EA* 63. [17] Ibid.

[18] *Early Auden*, 98. The 'Black Hole' recalls the 'buried engine room' which is a site of homosexual initiation in 'I chose this lean country' (*EA* 439–40).

of discussion, as the dawn-gust wrinkles the pools, I waken'.[19] 'The Black Hole' itself is fraught with homoerotic implications: it suggests a site—bodily as well as architectural—where illicit desire is brutally enacted to bring non-conformists into the group. Literally and figuratively beneath the rhetoric of the assembly hall, a more physical enforcement of group unity takes place in an act that, in the Prize-Day speaker's terms, is a ritual of perversion.

What, then, is the relation between the 'revolutionary' group movement of 'Argument' and the punishment/initiation of the perverted lovers in the Black Hole at the end of 'Address'? If the victims—the perverted lovers—are 'reborn' into a group movement to overturn their punishers, their own organization, rooted in homoerotic group identification, reflects their enemy's. The quasi-religious, quasi-political movement of 'Argument' embodies both a reaction against and a fulfilment of various impulses in 'Address for a Prize-Day'. In another passage in 'The Liberal Fascist' Auden wrote:

> By appealing to [loyalty and honour] . . . you can suppress the expression of all those emotions, particularly the sexual, which are still undeveloped; like a modern dictator you can defeat almost any opposition from other parts of the psyche, but if you do, if you deny these other emotions their expression and development . . . they will not only never grow up, but they will go backward, for human nature cannot stay still . . .[20]

Behind this passage is Freud's paradigm of sexual development, in which homosexuality is a normal stage to be outgrown. A school's authoritarian appeal to loyalty and sexual decency, Auden suggests, promotes exactly what it seeks to suppress. It forces sexuality 'backward' to an earlier stage—i.e. it produces the homosexual. 'Argument' and 'Statement' describe the result of this contradictory suppression and encouragement of same-sex desire in school, that crucial institution in forming the ruling class: a parabolic uprising in which homoerotic drives erupt into a movement of quasi-religious, quasi-political dimensions. But while it is ostensibly a mission of change, it has been shaped by the very structures it opposes.

The focus of this movement is a leader who never appears to the reader directly, but is somehow known to his followers:

> Speak the name only with meaning only for us, meaning Him, a call to our clearing. Secret the meeting in time and place, the time of the off-shore wind, the place where loyalty is divided. . . .

[19] *EA* 64.   [20] Ibid. 325.

On the concrete banks of baths, in the grassy squares of exercise, we are joined, brave in the long body, under His eye. . . .

Smile inwardly on their day handing round tea. (Their women have the faces of birds.) Walking in the mountains we were persons unknown to our parents, awarded them little, had a word of our own for our better shadow.[21]

In a sense, this is merely an oblique version of the standard gay adolescent coming-of-age narrative: boy meets boy and realizes his true, 'secret' identity, feels the erotic charge on the field and in the showers, and revels in his covert difference from parents and adult society at large. (The only element lacking is the conventional bourgeois guilt.) But this is also a narrative of some sort of revolution led by 'Him'—much as the church is called the Body of Christ, this speaker and his comrades are 'joined, brave in the long body, under His eye'.[22] In so far as this is merely schoolboy fantasy, then, Auden is implying that the homoerotic hero-worship of adolescence drives the desire for a strong-man to bring about political change.

After some rather obscure activities and a group litany, the final section of 'Argument' describes the leader's abrupt demise: 'Suspicion of one of our number . . . Friendly joking converting itself into a counterplot, the spore of fear. Then in the hot weeks, the pavement blistering and the press muzzled, the sudden disaster, surprising as a comic turn.'[23] One of the group has betrayed the leader, but why? and what does it mean? The answers can be found in Freud's analysis of libidinal ties within a group. Such ties, he says, exploit sexual desires inhibited from direct expression,[24] and we can see such inhibition directly reinforcing group loyalty in *The Orators*:

If it were possible, yes, now certain. To meet Him alone on the narrow path, forcing a question, would show our unique knowledge. Would hide Him wounded in a cave, kneeling all night by His bed of bracken . . . wearing His cloak receive the mistaken stab, deliver His message, fall at His feet, He gripping our moribund hands, smiling. But never for us . . . a league of two or three waiting for low water to execute His will.[25]

Up to now, the speaker of 'Argument' has been dutifully subsumed in the group, but here he begins to fantasize about exclusive bonds with the leader, 'meet[ing] Him alone', revealing 'unique knowledge'.

[21] Ibid. 64.

[22] Auden combines Freud's two main examples of libidinally based groups: the church and the army. See *Group Psychology and the Analysis of the Ego*, tr. James Strachey (London, 1922), 41–51.

[23] *EA* 68.   [24] *Group Psychology*, 118.   [25] *EA* 65.

In language of sexual desire and violence,[26] the speaker seems to merge with the wounded leader, 'wearing His cloak' and 'receiv[ing] the mistaken stab'. Exclusive erotic bonds with the leader conflict with the ties that bind the group together, ties whose sexual aim is inhibited. To pursue such desires would destroy the group and the leader who embodies it, and the speaker renounces his fantasy, accepting the group's mission 'to execute His will'.

The first-person plural pronouns here imply that the fantasy is typical, one to which any initiate may be subject. While there is no sense that the speaker of 'Argument' has an identity distinct from other initiates, this fantasy implies that individuation can arise in overcoming the inhibition governing homosexual desire for the leader. In fact, his death in the last part of 'Argument' is a betrayal of the group by an eruption of individuality: '*one* of our number' is the perpetrator. The results of the leader's death register in the bodies and behaviour of those once subsumed in the group: 'Love, that notable forked one, riding away from the farm, the ill word said, fought at the frozen dam, transforms itself to influenza and guilty rashes. Seduction of a postmistress on the lead roof of a church-tower, and an immature boy wrapping himself in a towel, ashamed at the public baths.'[27] Where desire had preserved the group, it now impels furtive individuation.

In 'Address for a Prize-Day' we saw how rhetoric enforces social unity and cognitive order, so it is odd that we never hear the leader speak in 'Argument'. 'Statement', on the other hand, conveys the rhetorical fall-out of his death. Unlike the often unfathomable tone of 'Argument', 'Statement' has the biblical air of a scripture codifying the leader's axioms after his death.[28] As such, its rhetorical aim—to define official, institutional truth—recalls the Prize-Day speaker's rhetorical exclusion of perverted love for the sake of group unity. But as John Boly has noted, 'Statement' ironically subverts group unity by portraying extreme individuality.[29] 'To each an award,' 'Statement' declares, 'suitable to his sex, his class and the power,' yet the 'awards'

---

[26] Cf. similar conjunctions of violence and homosexual desire in 'Control of the passes' and 'What's in your mind,' *EA* 25, 56.

[27] Ibid. 68–9. This quotation adapts lines from 'Because sap fell away', which tropes the failure of homosexual desire as a loss on the rugby field (Ibid. 441). Cf. Freud on those pursuing exclusive sexual bonds: 'The rejection of the group's influence is manifested in . . . a sense of shame' (*Group Psychology*, 121).

[28] See *Early Auden*, 101.

[29] See 'W. H. Auden's *The Orators*: Portraits of the Artist in the Thirties', *Twentieth Century Literature*, 27.3 (Fall 1981), 256–7.

suggest utter difference: 'One charms by thickness of wrist; one by variety of positions . . . One delivers buns in a van, halting at houses.'[30] The same may be said of their fates, some of which are heroic, but others ludicrous. As it reaches a rhetorical climax, offering Lawrentian prophecies in keeping with a group ethos, 'Statement' collapses into absurd disconnection: 'The leader shall be a fear; he shall protect from panic; the people shall reverence the carved stone under the oak-tree. The muscular shall lounge in bars; the puny shall keep diaries in classical Greek.'[31] The group's death by incurable singularity is rendered, finally, in 'Letter to a Wound', a love letter to the rift in an initiate's psyche left by the leader's death. It is a brilliantly smarmy, narcissistic paean to loss: 'The surgeon was dead right. Nothing will ever part us. Good-night and God bless you, my dear.'[32]

So far I have read 'The Initiates' as a parable of failed resistance, of revolt based on the same force as its enemy—that of homoerotic group bonds. If the perverted lovers threaten the body politic with irreducible difference, the revolution which follows 'Address' is undone by desire that individuates. To sum up, Auden sees same-sex desire as having contrary propensities: towards loss of self in group identity, and towards alienation of self from others. But here it is not only the ruling class that depends on homoerotic bonds, for the 'revolution' ends up mimicking its enemy's use of rhetoric to enforce social unity. That staple critical question—does *The Orators* imply that Auden was a fascist?—has two answers. Yes, for Auden here portrays all political power, whether dominant or resistant, as involving the erotically charged subjection of the individual to leader and group. And no, for he also depicts this subjection as a fundamentally oppressive exercise of power over difference.

If it is a mistake to try to pin down the politics of 'The Initiates' as fascist or anti-fascist, that is because the issue of Auden's seriousness is equally irresolvable. To see how 'The Initiates' employs a poetic of joking that exploits social and sexual difference, we must consider Auden's parable as itself a social act. 'Letter to a Wound' is the fictional epistle of a neurotic initiate, but it is also Auden's private joke. The wound in the letter is a psychic one, but once we know that Auden was treated for an anal fissure in 1930, certain passages take on a new meaning: 'Once, when a whore accosted me, I bowed, "I

---

[30] *EA* 69.   [31] Ibid. 71.   [32] Ibid. 73. See *Early Auden*, 101.

deeply regret it, Madam, but I have a friend." Once I carved on a seat in the park "We have sat here. You'd better not."[33] While Auden claimed the injury (also alluded to in the first of 'Six Odes') did not come from sexual activity, he called it in private the 'Stigmata of Sodom'.[34] A juvenile joke? Perhaps, but one can hardly re-read 'Letter to a Wound' without reflecting on it. If it is Auden diagnosing his homosexuality as neurotic self-infatuation, it also turns private knowledge into power over the unknowing reader. One recalls the epigraph to *The Orators*: 'Private faces in public places | Are wiser and nicer | Than public faces in private places.' 'The Initiates' opens with rhetoric which aims to control 'perverted lovers', who threaten social unity; 'Address for a Prize-Day' exemplifies public faces troubled by certain people's private places. Auden closes with a text that introjects a private face into a public book, and in doing so covertly, he exploits social differences among readers. Those in the know will read 'Letter to a Wound' differently from those who are not. So Auden's epigraph celebrates not only private social groups, but the signs by which gay people recognize each other in public—'Letter to a Wound' is, as it were, the written equivalent of the 'knowing gaze'.

What about the narrative of revolution in 'Argument' and 'Statement'? Much of Auden's early writing confronts us with a private landscape to which entrance is denied: 'Stranger, turn back again, frustrate and vexed: | This land, cut off, will not communicate.'[35] 'The Initiates' invites the reader into a private world where homosexual desire has political meanings, but Auden's avant-garde style keeps these meanings from becoming too obvious. His cryptic manner recalls 'Mortmere', the private fantasy world invented by Edward Upward and Christopher Isherwood in the 1920s. Taken as a parable about Auden and his friends, the failed revolution of 'The Initiates' implies, as John Boly argues, that the political pretensions of their writing are ineffective and immature.[36] Such homoerotic fantasies of revolt will hardly yield real change.

But the baroque obscurity of 'The Initiates' also suggests a different idea of socially oppositional writing. Twenty-five years after *The Orators*, Auden introduced John Ashbery's *Some Trees* (1956), observing:

From Rimbaud down to Mr. Ashbery, an important school of modern poets has been concerned with the discovery that, in childhood largely, in dreams

---

[33] *EA* 72.   [34] See *Early Auden*, 111.   [35] *EA* 22.
[36] Boly, 'W. H. Auden's *The Orators*', 256.

and daydreams entirely, the imaginative life of the human individual stubbornly continues to live by the old magical notions. Its world is one of sacred images and ritual acts . . . a numinous landscape inhabited by demons and strange beasts.[37]

The very childishness of the fantasy of revolt in 'The Initiates' cuts both ways. If Auden makes homoerotic leader-worship look immature, his writing itself belongs to that 'school of modern poets' like Rimbaud and Ashbery, whose work subverts normative 'adult' notions of reality and meaning. Indeed, the stylistic kinship of *Les Illuminations* and 'The Initiates' is apparent. Here is Rimbaud:

A swarm of gold leaves smothers the general's house.—You take the red road to reach the empty inn. The château's up for sale and the shutters are coming loose.—The priest must have taken away the key of the church. Around the park, the keepers' cottages are uninhabited. The fences are so high that you can only see the tree tops moving in the wind. Anyway, there's nothing to see there.[38]

Here is Auden:

The young mother in the red kerchief suckling her child in the doorway, and the dog fleaing itself in the hot dust. Clatter of nails on the inn's flagged floor. The hare-lipped girl sent with as far as the second turning. Talk of generals in a panelled room translated into a bayonet thrust at a sunbrowned throat, wounds among wheat fields.[39]

Both of these passages manipulate a tension between transparency of style and detail, on the one hand, and the lack of any obvious logical connection between details on the other. The weird portentousness of Auden's passage, so characteristic of his early poetry, comes from indeterminate significance in what is very precise imagery. Like much of Rimbaud's writing, the 'meaning' of Auden's passage cannot be conceptualized in terms of determinate reference and signification, so in applying these standards to *The Orators*, many early critics—predictably—found it obscure, confused, and immature.

The charge of 'immaturity' often serves as a code for 'homosexuality' among Auden's early critics, especially F. R. Leavis and Randall Jarrell. But it recalls Freud's connection between the techniques of jokes ('faulty thinking, displacements, absurdity, representation by

---

[37] Yale Series of Younger Poets 52 (New Haven, Conn., 1956), 13.
[38] 'Enfance' 2, *Complete Works, Selected Letters*, tr. Wallace Fowlie (Chicago, 1966), 217.
[39] *EA* 65.

opposite, etc.') and a child's linguistic play: '[H]e puts words together without regard to the condition that they make sense, in order to obtain from them the pleasurable effect of rhythm or rhyme . . . A private language may even be constructed for use among playmates.'[40] Like Mortmere, 'The Initiates' has the quality of a 'private language' whose jokes are missed by those who are not native speakers. It is joking at the expense of the 'public' reader, who is given a bizarre narrative in which tone and meaning are often impossible to pin down. In its frequent opacity, 'The Initiates' suggests that there are perspectives on and meanings within reality unavailable to understanding governed by public, adult norms. The ultimate point of 'The Initiates' is not whether it describes an assault against the ruling class for the sake of a particular cause—communist, fascist, or otherwise. The writing assaults our wish to understand—like homosexuality itself, it is a radical offence against sensibility and meaning.

III

If 'The Initiates' is partly a parable about the political pretensions of the Auden group, in 'Journal of an Airman' writing becomes Auden's chief concern; it is, after all, explicitly a written text, titled as such and given a fictional author. Indeed, I shall argue, the 'Journal' is a coded study of writing poetry, in which flying is a metaphor for the power in sexual deviance and in the social position of the homosexual poet. In the story of the Airman, Auden provides a biography of a homosexual poet and a theory of homosexual poetry, both its rhetorical (or anti-rhetorical) modes and its political aims. The 'Journal' is in fact a gloss to *The Orators* as a whole.

In his 1977 article on *The Orators*, Peter Firchow shows that Auden's Airman reflects John Layard's work on the Bwili, the sorcerers of Malekula, New Guinea.[41] A candidate is initiated in puberty by a Bwili who is his maternal uncle. The boy must be secluded from family and abstain from sex with women, but the climax of initiation is said to be his gradual dismemberment, during which he must continue to laugh as his limbs and head are cut off. If he keeps laughing,

---

[40] 'Jokes and Their Relation to the Unconscious' (1905), *SE*, vol. 8, 125.
[41] See above, n. 6. My reading of the 'Journal' is much indebted to Firchow's essay. See Layard, 'Malekula: Flying Tricksters, Ghosts, Gods, and Epileptics', and 'Shamanism: An Analysis Based on a Comparison with the Flying Tricksters of Malekula', *Journal of the Royal Anthropological Institute of Great Britain and Ireland*, 60.2 (July–Dec. 1930), 501–24, 525–50.

his body reassembles and he becomes a Bwili; if not, he dies.[42] Moreover, during initiation the boy is anally inseminated by ghosts. Having undergone ritual death and resurrection, Layard says, the Bwili 'has become one with the world of the resurrected dead,' with all the powers of a ghost when he is in his metamorphosed state.[43] He can take the form of a bird and fly, and he can also take the form of other animals, plants, and people. In disguise he often plays jokes on others (sometimes composing songs about his jokes), and while he cannot be killed when in disguise, he can kill others.[44] Layard also offers a psychological analysis of the Bwili by way of epilepsy: '[T]he purpose of epilepsy being to drown out one side—and that the adult side—of a conflict, the epileptic retains an infantile mentality, with the result that he is apt to be child-like in his tastes, irresponsible, roguish, and playful.'[45] Layard in turn connects epilepsy with homosexuality, another regressive disorder aimed at 'the suppression of the adult side of the conflict'.[46]

Like a Bwili, the Airman has been initiated (i.e. seduced?) by his maternal uncle, who he discovered at age sixteen was his 'real ancestor'.[47] Flying is Auden's modern version of the Bwili's ability to become a bird, and the Airman's poems recall an odd Bwili song Layard transcribes in his article. Like the Bwili, the Airman is involved with the dead—he worships his late Uncle Henry. Most importantly, the Airman is homosexual (he periodically refers to his lover, E)[48] and a practical joker. Joking is his main tactic in the war against the enemy.

The Airman analyses the enemy incessantly, but most importantly by means of discursive practices: 'Three terms of enemy speech—I mean—quite frankly—speaking as a scientist, etc.'; 'Three signs of an enemy letter—underlining—parentheses in brackets—careful obliteration of cancelled expressions.'[49] While clearly meant to be funny, such statements also define the enemy by his self-consciousness, his mental distance on what he says or writes. In the Airman's terms, the enemy suffers from 'self-regard', as opposed to 'self-care or minding one's own business'.[50] Enemy 'catchwords' are 'insure now—keep smiling—safety first',[51] for he minds other people's business, making

---

[42] Layard, 'Malekula', 507–8.   [43] Ibid. 523.   [44] Ibid. 509–10.
[45] Ibid. 520.   [46] Ibid. 524.   [47] *EA* 85.
[48] In the 1st edn. (1932) E is female, but in the 2nd (1934) and later editions, E is male. The only exception is a single pronoun Auden forgot to change in the 2nd edn.
[49] *EA* 81.   [50] Ibid. 73.   [51] Ibid. 82.

them self-conscious about their future, other people's reactions, and above all, their bodies. The enemy perpetuates alienation of mind from body: 'the enemy as philosopher' treats 'intellect–will–sensation as real and separate entities'.[52]

Since the enemy has elevated his private neuroses into a world-view, the Airman attacks by exposing the contingency of the enemy's ideas, revealing the enemy's truth as ideology:

The enemy's sense of humour—verbal symbolism. Private associations (rhyming slang), but note that he is serious, the associations are constant. He means what *he* says.

Practical jokes consist in upsetting these associations. They are in every sense contradictory and public, e.g. my bogus lecture to the London Truss Club.[53]

The enemy's central ideologies, the Airman implies, are sincerity and seriousness, but his verbal ticks ('I mean—quite frankly') belie his self-consciousness about them. His 'sense of humour' shows that he actually reasons through 'private associations', not logic. But the Airman's point is that the enemy *always* reasons this way: 'the associations are constant. He means what *he* says.' The Airman implies that the enemy takes his private associations to be reality, that 'truth' is just the collective agreement of those in charge. As Stan Smith puts it, 'Foremost among the Airman's subversive activities . . . is the undermining of language, particularly in those oral public forms that posit an audience of participating equals.'[54] The Airman's jokes flaunt *in*sincerity and *un*seriousness. They expose the enemy's 'truth' as collective agreement by revealing difference among those who seem equal and alike—'e.g. my bogus lecture to the London Truss Club'— an oration no more serious or sincere than Auden's 'Letter to a Wound'. This power to explain and subvert the enemy's cognitive processes is based upon the detachment and freedom from them symbolized by the Airman's flying. He has the 'hawk's view' of Auden's early work—the ability to see a culture from without. In this respect, his sexual deviance lends him a sense of privileged alienation from culture, something Auden himself must have felt. As we shall see, the Airman eventually realizes that his detachment is false—that he is infected by enemy thinking, just as the uprising of 'The Initiates' employed the rhetorical modes of those it fought. But we must first see how the Airman's joking is related to poetry and homosexuality.

[52] *EA* 76.   [53] Ibid. 78.   [54] Smith, 62.

While most of the Airman's journal is taken up with analysis of his own psyche and the enemy's, he also writes poems, which are all highly coded and might well be called jokes. The most revealing one is a sestina Auden later gave a title that is itself a sexual joke—'Have a Good Time':

> We have brought you, they said, a map of the country;
> Here is the line that runs to the vats,
> This patch of green on the left is the wood,
> We've pencilled an arrow to point out the bay.
> No thank you, no tea; why look at the clock.
> Keep it? Of course. It goes with our love.[55]

The poem allegorizes, as John Blair has said, the growth of the poet—a worker at the dyers' 'vats'. His elders tell him to 'wind up the clock' and to 'Keep fit by bathing in the bay,' but to avoid the 'flying trickster' in the wood. In fact, though, they are the enemy, for they treat 'intellect–will–sensation as real and separate entities'. The wood, Blair observes, signifies sensation, the bay a place to exercise the intellect, and the clock a device to assist the will.[56] Defying his elders, the young man gazes at the divers in the bay and enters the wood, where he 'Finds consummation . . . And sees for the first time the country', with 'water in the wood and trees by the bay'—he discovers that intellect, will, and sensation are interrelated.

But if we miss the suggestiveness of the poem's imagery we become the butt of the joke and end up among the enemy. The warning against the 'flying trickster', for example, recalls the antipathy of the Airman's mother toward his uncle, who was also a pilot. The 'consummation' the young man finds in the wood may be psychic, but it is expressed in obviously erotic terms, just as 'sensation' is depicted in the homoerotic sight of the distracting divers in the bay. So to read the poem only as an allegory of the poet's growth actually requires one to divorce intellect and will from sensation—thus contradicting the poem's allegorical point. It is another practical joke, in which the reader is forced into enemy thinking in order to decode the poem. The Airman's poem is another 'bogus lecture', subverting the enemy idea of truth transcending social differences among those who produce or consume signs. Such jokes are a favourite pastime of the Airman, and his 'Airman's Alphabet' extends this joking potential literally from A to Z:

---

[55] *EA* 77.   [56] *The Poetic Art of W. H. Auden* (Princeton, NJ, 1965), 80.

COCKPIT—   Soft seat
and support of soldier
and hold for hero. . . .
JOYSTICK—   Pivot of power
and responder to pressure
and grip for the glove.[57]

Like Auden's secret agent, the Airman is a figure for the homosexual poet, whose special insight into social and cognitive mechanisms of domination has subversive potential. This power is rooted, by implication, in the self-consciousness that comes with the closeted life in a homophobic culture. But looming here is a contradiction that undoes the Airman, for we have already seen how he idealizes *un*self-consciousness. It is the enemy, he says, who believes 'man's only glory is to think.'[58] 'THE ENEMY IS A LEARNED NOT A NAÏVE OBSERVER', he writes in the 'Journal', glossing 'Naïve observation' as 'insight' and 'Introspection' as 'spying'. The enemy embodies 'self-regard', not 'self-care', and his overweening intellect will pick out the oblique diagram in the Airman's '*Sure Test*', not the obvious, symmetrical ones.[59] In fact, the best word for the wrong diagram is Auden's code-word 'crooked', for the Airman's language in analysing the enemy mind implies that the enemy suffers from sick homosexual self-consciousness. Of course, all of the Airman's theories about the enemy point to his own reliance on thought, his own self-regard. Describing the aetiology of self-regard, he unwittingly recounts his own ancestry, which he later traces blithely to his maternal uncle: '*Note*—Self-regard . . . is a sex-linked disease. Man is the sufferer, woman the carrier. "What a wonderful woman she is!" Not so fast: wait till you see her son.'[60] This comment, of course, recalls the Freudian cliché that male homosexuality has something to do with mothers, just as the Airman's diagnosis of the enemy's 'self-regard' recalls the view of homosexuality as narcissism. The Airman has all the traits of the homophobe: his utter paranoia about the enemy—his belief that he can, as it were, tell one a mile away—invokes common notions about the identifiability of the pervert, whose depravity is 'written immodestly on his face and body'.[61]

[57] *EA* 79.   [58] Ibid. 78.   [59] Ibid. 74.   [60] Ibid. 73.
[61] Michel Foucault, *The History of Sexuality: An Introduction*, vol. 1, tr. Robert Hurley (New York, 1978), 43.

So if homosexuality is an empowering difference for the Airman, it also signifies the enemy's sickness. A corollary of this contradiction is that what produces the Airman's detachment also points to his complicity with the enemy, as seen in his problem with his hands: 'Only once here, quite at the beginning, and I put it back. Uncle Sam, is he one too? He has the same backward-bending thumb that I have.'[62] Here and elsewhere, it seems clear that the Airman suffers from kleptomania, but kleptomania seems itself a code. In a 1932 review, Auden refers to 'theft, that attempt to recover the lost or stolen treasure, love,'[63] an idea that fits nicely with the hints of masturbation in the Airman's self-recriminations. Moreover, the symptom the Airman sees in his Uncle Sam—that 'backward-bending thumb'—recalls Auden's trope of backwardness, which I have argued is a code for homosexuality. In fact, the passage glosses Auden's use of 'crooked' for 'homosexual'—a 'crook' is one who steals. The Airman steals, of course, in spite of himself—his hands will not follow orders. So the most important implication of his kleptomania is that he suffers from the enemy's splitting of 'intellect–will–sensation': he is at odds with his own desires.

The Airman's realization that the enemy has infected him comes when he suddenly understands his dream about E. In the dream, a river separates him from E, who is tied to a railroad tracks with the train on the way. But as the Airman shouts to the ferryman, his voice is drowned out by a crowd of football spectators behind him, and E killed. He then sees a newspaper photo of Uncle Henry, bordered in black, with the caption 'I have crossed it.'[64] In the dream, as John Boly says, the Airman's 'private self, which wants to save E, is repressed by . . . his public self, which heeds the roaring crowd.'[65] The dream allegorizes his refusal to admit his homosexuality publicly. But its very encoding as a dream points to the self-repression he ascribes to the enemy, who sets mind over body.

The Airman understands the dream only three days before he is due to attack the enemy:

Why, the words in my dream under Uncle's picture, 'I HAVE CROSSED IT'. To have been told the secret that will save everything and not to have listened . . .

1. The power of the enemy is a function of our resistance, therefore

2. The only efficient way to destroy it—self-destruction, the sacrifice of all resistance . . . .

---

[62] *EA* 79.   [63] *Early Auden*, 108.   [64] *EA* 85.
[65] Boly, 'W. H. Auden's *The Orators*', 253.

3. Conquest can only proceed by absorption of, i.e. infection by, the conquered. The true significance of my hands. 'Do not imagine that you, no more than any other conqueror, escape the mark of grossness.' They stole to force a hearing.[66]

His hands, that is, stole to express his own corruption: the harder he tried to control them, the more clearly he proved that his mind and body were not one. The only way to overcome this enemy-induced split, he reasons, is total self-abnegation. Until now, the Airman has rejected the verdict that his uncle's death was suicide. But his uncle's words in the dream—'I have crossed it'—suggest the verdict was right, that, as Edward Mendelson puts it, 'his uncle willingly crossed over the border that stood in the way of unity.'[67] The Airman puts his affairs in order, says goodbye to E, and flies off to die. His last words—'Hands in perfect order'—show his kleptomania cured.

But it is not clear how seriously to take the Airman's suicide. Does complicity with the enemy finally vitiate the Airman's agenda of subverting the enemy's single-mindedness and the ideology of univocality? And does his death mean that Auden rejects an oppositional homosexual poetic of joking? To be sure, the Airman's farewell to E suggests that homosexuality is the paradigmatic sign of infection with enemy self-consciousness, that it gives the lie to his ideal of organic self-integration. Since his desires are incurable, the only option is suicide. This is a disturbing reading, for it reaffirms the Prize-Day orator's view that death is the only cure for the pervert.[68]

In a sense, the Airman is killed by the enemy's ideology of sincerity, even though he knows it to be a lie. The enemy believes in univocality, that signifiers mean one thing, but the homosexual contradicts this proposition—that is what empowers the Airman. His jokes aim at exposing this lie, but he persists in an ideal of self-integration whose linguistic analogue is sincerity. Since he is caught in an irresolvable contradiction, sexual deviance mutates from a source of insight, into a sign of his own particular corruption—as if 'normal', socially condoned desire somehow meant *un*selfconsciousness, psychic unity, and sincerity. He thinks his uncle was cured by self-destruction, forgetting that his uncle was a trickster. 'I have crossed it' may mean that his uncle gave up resistance and crossed over to the enemy, but in the context

---

[66] *EA* 93.   [67] *Early Auden*, 109.

[68] Cf. the last part of 'It was Easter as I walked in the public gardens': 'We know it, we know that love | . . . Needs death, death of the grain, our death, | Death of the old gang' (*EA* 40).

of the dream, it can also mean that he crossed over his own river, as it were, and accepted his homosexuality. It never occurs to the Airman that his uncle's words might be duplicitious, and in the end, the Airman's abdication to the enemy, his fatal attempt at self-integration, is more duplicitous than he realizes. Complete self-abnegation would surely involve awaiting the enemy at home. Instead, in a gesture fairly easy to read in Freudian terms, he mans his plane and takes off—presumably to die rather explosively. We have already seen death serve as a trope for sexual initiation and consummation in 'The Initiates', leading to a kind of rebirth of the perverted lovers. The apparent death of the homosexual poet at the end of 'Journal' is too underdetermined for us to take at face value. It is, I suggest, another joke, with the Airman 'reborn' in Book III as a figure named 'W. H. Auden', who comes '[r]ound from the morphia' in the first ode.[69]

IV

After Books I and II, it is comforting to find in Book III poetry that declares a conventional generic allegiance. We know what to expect of 'Six Odes': that Auden will be addressing us *in propria persona*, seriously and directly on matters of personal or public import, for that is what odes do. Yet here more than anywhere in *The Orators*, the reader must consider how to 'take' these poems. Is Auden envisaging revolution at the end of the first ode? In the fifth ode, does he really hope that some day, 'All of the women and most of the men | Shall work with their hands and not think again'?[70] While the Airman's trouble with his hands makes it hard to take these lines seriously, much that we have seen makes 'yes' a plausible answer to both questions; *The Orators* is full of motifs of anti-bourgeois revolt, and the Airman is hardly a reassuring advocate for the life of the mind.

One way to exonerate Auden is to argue that he is not the speaker of the odes, that he stands apart laughing and expecting us to laugh.[71] Another way is to see them as simply reflecting Auden's political uncertainty.[72] But they are problematic only if we forget what *The Orators* has been suggesting thus far: that attempts to make words signify and refer univocally, free of contradiction, are really exertions of

[69] Ibid. 95.   [70] Ibid. 105.
[71] See Justin Replogle, *Auden's Poetry* (Seattle, 1969), 105–6; Joseph Warren Beach, *The Making of the Auden Canon* (Minneapolis, 1957), 84–92.
[72] See *Early Auden*, 111.

rhetorical power, and that such attempts always leave room for contradictions to undo them. The Airman uses this realization in his practical jokes, only to forget it in trying to save his identity from self-contradiction.

As something of an authorial stand-in, the Airman struggles with two opposed impulses in Auden's work: one towards resolving contradiction and the other towards accentuating it. The Airman 'dies', but 'Auden' is, as it were, reborn in Book III as a different poet with a different response to these problems. In naming his poems generically—'Six Odes'—Auden suggests a self-consciousness about form and convention his previous work has not implied. While these are not odes *on* anything very precise, the middle four are odes *to* various people: Gabriel Carritt, Edward Upward, John Warner, and Auden's pupils. Since such people would be unknown to the general reader, the odes ask to be read not as statements on certain personal issues but as public performances. They echo themes taken up already— groups, leadership, political change. But the questions the odes invite are not whether they are serious or sincere or persuasive, for they hardly resolve any of the issues *The Orators* has raised. Instead, we should ask whether they are capable, entertaining, moving, and so on. They invite judgement by aesthetic, not ideological criteria, for even as they heighten contradictions of meaning, they flaunt their formal and stylistic artifice. The 'Six Odes', in other words, show Auden moving from the homosexual poet as flying trickster, who exploits the public/private dichotomy for power over the reader, into a mode long favoured by gay writers—camp.

'Camp', Susan Sontag famously wrote, 'is esoteric—something of a private code, a badge of identity even, among small urban cliques.'[73] This is an appropriate place to begin, since so much of *The Orators* employs private codes. 'Letter to a Wound' relies, as we have seen, on a private joke, which resurfaces in the first ode, and 'Address for a Prize-Day' parodies the style of the headmaster at St Edmund's School. In one of his oddest poems, 'To return to the interest we were discussing,' the Airman tells an obscure 'fairy story' about 'a family called Do,' based on a vacation Auden spent with the family of his friend Gabriel Carritt.[74] But Auden overtly betrays his cliquishness in the odes in a way he does not elsewhere, precisely because he is 'speaking as himself' in poems with personal dedications.

[73] 'Notes on "Camp"', in *Against Interpretation* (New York, 1966), 275.
[74] See Carpenter, 125.

Exploring the private references, however, hardly elucidates the odes. The first one, 'Watching in three planes from a room', finds Auden dreaming in the recovery room after his operation. Various people wander in and out of the poem speaking ominously: 'The night-nurse', 'the Headmaster', and two friends. 'Stephen signalled from the sand dunes like a wooden madman | "Destroy this temple." ' In the next stanza his words come true—'It did fall'—but 'It' is never identified. Then,

> [I]n cold Europe, in the middle of Autumn destruction,
> Christopher stood, his face grown lined with wincing
> In front of ignorance—'Tell the English', he shivered,
>   'Man is a spirit'.[75]

Auden's tone here—and that of his friends—is so indecipherable that we cannot tell whether something profound is being conveyed or something trivial posing as profundity. As two recent critics have observed, the ode 'makes play of its cliquishness' by utterly indulging what the Airman calls 'self-regard'.[76] In a 'serious' reading, '"Tell the English . . . Man is a Spirit"' would imply the self-regard of Auden and his friends. But if one reads the ode this way, the grandeur of its ending is ludicrous:

> 'Have you heard of someone swifter than Syrian horses?
> Has he thrown the bully of Corinth in the sanded circle?
> Has he crossed the Isthmus already? Is he seeking brilliant
>   Athens and us?'[77]

To ask whether these lines herald a social saviour or demon misses their absurdity in context. We can read them seriously only if we take seriously the rhetoric of Stephen and Christopher, or see their 'self-regard' as warranting so mythic a saviour. The ode's tonal ambiguity makes more sense in light of the comment of a recent critic that camp rests on irony, 'incongruous contrast[s] between an individual or thing and its context or association.'[78] We see such incongruities in Auden's mixture of lofty and low subject-matter and diction that we cannot be sure whether private worries are being raised to the level of the public, or the public reduced to the silliness of the private.

---

[75] *EA* 95.

[76] Michael O'Neill and Gareth Reeves, *Auden, MacNeice, Spender: The Thirties Poetry* (London, 1992), 103.   [77] *EA* 96.

[78] Jack Babuscio, 'Camp and the Gay Sensibility', in *Gays and Film*, ed. Richard Dyer (New York, 1984), 41.

In each of the next five odes, the seriousness of the issues raised is compromised by incongruities of tone and diction, or an incommensurateness of form and content. In the sixth ode—'Not, Father, further do prolong'—Auden's fun in parodying the convoluted inversions of hymn syntax is quite at odds with the ode's message—a plea for clarifying deliverance by a deity who can 'with ray disarm, | Illumine, and not kill'.[79] Even as every 'maddened set we foot' ostensibly bespeaks moral sickness, Auden is showing off his metrical virtuosity. Just as the drag queen dons gender codes in order to subvert them, this poem's formal garb of supplication, so carefully but ludicrously arranged, undermines the association of homosexuality with passivity and weakness. These are all ideologies that *The Orators* has engaged with already (more or less seriously), but here they are embraced and defanged in camp. Similarly, the rhapsodic worship of power and the male body in the second ode and the longing for a leader in the fourth are indulged and satirized by addressing such impulses to harmless objects—a rugby team and a baby. Both the Sedbergh School XV and the infant John Warner embody union of mind and body, and what the Airman calls 'self-care'. But their elevation to heroic stature in such ostentatious style hardly advances serious political or psychological analysis.

V

Like his joking throughout *The Orators*, Auden's campy odes suggest that he is concerned with the relation of homosexuality to masculinity as much as with its political implications. In his 1929 journal Auden commented, 'All buggers . . . suffer under the reproach, real or imaginary[,] of "Call yourself a man." '[80] It is hard not to feel that 'The Initiates' is satirizing Auden's own political pretensions as dubious efforts to prove his manhood. Likewise, the Airman's fight against the enemy and his own hands only reaffirms his own lack of masculine strength. Every gesture, *The Orators* suggests, to prove one's manhood—to 'Call yourself a man'—is only another form of lying rhetoric proving just the opposite. But while *The Orators* supports such a reading, the Airman's jokes and Auden's writing, by corroding sincerity and integrity, also mock manhood and maturity, and the rhetorical invocation of these values for purposes of power. So at the same time,

---

[79] *EA* 110.   [80] Quoted in *Early Auden*, 59.

Auden links sexual deviance with antithetical values of play, insincerity, and childishness.

Moreover, *The Orators* suggests that such values can open up a different kind of world, one that, in Stephen Spender's words, 'we can only enter if we are prepared to accept it whilst we are reading about it.'[81] Spender's words recall the program of a poet whom I have mentioned already—Rimbaud, whose 'Adieu', in fact, is one text behind the Airman's 'death'.[82] If the poetry of *Les Illuminations* was a kind of linguistic alchemy, its potential for Rimbaud was, as one critic has argued, akin to that of sexual deviance. 'Homosexuality . . . in the program of Verlaine and Rimbaud, is one of a number of *disorderings of the senses* which free us from our everyday perceptions of the world.'[83] The more contradictory and strange passages in *The Orators* are also, I suggest, attempts at cognitive disruption. They are incoherent by conventional literary criteria, and they frustrate referential interpretation. In such passages we see Auden doing most openly what *The Orators* really does all the time, which is to give a view into a world perceived through the lens of sexual deviance. But even more challengingly, *The Orators* suggests that this other world intersects the familiar one of newspaper political rhetoric and school games, and it asks us to see within our 'real' world a queer other world that so contradicts an 'adult' sense of reality.

The Orators does not, finally, offer unequivocal statements about leadership or groups or political change, for Auden's model of the homosexual poet makes such pronouncements indefensible. This model follows from the intricate contradictions surrounding same-sex desire in this book, contradictions that undermine any pretence to cognitive and social detachment. It is society's orators—its 'real men'—who try to speak unequivocally, but in doing so they can only lie. *The Orators* suggests that the homosexual can know this truth, but only at the cost of admitting that it brings freedom in the recognition of complicity. These are solemn words perhaps at odds with Auden's spirit of fun in *The Orators*, for the recognition of contradiction is very much a source of play in this book. Even so, the political efficacy of such an aesthetic does seem questioned at the end of *The Orators*.

---

[81] 'Five Notes on W. H. Auden's Writing', *Twentieth Century*, 3 (July 1932), repr. in Haffenden, 102.

[82] *Early Auden*, 110.

[83] Paul Schmidt, 'Visions of Violence: Rimbaud and Verlaine', in *Homosexualities and French Literature*, eds. George Stambolian and Elaine Marks (Ithaca, NY, 1979), 235.

' "O where are you going?" ' the 'reader' asks, and the 'rider' (writer) answers, ' "Out of this house" '[84]—by which one might read, 'Out of this book'. In view of Auden's subsequent turn to more conventional style and form, it is hard not to see the 'Epilogue' as prophetic. Joking can seem a feeble weapon when 'maps can really point to places | Where life is evil now.'[85]

[84] *EA* 110.   [85] Ibid. 257.

'Everything Turns Away': Auden's Surrealism

DAVID PASCOE

IN August 1938, soon after returning from the Far East, Auden wrote from Brussels to tell Mrs Dodds of his experiences at the city's Palais des Beaux Arts. In the gallery, he explained, he was 'trying to appreciate Rubens. The daring and vitality take one's breath away, but what is it all ABOUT?'[1] Standing before the baroque images, he was claiming bewilderment; yet this is disingenuous about his critical aptitude, for Auden was not always so mystified by painters. In conversation some years later, he would offer throwaway comments on the history of art which are indispensable: 'it's impossible to represent Christ in art. We've got used to the Old Masters because they're formal, but in their day those pictures must have seemed outrageous';[2] and, in 1960, he felt expert enough to review *From Rococo to Cubism in Art and Literature*.[3] It is untrue that Auden 'cared little about the visual arts',[4] and 'Letter to Lord Byron' offered an opportunity to declare painterly allegiances:

> To me Art's subject is the human clay,
> And landscape but a background to a torso;
> All Cézanne's apples I would give away
> For one small Goya or a Daumier.[5]

Auden is suggesting that subject should be held in greater esteem than technique; but then, he always expected worldly information rather than abstraction: 'the first thing of importance is subject, and just as I would look at a painting of the Crucifixion before a painting of a still-life . . . so in literature I expect plenty of news.'[6] The dislike

---

[1] TLS to A. E. Dodds, 31 Aug. 1938 (Bodleian, MS Eng. lett. c. 464, fo. 21).

[2] Ansen, 70.

[3] 'The Problem of Nowness', *Mid-Century*, 18 (Nov. 1960), 14–20.

[4] *Early Auden*, 208.

[5] *EA* 185. Cf. the revelation made to Erika Mann from Iceland: 'borrowed two volumes of caricatures . . . and spent a very happy evening with Goya and Daumier and Max Beerbohm', *LFI* 123.

[6] *EA* 357.

of *nature morte*, his sense that it lacked subject, explains his hostility to 'Cézanne's apples'. Yet what he saw as indulgence was not always the fault of artist alone; hunger and greed drove many to distraction:

> The common clay and the uncommon nobs
> Were far too busy making piles or starving
> To look at pictures, poetry or carving.[7]

Goya, for instance, held Auden's attention in 1932, when, considering various foes, the Communist hopes that 'Cramp rack their limbs till they resemble | Cartoons by Goya':[8] graphic representations of the pain of 'making piles or starving'. Nor was Auden the only figure at the time to be affected by the work of Daumier, whose unflattering depictions of bourgeois life had brought praise from the Left. Blunt wrote that 'The line of Daumier, Courbet, the early Van Gogh, Meunier and Dalan is that of the real art of the growing proletariat, while that of the bourgeoisie continues towards the abstraction of the twentieth century'.[9] This was a standard distinction, often used to criticize Clive Bell's influential theories, which maintained that, on the basis of personal experience, one could suspend narrative, representational, or symbolic features and, instead, pursue the common characteristic in all objects of visual art: the stimulation of aesthetic emotions towards 'lines and colours combined in a particular way, certain forms and relations of forms'.[10] Many contributors to the debate about modern art, and, in particular, to the question of its potential for instigating social change, had been educated during the 1920s in Bell's liberal bourgeois culture; and, as a result, they had been made to reconsider their own aesthetics in the light of Communism:

As Marx and Engels replaced Fry and Bell on their bookshelves, many of those whose sense of the history of art had been governed by the criterion of 'significant form' now reconstructed that history in terms of a series of 'progressive' endeavours. Courbet replaced Cézanne as the typical heroic forebear of the modern artist, at least in the eyes of the avant-garde critics.[11]

In his appreciation of graphic art, Auden was, above all, a 'progressive' realist. He wrote a verse letter to William Coldstream, whom he had met at the GPO Film Unit, and recalled the time they discussed

[7] *EA* 187.   [8] Ibid. 123.
[9] Anthony Blunt, 'The "Realism" Quarrel', *Left Review*, 3.3 (Apr. 1937), 169.
[10] Clive Bell, *Art* (London, 1914), 209.
[11] Charles Harrison, *English Art and Modernism* (London, 1981), 307.

art over coffee 'Upstairs in the Corner House': 'And before the band had finished a potpourri from Wagner | We'd scrapped Significant Form, and voted for Subject'. According to Auden, Coldstream defined an artist as

> both perceiver and teller, the spy and the gossip
> Something between the slavey in Daumier's caricature
> The one called *Nadadada*.
> And the wife of a minor canon.[12]

But his terms are Audenesque: that precisely nineteenth-century colloquialism 'slavey'; and the idea of 'the spy and the gossip', encapsulated in the bizarre and acute social observation typical of the early poems. In fact, Coldstream frequently championed another nineteenth-century French artist, Degas, whose genius in depicting novel subject-matter lay, Coldstream believed, in creating the illusion of spontaneity; but it was an immediacy fabricated by means of painstaking research and careful execution. Coldstream told a friend in March 1933:

After Degas the camera. It must have been the great stimulus of Degas to have looked at Nature with as unbiased an eye as possible. If we are quite honest can't we say that these shapes, so strange and unexpected, which we find in Degas' paintings, the wide foregrounds, the cigar in the hand more important than the face, the light on the tumbler more geometric than the walls caught unawares, can't find these qualities in any snapshot?[13]

And, in September 1936, he wrote again: 'I've got a craze for doing heads and faces—it's the result of having had to take a job I'm sure—any way I count it the reward of virtue to be able to want to paint people'.[14] His stint working alongside Auden at the Film Unit had made him aware of the importance of subject; yet, transferred to the idiom of his own work, it was not a question of the merely routine transference of information from the real world onto the canvas. Coldstream had to assure himself of the accuracy of his own perception of certain human dimensions; yet, equally pressing was the need to demonstrate that certain fixed points in a composition had pre-existed in other painters.

Take the portrait of Auden that Coldstream painted on a visit to

[12] *LFI* 223.
[13] Quoted in Bruce Laughton, *The Euston Road School* (Aldershot, 1986), 110.
[14] Ibid. 118.

the Downs School in June 1937.[15] The subject sits reading in Maurice Feild's house, his head gently supported by the right hand as he gazes intently towards the desktop. The face is delicately painted, its dimensions precise and humane; yet it seems precariously perched on an oddly two-dimensional body, whose physiological shape is concealed beneath a sack-like jacket. It may be that the pose alludes to Courbet's famous depiction of Baudelaire in *L'Atélier du peintre* (1855); but in the strange prominence of the hand, the composition is closer to Ingres.[16] Further, the relation of the figure to the curve of the table-top may allude to 'Degas's way of treating space when he was seated close to the model';[17] hence, space is suggested (rather than depicted) by placing figures off-centre and objects in the foreground, a juxtaposition which creates fluid perspective. Having experienced Coldstream's careful composition—his punctiliousness over artistic antecedents—Auden, in verse greetings written in Brussels during December 1938, hoped that 'Bill . . . might learn to paint faster'.[18]

Among literary critics at the time, Geoffrey Grigson was the most comfortable with the visual arts, and so, in the autumn of 1938, he passed judgement on what he felt to be Auden's wayward championing of Coldstream's work. 'This plumping for subject in art is all very well; art can do again with subject' he wrote, but,

Subject in the art of William Coldstream and Graham Bell and others would be easier to stomach and commend if the art were more pronounced. It would be better if we could be sure that they had come to subject by way of painting, by seeing and formalising and not by the convenient short-cut of thinking about Degas and having talks with Mr Auden.

Grigson then shifts tack, and gathers momentum:

Mr Coldstream may be cute, he may be intelligent, he may talk very well; but cuteness, intellect and talk are no substitutes for eyes, and from what I have seen of it, I believe that Mr Coldstream's painting is a blind man's painting—clever, correct, well-informed, academic and frozen. In other words, it is a mixed mannerism by the everlasting student.

---

[15] The portrait was begun on 17 June 1937, and is now held at HRC. Also present during the weekend were Hedli Anderson and Benjamin Britten, who were working on the blues music for *The Ascent of F6*. See Humphrey Carpenter, *Benjamin Britten: A Biography* (London, 1992), 106.

[16] On this topic, see Norman Bryson, *Tradition and Desire from David to Delacroix* (Cambridge, 1984), 157–75.

[17] Laughton, *Euston Road School*, 121.   [18] Quoted in Carpenter, 248.

Coldstream's allusiveness, designed to bolster the objectivity of his work by shaping its subject, is derided. Turning his attention to Auden, Grigson notes, personally, that the poet is 'short-sighted', but adds that 'eyes seem to matter less in this business than ideas'. He suggests that Auden 'compare himself, painted by Coldstream to Johnson painted by Reynolds' and continues:

He may like his Daumiers and his Goyas—so do Picasso and Henry Moore—but he might ask himself a question. Realising that he has many of the most sensitive and visually expert persons in England against him in this business, he might ask how much he knows and feels for (i) Mantegna (ii) Uccello (iii) Poussin (iv) Rembrandt (v) Delacroix (vi) Constable (vii) Seurat (viii) Picasso. If his answer is unsatisfactory, let him send up the maroons and spend two minutes' reflective and silent humility, and then ask another question: *Shall I give tongue to my inexperience and commit myself to what may be bad, or, my position and influence being what they are, content myself with my own opinion and admire in silence?*[19]

Grigson, accentuating his own greater expertise, suggests that Auden's criticism of art is at best misinformed and at worst senseless; and given Auden's position as a cultural commentator—a special issue of *New Verse* had been dedicated to him in 1937, the same year in which he received the King's Gold Medal for Poetry—his dabbling amounted, in Grigson's view, to dangerous opinion-forming.

Clearly Grigson did not realize that championing Coldstream was part of a larger conflict in Auden's mind between the claims of Realism and Surrealism; a conflict which had, for several years, been taking place in various areas of contemporary European culture. In June 1936 Auden and MacNeice travelled to Iceland and remained there until 10 September. During this period, Byron was informed about the mechanics of reputation:

> Because there's snobbery in every age,
>> Because some names are loved by the superior,
>> It does not follow they're the least inferior:
> For all I know the Beatific Vision's
> On view at all Surrealist Exhibitions.[20]

That 'For all I know' may be an honest admission of bafflement in the face of discussions of the spirituality of modern art; but it also

---

[19] Geoffrey Grigson, 'Remarks on Painting and Mr Auden', *New Verse*, NS 1.1 (Jan. 1939), 17–19.
[20] *EA* 178.

announces Auden's absence from the artistic event of 1936, the International Surrealist Exhibition held at the New Burlington Galleries from 11 June to 4 July. The show caused a sensation on the opening day and some of the more inane of the 400 exhibits became justly famous.[21] A painting of a woman, decorated with an imitation bird attached to her forehead by a piece of sponge, was smuggled in and hung for a short time, the perpetrator of this *objet d'art* calling himself D. S. Windle. At the other extreme, Joan Miró's assemblage *Poetic Object* (in which a stuffed parrot sat atop a bowler hat, on the brim of which perched a dead fish) caused something of a stink. Because of its unpleasant odour, the bloater was removed by Paul Nash, and eventually replaced with a celluloid one.[22]

From Iceland, MacNeice's Hetty writes to Nancy to inform her that she woke at 6.30 with a 'dream couplet' running in her head: 'I wonder would the Surrealists pay me anything for that?'[23] and in their mischievous 'Last Will and Testament', Auden and MacNeice declared: 'the Surrealists shall have | J. A. Smith as an Objet Trouvé in disguise'.[24] Janet Adam Smith, assistant editor of *The Listener* until her marriage to Michael Roberts in 1935, was a great champion of the Audenesque in the magazine's pages; and, as such, her status as a found object would have been ambiguous to the unwitting experimentalist.[25] Auden himself became an *objet trouvé*, when the London Gallery's show of Surrealist Objects, which began at midnight on 25 November 1937, presented him in the spirit of the movement. The exhibit was described as 'a glass witch ball' on to which were stuck moustaches of different colours. 'There was a paper frill on top encircling a trotter which held a cigarette between its nails. It was labelled with a newspaper cutting: "Auden receives royal medal"'.[26] This jibed at what was seen as Auden's pig-headed acceptance of the King's Gold Medal and, perhaps, at his fondness for disguising himself with false beards.

[21] On the impact of the exhibition, see Alan Young, *Dada and After* (Manchester, 1981), 170–87.

[22] See Julian Symons, *The Thirties: A Dream Revolved* (London, 1975), 85–91.

[23] *LFI* 177.   [24] Ibid. 243.

[25] In 1935 Smith edited *Poems of Tomorrow*, a selection of verse from *The Listener* which included 'The Witnesses' and 'A Bride in the 30s'. It may also be possible that Auden had seen, or heard of, Smith's suspicious review of David Gascoyne's *Man's Life is This Meat* in which she observed that 'Often his nouns and adjectives pair off as comfortably as in the most conservative verse', 'Books of the Quarter', *The Criterion*, 15 (July 1936), 730–4.

[26] Geoffrey Grigson, untitled notice in *New Verse*, 28 (Jan. 1938), 14.

Such collage was crucial to Surrealist art, displacing one realm of convention to arrive at another, more specific, understanding. The movement aimed to discredit the conventionality of the Thirties by attacking the object, the basic ineluctable component of that reality; indeed, its *raison d'être*. The easiest step in this offensive was to remove the object from its habitual surroundings; more difficult was to alter the angle from which it was customarily perceived. In 1932 Louis Aragon announced the morals of collage and argued that scissors and paper formed the only palette that did not return the artist to school.[27] David Gascoyne, who wrote the first full-length account of the movement for an English audience, averred: 'All that is needed to produce a Surrealist picture is an unshackled imagination and a few materials: paper or cardboard, pencil, scissors, paste, and an illustrated magazine, a catalogue or newspaper. The marvellous is within everyone's reach.'[28] Hence, the object became simply a given; not even a commodity of social circulation, but rather the thing of unforeseeable and continuing poetic adventure, yet 'within everyone's reach'. At the London Exhibition, a woman wandered through the gallery dressed in a white gown, her face enclosed in a veil of roses. This 'Surrealist Phantom' wore long black gloves and, in one hand, carried a model human leg covered with roses; in the other, a raw pork chop was held. Unfortunately, the show took place during a heat wave and the woman, Sheila Legg (hence the leg?), soon had to abandon the meat.

Yet the arbitrariness displayed here—so beloved of Surrealists—was not a chance occurrence; instead it had been routinely instigated as an aspect of a technical strategy. Surrealism demanded the surrender of exteriority, that image of an independent, objective, universal nature which meant to provide art with its materials and rules. Simultaneously, however, the veneration of the accidental also announced the need to regard some aspects of private and public life as subject to control, planning, and design, though only in the interests of oppression. Therefore, when Auden talked of the 'surrealist police', that 'two-edged'[29] phrase hinted both at the terrors and the fabrications of totalitarianism. In the London Exhibition's catalogue, Herbert Read wrote: 'Because our art and literature is the most

[27] Louis Aragon, 'La peinture au défi', in *Écrits sur l'art moderne*, ed. J. Ristat (Paris, 1981), 43–4.
[28] David Gascoyne, *A Short Survey of Surrealism* (London, 1935), 106.
[29] *Early Auden*, 208.

romantic in the world, it is likely to become the most superrealistic.'[30]
Auden, who had slated Read's defence of Shelley earlier in the year,
could not agree with this claim.[31] His parable, 'The Sportsmen',
printed in *New Verse* in September 1938, depicted modern society as
an increasingly wooded country in which the sportsman (the artist)
has been required to scrap his favoured pastime, duck-shooting, (basic
art-forms which satisfied early modern society), and instead adopt
more urbane sports (the modern art of recent times) until the prolif-
eration of trees renders this impossible. However, in 'a far country
[Europe] where the inhabitants had cleared the land of timber . . . the
duck had once more become plentiful and shooting parties were again
in fashion'. Efforts to emulate this example by cutting down the trees
are prevented by vested interests, and so the sportsmen fabricate fake
birds with which they attempt to dupe the locals: 'Some of the
younger villagers who had never seen a duck except in a museum
were impressed, and praised the sportsmen for their skill'. The 'older
and wiser', however, are not fooled and observe: ' "These are not
duck; they are only clay and old newspapers" '.[32] The creation of such
objets d'art from 'old newspapers', which contain reported rather than
experienced events, implies that the parable is directed at the intellectual duplicity of the Surrealistic genius in Europe in the thirties: a
genius which venerated the haphazardness of collage, and whose subject was never genuine, always vicarious.

During the decade, Auden, too, was often described as a quasi-
Surrealist. Empson perceived a particular style working through *Paid
on Both Sides*: 'when John has just ordered the spy to be shot, a sort
of surrealist technique is used to convey his motives'. The play, he
concluded, 'puts psychoanalysis and surrealism' into 'their proper
place'.[33] An anonymous reviewer in 1932 described Auden's ' "surréaliste satire" ' as a 'mere dribble of disconnexions';[34] while for
Malcolm Cowley, 'some pages of Auden . . . have the irresponsible
savagery of the Dada manifesto'.[35] Hugh Porteus, too, felt that 'a
modified surréaliste technique, even though it is employed in a comic

[30] Cited in Symons, *Thirties*, 85.

[31] 'Psychology and Criticism', *New Verse*, 20 (Apr.–May 1936), 22–4.

[32] *EA* 370.

[33] William Empson, 'A Note on W. H. Auden's *Paid on Both Sides*', *Experiment*, 7
(Spring 1931), 60–1.

[34] Anon., '*The Orators*', *Times Literary Supplement*, (6 June 1932), 424.

[35] Malcolm Cowley, rev. of Auden, *Poems* (New York, 1934) in *New Republic*, 80 (26
Sept. 1934), 189–90.

capacity, seems to me to spoil huge chunks of his major works';[36] and Prokosch blamed Auden's memory for sometimes giving 'a surrealist sheen to his poetry'.[37] Hence, in discussions of *The Ascent of F6*, it became commonplace to report the 'surrealist presentation of Ransom's hysteria under the stress of approaching the summit'.[38] More recently, it has been argued that Auden 'availed himself of certain surrealist devices in order to make his didactic points', his favourite trick being 'the catalogue of objects that have no rational connection with each other'; a trick whose purpose was to imply that 'a dream-logic holds these objects together in the bourgeois unconscious, and that therefore they possess a significance denied to rational products'. So, for Paul Ray, in 'Casino', the comparison of 'the casino hall absorbing the gambler's prayers to the night taking up the cravings of lions in dens, is one, I submit, that he learned from the Surrealists.'[39]

Auden claimed that his only knowledge of Surrealism derived from 'Mr Gascoyne's books, a few French writers like Breton and Aragon, some paintings of Dali, Ernst, and others, and from the pages of the *Minotaur* [sic]. I have never met a surrealist.'[40] His knowledge was vicarious; indeed, he wanted it to remain so. In late 1936 he expressed misgivings about the imminent trip to Spain: 'I do hope that there are not too many surrealists there'.[41] This was only half joking; for such people were not simply to be avoided, but to be bested. He considered their goals to be at once trivial and totalitarian; ignorant and knowing; and, as such, products of a cynical duplicity. Before leaving for Iceland, Auden wrote (under the pseudonym of 'J.B.') a piece entitled 'Honest Doubt' for Grigson's journal, and in it asked some 'aesthetic and political' questions of the Surrealists. He was interested in receiving answers to an awkward political question: if the movement rejected the use of reason and the conscious faculties through all stages of creativity, how was this veto to be reconciled with the position of importance accorded to both by Communism and psychoanalysis, 'both of which are profoundly rational, believing,

[36] H. G. Porteus, 'W. H. Auden', *Twentieth Century*, 4 (Feb. 1933), 14–16.

[37] F. Prokosch, contribution to 'Twelve Comments on Auden', *New Verse*, 26–7, (Nov. 1937), 24.

[38] A. R. Humphreys, '*The Ascent of F6*', *Cambridge Review*, 58 (30 Apr. 1937), 353–7.

[39] Paul C. Ray, *The Surrealist Movement in Britain* (Ithaca, NY, 1971), 272–5.

[40] J. B., 'Honest Doubt', *New Verse*, 21 (June–July 1936), 14–16.

[41] ALS to A. E. Dodds [8 Dec. 1936], (Bodleian, MS Eng. Lett. c. 464, fo. 10).

certainly, in unconscious forces, economic or instinctive, as the driving forces in life, but also in the necessity for their conscious recognition and rational understanding and guidance?'[42] In challenging the Surrealists' declaration that their arbitrary actions were revolutionary, Auden was implying that conscious analysis and wilful responsibility were required by any revolutionary art.

Such questions he termed 'political'. Under the heading 'aesthetic', Auden asked: 'is genuine surrealist writing always and absolutely automatic, and never consciously worked over?' and, in addition, 'at what point does it cease to be surrealist?' He had always been concerned about the willed nature of *objets d'art* which claimed to be spontaneous and so saw an irony in the Surrealists' emphasis on the *orderly* disordering of the senses. In 1935 he noted that 'Even the most surrealistic writing or Mr James Joyce's latest prose shows every sign of being non-automatic and extremely carefully worked over'.[43] Certainly, in *Finnegans Wake* and other examples of 'night' writing, it is significant that the unconscious took care to compose itself in recognizable syntactical units. Even the Surrealists grew aware of the difficulty in gauging the extent of conscious intervention in supposedly unconscious performances, and automatic writing became less common as the decade continued. Following up his original 'aesthetic' question, Auden sought to know how Surrealists distinguished 'more from less valuable activity'. In other words, could the difference be told between a patent absurdity and a profound one? As instances of profundity, Auden cited 'the best kind of surrealist writing': 'Lewis Carrol [*sic*], Edward Lear, and Rimbaud in *Les Illuminations* . . . highly repressed individuals in a society with very strong taboos.' In a relatively self-aware and liberated community, however, a 'lack of pressure' would 'leave you material without form';[44] for Auden, 'material without form' might have served as a working definition of most Surreal art in the Thirties, and one which reached its embodiment in Dali's rescue from the diving-suit he had decided to wear to lecture at the London Surrealist Exhibition of 1936.[45]

Auden stayed in Brussels until the end of September 1938, working on the sonnet sequence, *In Time of War*, and then spent the autumn in England, lecturing on his experiences in China and assisting in the production of *On The Frontier* which opened in November. He returned to the Continent in early December, lecturing in Paris and

[42] 'Honest Doubt', 16.   [43] *EA* 337.   [44] 'Honest Doubt', 15.
[45] See the account in Symons, *Thirties*, 86.

meeting David Gascoyne, who described Auden as 'disguising only with a difficultly acquired social manner the petulance and embarrassment of an adolescent'.[46] By the middle of the month, he was staying with Isherwood at 70 Square Marie Louise, in a flat overlooking an ornamental lake adorned with real ducks: 'a very nice Ibsen set'. The two friends were finishing work on *Journey to A War* which would be published in the spring; but Auden wrote on 15 December: 'I have upset my tummy somehow and sit gloomily in the window, imagining that the house is being watched. I hope the muses are going to be kind and visit me.'[47] They did. Within days Auden began an astonishing group of poems which responded to the meditations on artistic responsibilities that had been taking place in his work over the previous two years. The poems, most of which were first published in *New Writing* in spring 1939, were 'The Capital', 'Brussels In Winter', 'Gare Du Midi', 'Palais des Beaux Arts', 'A. E. Housman', 'The Novelist', and 'The Composer'.[48] Most significantly, he also wrote about Lear and Rimbaud.

The poem on Lear, which may have originated as the by-product of a review Auden wrote for a Birmingham journal in October 1938, shows how 'a dirty landscape-painter who hated his nose' eventually 'became a land',[49] where the verb connotes both the development, and the suitability, of an Audenesque hero.[50] Rimbaud was a model too; yet in his vaunting poetry as a 'dérèglement des tous les sens', (which Auden rendered as 'senses systematically deranged',[51]) he also provided the Surrealists with a hero: a figure who renounced the world of art and sought direct action. Auden always held Rimbaud in high esteem; but for different, more personal, reasons. In 1940 he figured him as 'the adolescent with red hands, | Skilful, intolerant and quick, | Who strangled an old rhetoric';[52] and who helped to free truth from its entrapment in art by carrying the experience of poetry

---

[46] David Gascoyne, *Collected Journals, 1936–1942* (London, 1991), 229.

[47] TLS to A. E. Dodds, 15 Dec. 1938 (Bodleian, MS Eng. Lett. c. 464, fo. 25).

[48] Along with 'Rimbaud', these constituted the 'Eight Poems' that were published in *New Writing*, 2 (Spring 1939), 1–6. 'Palais des Beaux Arts' was retitled 'Musée des Beaux Arts' for *Another Time* (1940).

[49] *EA* 239.

[50] A review of the *Collected Verse of Lewis Carroll* and *The Lear Omnibus* appeared as 'Nonsense Poetry' in *The Town Crier*, NS 995 (28 Oct. 1938), 2. Fuller has shown the extent of Auden's debt in this poem to Angus Davidson's biography *Edward Lear* (Harmondsworth, 1938). See John Fuller, *A Reader's Guide to W. H. Auden* (London, 1970), 123.

[51] *EA* 237.   [52] *NYL* 23.

into real life. This murderer was driven by memories of his *enfance terrible*: 'in that child the rhetorican's lie | Burst like a pipe'.[53] Yet, as Isherwood reports, that image also refers to 'a domestic accident'; the radiator in Auden's room burst and he had to sit in his overcoat: 'the cold had made a poet'.[54]

The chilly boulevards of the Belgian capital captivated Auden's imagination. Like a *flâneur* he sought out not just the 'Quarter of pleasures where the rich are always waiting,' nor the art gallery, but also 'unlighted streets' which 'hide away the appalling'.[55] He knew that even at its most disturbingly urban, the surrealist city was a place of enchantment. 'Brussels in Winter' seems to recall the Paris of Baudelaire who asked 'Quelles bizarreries ne trouve-t-on pas dans une grande ville, quand on sait se promener et regarder?';[56] or the metropolis shown to Breton by his mysterious heroine, Nadja; or the topography traced in Aragon's description of the Passage de l'Opéra in *Le Paysan de Paris* (1930). In each case, characters walk in no particular direction, but look only for the moment of discovery, the unattainable, the dark. Through random juxtapositions, unpredictable events and labyrinthine twists, such scenes defined the ultimate possibilities of the experience Auden wrote about:

> Wandering the cold streets tangled like old string,
> Coming on fountains silent in the frost,
> The city still escapes you . . .[57]

This is irregular, haphazard, and oddly alluring. At first, given the proximity of the rhyme, it sounds like the 'wandering' speaker is 'tangled like old string'; and that he is 'silent in the frost' like the 'fountains'. The vaguely poised present participles are so confusing that even the phrase 'the city still escapes you' does not make clear whether 'you' or 'the city' is the subject of the verb; and that central 'still', midway between adjective and adverb, finely fixes the scene between the dead of night and an everlasting life of roaming. The speaker encounters those who have never stopped moving, 'the homeless and the really humbled', travellers or refugees, who 'in their misery are all assembled'. Again, in 'assembled' there is the tension between active and passive voices which signifies, simultaneously, a

---

[53] *EA* 237.   [54] *EA* 237; *C&HK* (UK), 245.   [55] *EA* 235–6.

[56] Charles Baudelaire, *Œuvres complètes*, ed. Claude Pichois, 2 vols. (Paris, 1975), vol. 1, 355.

[57] *EA* 236.

drifting and a state of attention. At first, the word makes their plight
sound institutionally formalized; but it also renders them as *objets
trouvés*, like Miró's assemblages. Then comes the central line: 'The
winter holds them like the Opera'. The image is brilliantly
enthralling; it both grips with the suspense of their animation and
with a sense of their entrapment. For is 'the Opera' a building; or is
it a work by Puccini about dying in winter in a Francophone capital
city?

The line has been instanced as typical of Auden's Surrealist voice,
since in it 'things are associated within images that have no common
ground';[58] yet it may just be that 'a phrase . . . packed with meaning
like a van'[59] needs to be unloaded at the point of delivery. Certainly,
it is in such a context that 'Musée des Beaux Arts' must be seen, for
it is a consignment of paintings by the Flemish master Pieter
Brueghel. It has been noted that, as well as commenting on Icarus,
Auden also alludes to *The Numbering at Bethlehem* and *The Slaughter
of the Innocents*, both panoramic studies of terror and repression.[60]
For art critics now, Brueghel's distinction is easy to characterize as a
combination of the quotidian and the unique, the general mapping
and the specific action. Svetlana Alpers argues: 'The mapped view
suggests an encompassing of the world, without, however, asserting
the order based on human measure that is offered by perspective pictures. By depicting human behaviour in this unlikely setting . . .
Brueghel can suggest the endless repetitiveness of human behaviour'.[61] Of *Icarus*, Norman Bryson observes: 'Brueghel's image implies
that in fact what runs the world is repetition, unconsciousness, the
sleep of culture: the forces that stabilize and maintain the human
world are habit, automatism and inertia.'[62] Things do not change
from age to age; and the community of suffering seen under such an
aspect, but observed with such care, has a special poignancy. In this
regard Brueghel's *Icarus* employs a special device: the furrows of clay

---

[58] Ray, *Surrealist Movement in Britain*, 272.   [59] *EA* 236.

[60] Arthur Kinney, 'Auden, Brueghel, and "Musée des Beaux Arts"', *College English*,
24 (Apr. 1963), 529–31. See also Maurice Charney, 'Sir Lewis Namier and Auden's
"Musée des Beaux Arts"', *Philological Quarterly*, 39 (Jan. 1960), 129–31; Max
Bluestone, 'The Iconographic Sources of Auden's "Musée des Beaux Arts"', *Modern
Language Notes*, 76 (Apr. 1961), 331–6; Michael Riffaterre, 'Textuality: W. H. Auden's
"Musée des Beaux Arts"' in Mary-Ann Caws, ed., *Textual Analysis* (New York, 1986),
1–14; and John E. Coombes, 'Constructing the Icarus Myth: Brueghel, Brecht and
Auden', *Word & Image*, 2.1 (Jan.–Mar. 1986), 24–6.

[61] Svetlana Alpers, *The Art of Describing* (London, 1983), 144–5.

[62] Norman Bryson, *Looking at the Overlooked* (London, 1991), 140.

which wind out down the contours of the field of vision until they encounter the barely visible figure of the corpse among the trees on the left. The sense of sequence created by the continuity of these folds of earth is, at the same time, broken by their discontinuity. It is as if the lives in this picture aim for isolation, even insulation. Its characters look anywhere except at each other, just as they studiously ignore the corpse in the woods and the boy falling from the sky. The painting's structural properties reinforce the surreal incoherence; yet its attributes are also fastidious, as objects are juxtaposed with a kind of lateral logic which precludes any shame, but offers no comfort.

Auden's technique mirrors Brueghel's. Take his pronouns. 'It' (l.3) refers to 'suffering'; at its reappearance (l.7) 'it' may allude to 'suffering' or to the 'miraculous birth'. Either way, 'it' has become evasive. Similarly compromised is 'they' (l.9), which may point to the children, just mentioned; but, in fact, 'they' refers to the 'Old Masters': the sad truth is they endure longer than children. Mendelson notes that 'beneath the apparent surface disorder a deeper pattern of connectedness gradually makes itself felt,'[63] and he astutely instances the 'unassertive rhymes'. More obvious, though, are the present participles which are scattered throughout the poem's two long sentences: 'Suffering', 'eating', 'opening', 'walking', 'waiting', 'skating', 'disappearing', 'falling', all signal continuing action. Consequently, the verbal endings are echoed in adjective and noun: 'everything'; 'something amazing'. The glut of gerunds is reminiscent of '1929':

> Coming out of me living is always thinking,
> Thinking changing and changing living,
> Am feeling as it was seeing—
> In city leaning on harbour parapet
> To watch a colony of duck below . . .[64]

As then, so in 1938: sensibility and sight are crossed, so that subject and object are confused in the contemplation of winged creatures.

This technique is deployed to equally casual effect in the second section where 'everything turns away | Quite leisurely from the disaster.'[65] The habit of ignoring obvious responsibility creates potential directions for the Audenesque which can move it from the realm of seeing into fantastic configurations, the surreal and the comic. He gazes at the picture, yet everything looks away from him:

[63] *Early Auden*, 363.   [64] *EA* 37.   [65] Ibid. 237.

> the ploughman may
> Have heard the splash, the forsaken cry,
> But for him it was not an important failure; the sun shone
> As it had to on the white legs disappearing into the green
> Water; and the expensive delicate ship that must have seen
> Something amazing, a boy falling out of the sky,
> Had somewhere to get to and sailed calmly on.[66]

This is deliberately reserved, its grammar and syntax showing the bliss of ignorance: 'may' is reluctant to commit itself to its true verbal obligations, and hedges; while the qualification, 'for him', attempts to make amends by suggesting that not all choose to be as unvigilant, as 'leisurely', as the ploughman at work. None the less, followed by the near paradox of 'important failure', which suggests that only an insufficient harvest would animate a farmer's grief, Auden implies that actions are regulated by larger structures than the human or the personal. By combining the traditional theme of the seasons with an extensive mapped view of suffering, a yearly cycle is offered rather than a local dimension. The sun shining, 'as it had to', so reminiscent of the dead rhythms of the opening sentence of Beckett's *Murphy*, published in March 1938 ('The sun shone, having no alternative, on the nothing new'),[67] suggests that, even though partly responsible for the crash, a heavenly body has no choice. The style is complex, deliberately unknowing, yet in identifying disaster, Auden realizes the difficulties in moralizing rather than attitudinizing; in questions of art it was as exhausting for him to occupy the moral high ground as for Brueghel. The final lines of the poem, with their insistent sibilants, attempt to anchor the picture; yet they only prove that the impulse to fabricate new forms melts along with the waxy wings, while earthbound routine continues ignorantly 'on'. With that as his last word on the picture, Auden suggests that the world relies only on blank repetitions to further an artist's creations.

After all, Brueghel's literary source was Ovid (*Metamorphoses* 8. 217–28); and in some ways, too, the tale of Icarus might be surreal, for it concerns the fabrication of wings by the fabulous artificer, Daedalus, the gaoler of that surrealist icon, the *Minotaure*.[68] One might also note that fake birds were a staple of the Surrealist

[66] Ibid.   [67] Samuel Beckett, *Murphy* (London, 1938), 1.
[68] *Minotaure* was founded in Paris in 1933 and soon became a Surrealist journal. It was especially famous for its cover art by Miró, Magritte, Dali, and Masson, all of whom contributed works on the theme of the Minotaur myth.

Movement; and that Ernst's most characteristic collages feature humans growing wings.[69] In Auden, another trapped monster, the Sphinx, asks '"Am I to suffer always?" Yes', comes the reply; and the same affirmation heralds an air-raid in Manchuria: 'Yes, we are going to suffer, now; the sky | Throbs like a feverish forehead.'[70] In Brussels in the winter of 1938, suffering was on Auden's mind; he had witnessed it in a Chinese field hospital six months earlier and had not recovered. Of the wounded civilians, he observed, 'They are and suffer', where the first verb signals an existence, but nothing more. Meanwhile 'we stand elsewhere'. Ultimately, suffering cannot be 'shared': 'only happiness . . . And anger, and the idea of love.'[71] Hence, in the first published version of 'Brussels in Winter', line 7 read, 'And in their suffering are all assembled'; but because it implied a possible fabrication of their situation, an artistic misrepresentation, the noun was subsequently altered to 'misery'.

'About suffering they were never wrong, | The Old Masters;' but the vocal possibilities of this opening line, a dying fall on the second word, might imply that they may have been incorrect about other matters. Moreover, though 'suffering . . . takes place', in *Icarus*, at least, it does it not take the place of life. In art, Auden expected plenty of news; yet here is a poem about a painting in which 'disaster' is nothing new. So is the depiction of the 'human position' of 'suffering' synonymous with the validity of human interest? But in this respect, to be 'human' is not quite to be 'humane'; and the poem considers the difference between the adjectives as exemplified in their primary human subject. Auden records both his response to a work of art and to a memory, as the painting's energies are assimilated into the plot of his own life. Indeed, he answered Brueghel not vicariously as an art critic might, but as an individual who had experienced suffering; who had been on the 'expensive delicate ship' when it turned away from the war in Manchuria. He wrote later that 'the metaphor of the ship is only employed when society is in peril'; the ship is 'a metaphor for society in danger from within or without,'[72] and throughout the period, it appeared in his work. In *The Dance of Death* 'the ship of England crosses the ocean';[73] but 'the state ship that deliberately chooses the high sea is the state in disorder, the Ship of

---

[69] See, for instance, Max Ernst, *Une Semaine de bonté ou les sept éléments capitaux* (Paris, 1930).

[70] *EA* 232, 256.

[71] Ibid. 258.

[72] *The Enchafèd Flood* (London, 1951), 19.

[73] *PDW* 92.

Fools'.[74] Hence, in 'Atlantis', dating from January 1941, the Questing Hero is told that 'Only the Ship of Fools is | Making the voyage this year, | As gales of abnormal force | Are predicted.'[75] The spiritual journey presented here was, in effect, away from a war in Europe; and, as such, antithetical to that described a few years earlier in 'The Ship', a poem written *en route* to a conflict in the Far East:

> The streets are brightly lit; our city is kept clean:
> The third class have the greasiest cards, the first play high;
> The beggars sleeping in the bows have never seen
> What can be done in staterooms; no one asks why.[76]

This ship was 'mankind and human society moving through time and struggling with its destiny;'[77] but in 1938, that destiny was terrifyingly near: 'It is our culture that with such calm progresses | Over the barren plains of a sea.'[78] This deadly calm, so close to complacency, Auden reflected on in 'Musée des Beaux Arts', which, it should not be forgotten, was written in the aftermath of the Munich Crisis.

Like 'suffering', 'expensive' was another word on his mind at this time, because it asked questions about human and artistic values. In Sonnet VIII of *In Time of War*, civilized man 'lived expensively and did without,'[79] the contradiction implying the depth of his self-deception; while in 'Dover', the aircraft that 'fly in the new European air' are 'expensive and lovely as a rich child's toy',[80] and so all the more likely to be discarded, and replaced by others. 'Musée des Beaux Arts' has the 'expensive delicate ship', where the delicacy exists both because of, and despite, its expense. A massive outlay should produce a correspondingly solid vessel, but Auden looks at the filigree of the rigging and sees an *objet d'art*. Like some 'dreadful martyrdom', this craft must 'run its course | Anyhow'; but the arbitrariness of that last word may imply the means by which 'the poem seeks to incorporate the ship—problematic . . . mysterious, *unreal*—into a metaphysic of tragic unity'.[81]

Auden, then, read Brueghel's quasi-surreal picture as realistically as he could, investing it with the significance, the subject, of his own life. Yet, as ever, he needed Isherwood's pragmatism to make the connection between experience and art. In Brussels, both ill, they

---

[74] *Enchafèd Flood*, 20.   [75] *CP91* 315.   [76] *EA* 232.
[77] *Enchafèd Flood*, 61.   [78] *EA* 232.   [79] Ibid. 254.
[80] *EA* 223.   [81] Coombes, 'Constructing the Icarus Myth', 26.

completed *Journey to a War*; and Auden would have encountered, perhaps for the first time, Isherwood's account of their departure from Wenchow in their 'expensive delicate' steamer:

A cabin port-hole is a picture-frame. No sooner had we arrived on board than the brass-encircled view became romantic and false. The brown river in the rain, the boatmen in their dark bat-wing capes, the tree-crowned pagodas on the foreshore, the mountains scarved in mist—these were no longer features of the beautiful prosaic country we had just left behind us; they were the scenery of the traveller's dream.[82]

This passage would have placed Brueghel's painting in a human perspective for Auden; but one realistic enough to overcome the surrealism of those 'dreams' he might have experienced as one escaping a war.

[82] *Journey to a War*, with Christopher Isherwood (London, 1939), 234.

Persuasions to Rejoice: Auden's Oedipal Dialogues with W. B. Yeats

STAN SMITH

W. H. AUDEN wrote to Stephen Spender in 1964:

I am incapable of saying a word about W. B. Yeats because through no fault of his, he has become for me a symbol of my own devil of unauthenticity, of everything which I must try to eliminate from my own poetry, false emotions, inflated rhetoric, empty sonorities . . . His [poems] make me whore after lies.[1]

Yeats, as a poetic father-figure, is here associated with that 'Father of Lies', the devil of rhetoric and political propaganda, who, Auden says in *Secondary Worlds*, 'does not ask for a free response to his spell; he demands a tautological echo', and has therefore to be rejected in the name of the authentic, non-instrumental language of poetry.[2] But poetry for Auden is also necessarily of the Devil's party, an equivocal and treacherous mode of utterance perpetually betraying its user: 'The Devil, indeed, is the father of Poetry, for poetry might be defined as the clear expression of mixed feelings. The Poetic mood is never indicative.' In this same note in *New Year Letter*, Auden's solution is to transform moral equivocation into artistic virtue: 'All knowledge that conflicts with itself is Poetic Fiction'.[3] In the elegy 'In Memory of W. B. Yeats', written in February 1939, the month after Yeats's death, published in *The New Republic* on 8 March, and in a fuller version in *The London Mercury* in April of the same year, Auden initiates his argument with the older poet's rhetorical postures, and what they imply for the truthfulness of 'Poetic Fiction' as a mode of knowing.[4]

Yeats's '[The] Man and the Echo', written and revised between July and October 1938, had already appeared in both *The Atlantic*

---

[1] Quoted in *Early Auden*, 206. Mendelson's book offers an excellent, succinct account of Auden's poetic dealings with Yeats.

[2] *SW* 126–30.   [3] *NYL* 119.

[4] *New Republic*, 98.1266 (8 Mar. 1939), 123; *London Mercury*, 39.234 (Apr. 1939), 578–80, first collected in *Another Time* (New York and London, 1940), repr. in *EA* 241–3.

Monthly and *The London Mercury* in the very month of his death. There, in uncharacteristically self-questioning mood, the ageing poet, for whom death is now only a matter of time, speaks of 'All that I have said and done' now 'Turn[ing] into a question till | I lie awake night after night | And never get the answers right.'[5] Indeed, question and response is the very pattern of the poem, as the poet consults the oracle in the rocky cleft of Alt only to receive in reply the foreshortened echo of his own enquiries, the night turning his words back upon him in a mockery of all that he has done and said. The sequence culminates in a rhetorical question which answers its own grandiose prospect of immortality with a further question that simply reinstates the uncertainties of the mortal present:

> O Rocky Voice
> Shall we in that great night rejoice?
> What do we know but that we face
> One another in this place?

This self-rebuff leads Yeats to lose his theme, so that the poem ends in the diminuendo of a stricken rabbit's cry, implying that the death of the poet is no more meaningful than the casual slaughter of a beast of the field by hawk or owl.

Auden's poem, appearing in the same journal three months later, must be seen as a direct and unexpected response to Yeats's rhetorical questionings. Yeats proceeds by anxious questions which he does not expect to have answered. Auden responds with assertions and exhortations which, at times, come close to imperious commands. In a final section which echoes the predominantly trochaic tetrameter couplets of Yeats's poem, the antepenultimate stanza deploys the same rhyme Yeats uses in 'Man and the Echo' to present an apparently unequivocal answer to the older poet's questions:

> Follow, poet, follow right
> To the bottom of the night,
> With your unconstraining voice
> Still persuade us to rejoice.[6]

Whereas Yeats had spoken of man pursuing his thoughts until, 'all work done, [he] dismisses all | Out of intellect and sight | And sinks at last into the night', Auden extends that active pursuing into the

---

[5] W. B. Yeats, *The Poems*, ed. Richard J. Finneran, rev. edn. (London, 1990), 345–6.
[6] *EA* 243.

grave itself (though, now, Yeats's metaphysical 'night' has become that midnight of the century, the political darkness of a Europe about to plunge into war).

Yeats had foregrounded the duties of the human intellect in the second long affirmative section of the Man's address to the darkness. 'The spiritual intellect's great work' cannot be shirked by sickness or suicide, or evaded in love and drink,

> And till his intellect grows sure
> That all's arranged in one clear view,
> [He] Pursues the thoughts that I pursue . . .
> And sinks at last into the night.

Yet this affirmation is undercut by the Echo's curt response (which could be either command or confirmation): 'Into the night'. By contrast, Auden's poem has no illusions about the power of intellect to measure the whole, arrange it in one clear view, in an image which calls up other echoes of Yeats at his most abject:

> In the nightmare of the dark
> All the dogs of Europe bark,
> And the living nations wait,
> Each sequestered in its hate;
>
> Intellectual disgrace
> Stares from every human face,
> And the seas of pity lie
> Locked and frozen in each eye.

If the rhyme of 'disgrace' and 'face' renders negative that exchange of looks evoked in Yeats's last question ('What do we know but that we face | One another in this place?'), the barking dogs, mediated by the midnight when 'no dogs barked' of 'The Three Bushes' and 'To Dorothy Wellesley' (both poems originally published in *The London Mercury*, in January 1937 and March 1938 respectively),[7] pick up and link the indignity of age ('tied to me | As to a dog's tail') lamented in 'The Tower' and the vision of civilization sinking, its great battle lost, in 'Long-Legged Fly' ('Quiet the dog').[8] This last poem, written between November 1937 and April 1938, first appeared in the same issue of *The London Mercury* (April 1939) as Auden's elegy. Whether the editors had given Auden prior sight of Yeats's poem is a matter

---

[7] Yeats, *Poems*, 296–8, 304. [8] Ibid. 194–200, 339.

of conjecture, but the correspondence is striking, and it seems reasonable to infer deliberation.

Auden's lines, for all the extremity of which they speak, are not despairing. On the contrary, there is an insouciant existential gaiety to them like that of which Yeats spoke as the proper approach to death—the death of civilizations as well as individuals—in 'Lapis Lazuli' (first published in *The London Mercury* in March 1938) and 'The Gyres' (*New Poems*, 1938). In the latter, confronting a world in which 'numb nightmare ride[s] on top', the poet draws solace from the same oracular source: 'What matter? Out of Cavern comes a voice, | And all it knows is that one word "Rejoice!" '[9] Auden's command to the poet is strangely doubled in 'In Memory of W. B. Yeats', just as Yeats's echoic technique, emulating any number of Renaissance poems, doubles language back upon itself in a spurious mutuality in which the poet is really only talking to himself. (Perhaps Auden is recalling this when he speaks in *Secondary Worlds* of the propagandist demanding not 'a free response' but 'a tautological echo'.)

In one sense, Yeats is now, in Auden's poem, himself identified with Rocky Voice, the words of a dead man persuading us to rejoice from beyond the grave. The difference between persuasion and command is, however, a significant one. If anyone is doing the commanding here, it is Auden. In that sense, Auden himself identifies vicariously with Rocky Voice, for, in commanding Yeats to persuade *us* to rejoice, he is also, at a remove, echoing Rocky Voice's command that Yeats himself rejoice. Again, whereas Yeats's verbal echoings enforce closure, Auden's doubling here is open-ended, striking out into what the 'Prologue' to *New Year Letter* was shortly to call 'the unknown unconditional dark' of history, setting up an endless succession of poets who will in turn obey and pass on these commands.[10] If Auden urges 'Follow, poet, follow', it is deliberately unclear who precisely is addressed. Is it (taking up the line 'Pursues the thoughts that I pursue') the already dead Yeats who is being urged not to sink at last into the night? Or is it the living poet who is Yeats's successor—Auden himself perhaps—who is encouraged to follow his mentor, and rejoice even in the face of numb nightmare? Or is it also other, younger poets who will in turn succeed Auden, when he too has joined Yeats in the dark Cavern of eternity? In other words, is this elegy not also a bid for the poetic succession?

[9] Yeats, *Poems*, 293.   [10] *NYL* 14.

Poetry's function in these lines seems to be as the source of end-lessly renewed gaiety, persuading us to rejoice even in the face of the holocaust. Yeats survives, in traditional terms, as a sequence of verbal effects, those poems spoken of in the opening movement which out-live their creator, 'the words of a dead man | . . . modified in the guts of the living'. But poetry is not defined here as pure disinter-ested utterance. Rather it is a series of rhetorical devices, aimed at an effect: at persuasion. This emphasis seems rather to contradict the poem's later assertion that 'poetry makes nothing happen', and Auden's insistence on distinguishing, in the notes to *New Year Letter*, between poetry and propaganda. The apparent contradiction can be understood if we see that the confident affirmation 'poetry makes nothing happen', in a section which was added to the *London Mercury* text (it doesn't appear in the *New Republic* version), is a direct response to one of Yeats's key questions in 'Man and the Echo'. For the first questions in this poem concern Yeats's distress and guilt, as the author of *Cathleen ni Houlihan*, for the Easter Uprising and all its consequent misery:

> Did that play of mine send out
> Certain men the English shot?
> Did words of mine put too great strain
> On that woman's reeling brain?
> Could my spoken words have checked
> That whereby a house lay wrecked?
> And all seems evil until I
> Sleepless would lie down and die.

By 1939 Auden shared a similar anxiety, for, as he veered towards pacifism, he had become more and more distressed (as his notorious rewriting of 'Spain' later that year was to reveal) about his own pro-paganda role in sending men to commit 'the necessary murder' on behalf of the Spanish Republic. The revised version of this poem, 'Spain 1937', the added date carefully dissociating the author from his past,[11] was to appear immediately before the Yeats elegy as the first poem in a section of 'Occasional Poems' at the end of *Another Time* in 1940. When Auden speaks of 'intellectual disgrace' staring in every

---

[11] I am indebted to Nicholas Jenkins for this observation. I have argued elsewhere for a historical relation between Yeats's 'Long-Legged Fly', the Spanish Civil War, and Auden's 'Spain' (see Stan Smith, 'Missing Dates: From "Spain 1937" to "September 1, 1939"', *Literature and History*, 13.2 (Autumn 1987), 155-74). Yeats's poem may well have influenced the Auden revisions.

human face, it is in part his own disgrace that he confronts. But if 'poetry makes nothing happen', then the poet is exculpated from that kind of responsibility for time. Whatever he says in the realm of practical politics has no effect. So Yeats and Auden, like Kipling and Paul Claudel, will be pardoned for their eccentric political 'views' (a word which recalls Yeats's desire to see that 'all's arranged in one clear view'). By persuading us to rejoice (to utter, not to act) poetry actually releases us from prison, turning a world of consequence ('curse', 'unsuccess', 'prison') into an order of language ('verse', 'rapture', 'praise') which is self-sufficient and issueless. Auden attempts here to complete that task Yeats had set for intellect in 'Man and the Echo': 'Nor can there be work so great | As that which cleans man's dirty slate.' Art exonerates history, wiping clean 'man's dirty slate' as, in such poems as 'The Circus Animals' Desertion', 'the sweepings of a street' are transformed into 'masterful images' which 'grew in pure mind'.[12] This poem, with its fretting about the destruction of the soul by political 'fanaticism and hate', and 'Politics', with its pointed contrast of personal desire with the inhuman fixity of 'Roman . . . Russian . . . Spanish politics',[13] were in fact published alongside 'Man and the Echo' in both *The Atlantic Monthly* and *The London Mercury* in January 1939, commanding Auden, one could almost say, to a personal response. But 'In Memory of W. B. Yeats' compounds this response with a further, plangent echo of Yeats at his own most elegiac, calling up those 'dear shadows' summoned in 'In Memory of Eva Gore-Booth and Con Markievicz'. There Yeats remarks: 'The innocent and the beautiful | Have no enemy but time.'[14]

In endorsing this Auden expands it into the trope of poetic survival:

> Time that is intolerant
> Of the brave and innocent,
> And indifferent in a week
> To a beautiful physique,
>
> Worships language and forgives
> Everyone by whom it lives.

The poem speaks of 'writing well' as the 'strange excuse' with which time will pardon Yeats's political views, as it has already pardoned Kipling and will pardon Paul Claudel. A syntactical ambiguity elides

---

[12] Yeats, *Poems*, 346–8.   [13] Ibid. 348.   [14] Ibid. 233–4.

the difficulties here. If it is language that lives by their writing, then poets such as Yeats and Auden need not feel guilty about any effects that might follow in the historical world from the ideas their writing contains. For poetry is not propaganda, it 'makes nothing happen'. If, however, it is 'time' that lives by this 'writing well', then we are back with the anxious questions about responsibility for history of 'Man and the Echo'.

Auden's other obituary for Yeats, the essay published in *Partisan Review* in the spring of 1939, 'The Public v. the Late Mr William Butler Yeats',[15] expands the argument of the poem. The article is conceived as a trial divided between a Public Prosecutor and a Counsel for the Defence, the former indicting Yeats's 'feudal mentality' and propaganda for fascism, the latter concluding that Yeats justified himself as a maker of 'verbal structures' which have the perennial 'power to make personal excitement socially available' and thus transcend any propaganda effects they might have in their immediate context. Auden's phraseology explains the 'strange excuse' offered in the poem:

For art is a product of history, not a cause. Unlike some other products, technical inventions for example, it does not re-enter history as an effective agent, so that the question whether art should or should not be propaganda is unreal. The case for the prosecution rests on the fallacious belief that art ever makes anything happen.

Nevertheless, in 'the field of language' the poet remains 'a man of action', and here the increasingly 'democratic style' of Yeats's later verse is 'the diction of a just man, and it is for this reason that just men will always recognise the author as a master.' This does not fully resolve Auden's dilemma, but it elucidates the conclusion of his elegy, where he claims that Yeats's work will continue to 'In the prison of his days | Teach the free man how to praise'. The poetic voice, that is, though it does persuade, is 'unconstraining' in its persuasions. Indeed it succeeds in persuading precisely because it invites us to a 'free' act.

Yeats's elegy for his two nationalist women friends had spoken of them now knowing it all, having transcended in death 'All the folly of a fight | With a common wrong or right'. In Auden's elegy, Yeats's poetry itself represents this higher, reconciling knowledge for a world

---

[15] 'The Public v. the Late Mr William Butler Yeats', *Partisan Review*, 6.3 (Spring 1939), 46–51, repr. in *EA* 389–93.

confronting the 'intellectual disgrace' of global conflict, where 'the living nations wait, | Each sequestered in its hate'. Yeats's own ambivalent relationship to the destructive nationalisms of Ireland and contemporary Europe is discussed at length and with some discrimination in the judicious and judicial prose of the obituary essay. Significantly, when Auden assumes the voice of 'Poetic Fiction' to deal with the same topic, he is much more aware of 'mixed feelings' and 'self-contradiction', finding it necessary to invoke the subversive authority of other Irish voices ('Nightmare of the dark' recalling, for example, Stephen Dedalus's famous comment on history as nightmare in *Ulysses*, finally published in an unlimited, uncensored edition as recently as 1937).[16]

In this rich intertextual medley, Auden's voice finds its own distinctive tone, 'The words of a dead man | Are modified in the guts of the living'. In its various echoes of its Irish predecessor, Auden's poem takes up and extends Yeats's debate with death and historical responsibility in 'Man and the Echo'. Examining Yeats's record, the elegy, in the words of Yeats's poem, 'stands in judgment on his soul, | And, all work done, dismisses all'. Yeats's judicial metaphors help to explain the insistent legal imagery of Auden's poem. If Yeats is to be 'punished under a foreign code of conscience', this is because history imports alien values into the guiltless order of art. In the historical world, we are all in prison, 'each in the cell of himself . . . almost convinced of his freedom'. But in fact the poet will be 'pardoned' because 'In the prison of his days' he will 'Teach the free man how to praise'. The silliness and 'human unsuccess' of the man are pardoned, forgiven, because poetry transforms 'curse' into the 'verse' in and with which it rhymes. Auden's own poem in turn becomes an echo of Yeats's echoes, itself a 'verbal structure' which self-reflexively 'Worships language and forgives | Everyone by whom it lives.' In offering a kind of rhyme for Yeats's, Auden's poem modifies the words of a dead man and becomes a commentary on itself as much as on its object.

Auden's courtroom metaphors, developed in 'The Public v. the Late Mr William Butler Yeats' to the extent that he assumes the roles of prosecuting and defence counsel, judge and jury, finally acquitting

---

[16] James Joyce, *Ulysses* (London, 1937). There are some remarkable precedents for Auden's poem in the passages where Stephen reflects on the nightmare of history, and, in particular, reflections on the 'mouth'/'south' rhyme in a passage which 'rhymes' 'the whole bloody history' of Irish nationalism with the forms of fiction; see 127–9.

Yeats as 'a just man', point forward to that moment in *New Year Letter* where Auden speaks of himself appearing before a 'summary tribunal' where he is 'Both prosecution and defence', passing no sentence but his own for the 'crime' of adopting 'The preacher's loose immodest tone'.[17] Absolving Yeats of guilt in this elegy, Auden forgives the older poet as a surrogate, a scapegoat even, for his own crimes. But the pardon he vicariously proclaims on behalf of 'Time' (that devouring patriarch) also constitutes an act of usurpation which deposes the older poet, in a tone which is as much triumphalist as respectful, emptying the Irish vessel of its poetry in order to fill it with his own. The final call to 'Follow, poet' could be addressed as much to himself as to Yeats. Auden will follow (succeed) Yeats by in his turn persuading us, like the poems he praises, to rejoice in and learn from his own verses. In doing so, he establishes his claim to supplant Yeats ('human unsuccess' establishing a poetic succession), writing Yeats's obituary in an act of homage which is also an oedipal celebration of triumph over the Father of Lies.[18]

[17] *NYL* 21–4.
[18] 'Greatness Finding Itself' (1960), repr. in *FA* 79–87, offers Auden's own lucid exposition of the Freudian concepts I am deploying here and is of considerable relevance to this and the other poems in section III of *Another Time*, in particular 'In Memory of Ernst Toller', 'September 1, 1939', and 'In Memory of Sigmund Freud'.

The Achievement of Edward Upward

KATHERINE BUCKNELL

IN his notoriously doctrinaire 'Sketch for a Marxist Interpretation of Literature' (1937) Edward Upward insisted that a writer 'must first of all become a socialist in his practical life, must go over to the progressive side of the class conflict' if he wishes to do his best work. But he also pointed out that becoming a socialist will not necessarily make him a good writer: 'The quality of his writing will depend upon his individual talent.'[1] The quality of Upward's writing has been controversial. Praise has come, both early and late, from his close friends, especially Stephen Spender and, above all, Christopher Isherwood, whose admiration for Upward's writing is inseparably mingled with their admiration for the moral seriousness with which he has upheld his political beliefs. This has tainted Upward's reputation. Valentine Cunningham has called Upward 'the glaring example' of a writer unjustly 'boomed', complaining that his hefty three-part autobiographical novel *The Spiral Ascent* 'simply *bores* you'.[2] Before Cunningham, the informed view, put by John Lehmann and Samuel Hynes, was that Upward had sacrificed a uniquely promising imaginative talent to his Marxist ideology.[3] But more recently Frank Kermode has suggested that *The Spiral Ascent* is undervalued, both for the virtues of its style and form and also because it shares the attributes of 'literature which achieves permanence' in that it transgresses the important frontier of class.[4] Surely Frank Kermode is right that *The Spiral Ascent* will achieve permanence, if not for these reasons alone. *The Spiral Ascent* is at the very least a record of an intelligent life devoted largely to the Communist Party of Great Britain, and we will turn to it to find out what that life, briefly the chosen one of many artists and intellectuals of the period, was like.

For a biographical sketch of Upward and an account of his friendship with Auden, see Appendix, 184–6.

[1] 'Sketch for a Marxist Interpretation of Literature', in *The Mind in Chains: Socialism and the Cultural Revolution*, ed. C. Day Lewis (London, 1937), 52.

[2] Cunningham, 147, 302.

[3] Lehmann, *The Whispering Gallery* (London, 1955), 244 and Hynes, 317.

[4] *History and Value* (Oxford, 1988), 22; see also 53–7.

But *The Spiral Ascent* is also an important spiritual autobiography which, for all its radical ambition to create a new kind of Marxist realism, has roots in a native English tradition of plain writing that testifies to the personal experience of religious and political belief or disillusion. If we regard it in the light of that tradition, as well as in the light of Upward's Marxist-Leninist theories, we will better understand it and more accurately appraise its value. *The Spiral Ascent* was never meant to entertain; it was meant to explain, to edify, to demystify, and perhaps to inspire. Purposively suspicious of over-fine writing, Upward's style is stubbornly and self-consciously plain, sometimes even bleak, in order to be morally trustworthy. Yet at the same time, the dialectical design of the trilogy is immensely ambitious and rich.

The phrase 'individual talent' in Upward's 'Sketch for a Marxist Interpretation of Literature' suggests a comparison with T. S. Eliot's 'Tradition and the Individual Talent' (1919). Eliot had said that the artist must begin by surrendering himself to tradition; however, in 1937 Upward was concerned not with the past, but with the future. He proclaimed that the writer must be prepared to give up even his writing and possibly 'life itself'[5] to the cause of the workers. For a time, Upward did give up his writing. But he never gave up *trying* to write, and it is clear from *The Spiral Ascent* as well as from other published remarks[6] that he chose to bury himself in Party work not only to hasten the revolution, but also because he wrote only with great difficulty and the struggle was driving him to the edge of sanity. His manuscripts (which are now in the British Library) include countless abandoned fragments, especially from the 1940s and 1950s, and they reveal that his habit of harsh self-criticism began early, in the margins of his juvenilia, along with painstaking, even obsessive, redrafting. He says that his diaries further attest to his persistent efforts.[7] His standards were killingly high, which is partly why Isherwood, Auden, and Spender so looked up to him in youth. Upward eventually left the Communist Party in 1948; it had fallen, in his view, from true Marxism-Leninism into revisionism, and he believes that he was forced out because he refused to modify his strict revolutionary principles. As a result he faced not only the pain of

---

[5] 'Sketch', 53.

[6] See 'A Conversation with Edward Upward', *The Review*, 11–12 (1964), 65–7.

[7] ALS, 2 Feb. 1992, to Katherine Bucknell. The diaries are promised to the British Library on Upward's death.

political disillusionment and isolation, but also the severe challenge of once again struggling to fulfil his prematurely celebrated literary talent. The burden was immense and he finally suffered a complete neurotic breakdown, its paralysing effect made more dreadful by the knowledge that one of his younger brothers was permanently insane in an institution.

Remarkably, after nearly twenty years of self-sacrifice as a Marxist and growing self-doubt as a writer, Upward emerged in the 1960s as a master of the plain style. He achieved this mastery by giving himself up, after all, to literary tradition. His models have no place in Eliot's canon, and few contemporary writers have much noticed them: Bunyan, Defoe, Cowper, W. Hale White (*The Autobiography of Mark Rutherford: Dissenting Minister, Mark Rutherford's Deliverance*), Robert Tressall (*The Ragged Trousered Philanthropists*), and Gissing (at fifteen Upward admired *The Private Papers of Henry Ryecroft*, still an influence, but now he prefers the style of *New Grub Street*[8]). These are mostly prose writers, plain stylists, and autobiographers of sorts, all struggling as Upward did with the bitterness of failed ambition or political disillusionment, or the agony of spiritual crisis. Many of them are dissenters, some are sceptics or atheists striving to understand how man is to help himself to a better life in a world where the possibility of any other help is in doubt. For some, writing, in solitude or retirement, serves as a kind of self-cure.

In this vein, Upward's greatest model is Wordsworth. The third and most engrossing volume of *The Spiral Ascent*, called *No Home But the Struggle*, is modelled on *The Prelude*. It charts the growth of Upward's mind in a narrative that shuttles continually backwards and forwards in time, describing on the one hand the reclusive, outwardly dull simplicity of Upward's retirement in late middle age to a family house on the Isle of Wight and recollecting on the other hand his excited, even manic, youthful experiences on the Isle of Wight and elsewhere which are triggered again in memory by his return to the setting where he spent so much of his childhood. The circumstances of Upward's retirement are like those of Gissing's Henry Ryecroft in Devon, but his episodic memories of youth, like Wordsworth's spots of time, brim with lost emotional intensity, and invigorate his account of old age and seclusion. Alan Sebrill, the Upward character, learns to seek out these recollections, which at first occur accidentally, in order

---

[8] ALS, 2 Feb. 1992, to K. B.

to drain from them their latent poetic power. The process typically begins with a Wordsworthian walk along the seacliff:

It's not true that I've lost the ability to be poetically excited by this place. I am disregarding what happened only two days ago as I was walking along the cliff path in the afternoon. I saw the building which looks like a small power-house and which stands half-screened now by a row of holm-oaks about a hundred and fifty yards inland from the cliff edge. I remembered the impression it had made on me as a boy of sixteen and the poem I had conceived about it then. I remembered not so much the poem itself as the extraordinary exhilaration this supposed powerhouse—it is an ice-cream factory now, whatever it may have been forty-four years ago—had aroused in me because of the strangeness of its presence there not far from the cliff edge with no other tall-chimneyed building visible inland for miles around, and because of the look its large round-headed windows had given of being an apparition from the mid-nineteenth century, half Beulah chapel and half industrial mill, and because of the heavy flywheel and glistening piston and whirling brass-balled governor and big horizontal boiler I had imagined to be concealed behind the long high stretch of windowless wall below the windows. In remembering that past poetic exhilaration I felt a similar exhilaration, as an iron core is magnetised by the electric current running through a coil of wire that surrounds it. The old poetic life gave potency to the new; and through my surroundings here it will do so again, often. That is why I have come to live here.

Must I passively wait for the next time when the past will vivify the present? What is to prevent me from deliberately—this morning, this instant—stimulating poetic imaginativeness in myself by thinking of other occasions here years ago when I felt the kind of excitement that the sight of the power-house near the cliff path gave me?[9]

The Prelude solved for Upward a great technical problem. His prose poems written in the early 1930s ('The Colleagues', 'Sunday', 'The Island') are tense with visionary excitement, but only in his novel *Journey to the Border* (1938) was he able to sustain a narrative of much length. And even *Journey to the Border* turns on a single instant of vision: the tutor's recognition that he must join the workers' movement. The story is a Marxist rewrite of *Pilgrim's Progress*—as it happens, Upward says that *Pilgrim's Progress* was the first book that he read by himself as a child.[10] But *Pilgrim's Progress* is based on the belief that we can leave this world for a better one; its climactic event is death and its sequel is simply an exact repetition, by his wife and children, of Christian's journey. It offers no literary method for pro-

[9] *Spiral*, 508–9.   [10] Conversation with K. B., 19 July 1988.

longing the excitement of conversion or integrating it into the ongoing Marxist struggle to change this world into a better one. It was not until he read (or reread) *The Prelude* in maturity, that Upward saw how to cross and cross again not Kermode's important frontier of class, but the internal frontier between vision and disillusion, past self and present self, bourgeois self and Marxist self, continually rediscovering and reanimating his developing political and poetic convictions, and thereby charting the relationship between them. This gives the third volume of *The Spiral Ascent* a dynamic intensity which retrospectively reshapes the reader's understanding of the first two volumes and which crowns the work.

Upward attended I. A. Richards's lectures in Cambridge in the 1920s and was both gripped and antagonized by Richards's assertions that imaginative literature, because it deals in emotion, does not refer to reality. Upward felt that he could no longer write if his writing had nothing to do with the real world. Then, in the 1930s, he read Lenin's *Materialism and Empirio-Criticism*, and there he found satisfactory philosophical reassurance that emotions do reflect material reality. Lenin's book is framed as a critique of Ernst Mach, a proponent of empirio-criticism who spawned a revisionist movement in Marxism, but *Materialism and Empirio-Criticism* has the larger aim of distinguishing the true materialism of Marx and Engels not only from Machian empirio-criticism which Lenin regarded as idealist, but also from many other versions of idealism as well. Hence Lenin begins his critique in 1710 with Bishop Berkeley, in whose philosophy he argues Machianism had its unacknowledged idealist precursor. Over and over again Lenin returns to the fundamental epistemological question of the relation of thinking to being, asserting that throughout the writings of Marx and Engels, being precedes thinking, matter precedes sensation, the physical precedes the psychical, rather than the other way around. In true materialism, according to Lenin, man's sensations and perceptions are a reflection of things; moreover, these sensations and perceptions are represented not by arbitrary signs and symbols, but by copies, mental images, mirror reflections of the world.[11] Lenin's arguments can be easily recognized as the basis for Upward's 'Sketch for a Marxist Interpretation of Literature', where Upward takes on I. A. Richards directly, insisting that:

[11] V. I. Lenin, *Materialism and Empirio-Criticism: Critical Notes Concerning a Reactionary Philosophy* (completed 1908), tr. David Kvitko (London, 1927). See introd. and chs. 1, 3.2, 4.6.

Imaginative writing, no less than scientific theory or any other form of intellectual activity, reflects the material world—but reflects it in a special way. Literature, like science, generalises about the world, but its generalisations are more emotional and less intellectual than those of science. Whereas science translates material reality into terms of thought, literature translates it into terms of feeling.[12]

Such arguments enabled Upward to write *Journey to the Border*, yet he then published nothing for over twenty years. At first this was partly because he had nothing to say. He believed he had to live the life of a Party member before he could write about the class struggle. *Journey to the Border* took him about five years to complete, and while he was working on it he told Isherwood that Party work was consuming most of his spare time; this work was, he wrote, 'worthless to the party but will be very valuable someday to my writing.'[13] A few years after this letter, in his 'Sketch for a Marxist Interpretation of Literature', he emphasized the importance of actually changing the material world and he linked this closely to the necessity of rejecting fantasy in literature; fantasy was an outmoded style, out of touch with reality:

a modern fantasy cannot tell the truth, cannot give a picture of life which will survive the test of experience; since fantasy implies in practice a retreat from the real world into the world of imagination, and though such a retreat may have been practicable and desirable in a more leisured and less profoundly disturbed age than our own it is becoming increasingly impracticable to-day . . . to-day not only does the possibility exist of radically changing material conditions, but men cannot much longer console themselves with fantasies about a world which is daily drifting towards a war of unprecedented destructiveness.[14]

This statement describes better than any other the change in Upward's writing that has led his critics to lament that he sacrificed the fantastic style of his early surrealistic writing for the sake of his new found Marxism. But surely it was not a sacrifice; surely he turned to Marxism because he had privately lost faith in his imagination and in his talent as a writer. Mortmere itself had gradually become inaccessible to him. In September 1934 he wrote to Isherwood, 'I have lost the art of working up a romantically sinister atmosphere with conviction,' and later the same year, 'When our

[12] 'Sketch', 43–4.
[13] AL, Monday [probably spring 1933]; private American collection.   [14] 48–9.

incomprehensible Mortmere language seems most called for I am no longer able to write it.'[15] Naturally Upward might have simply outgrown Mortmere, but this would not altogether account for the change in his style, especially since he had none the less continued to draw in his 1930s fiction on the gift for fantasy which he had first schooled in Mortmere. The theories of I. A. Richards so shook him in the mid-1920s because Upward feared they might be true; for a time he could not see any connection between his imaginative writing and the real world. He says he felt he could not live, let alone write, without a logical and coherent account of existence. His letters to Isherwood from this period are full of talk, mostly joking, of suicide; still, his life had for a time no certain aim. Marxism offered him a guarantee that the material world existed and that he had a role to play in it; moreover Lenin's *Materialism and Empirio-Criticism* in particular assured him that his emotions and his ideas did reflect reality. When he found himself unable to write, Upward was in despair, and in turning to Marxism he was turning for salvation to a life he believed might eventually provide him with a new subject for his art and thereby rehabilitate his imagination.

Yet even his new theoretical orthodoxy was not enough; once *Journey to the Border* was complete he still could not write. And it is of great significance that when he did begin to write again many years later, it was on exactly the same theoretical basis that he had established in the 1930s; there was nothing wrong, for Upward, with his theories. In fact, the theories are baldly restated near the end of *The Rotten Elements* in a dialogue in which Alan Sebrill, complaining about the quality of contemporary Soviet literature, refers to *Materialism and Empirio-Criticism* to emphasize (as Upward had done in his 'Sketch for a Marxist Interpretation of Literature'[16]) the importance of 'emotional truth' in art. In the end, Sebrill is forced to admit that Lenin never used this precise concept; it is Sebrill's own logical extension of Lenin's argument: 'But if emotions reflect reality they can surely reflect it with a greater or lesser degree of truth'.[17] For Sebrill, 'emotional truth' is crucial to all art, and although he tries to attribute it to or associate it with Lenin's materialism, it has at least as much to do with Wordsworth as with Lenin. Emotional truth is

---

[15] AL, 2 Sept. 1934; TL, 23 Dec. 1934; private American collection.
[16] 'The writer's job is to create new forms now, to arrive by hard work at the emotional truth about present-day reality,' (54).
[17] *Spiral*, 490.

central to Wordsworth's work. In *The Rotten Elements* Sebrill begins reading Wordsworth's *The Excursion* just before the last, worst phase of his illness because he wants 'to find what similarities there were between Wordsworth's disillusionment with the French Revolution and the disillusionment of twentieth-century intellectuals with the Russian Revolution'.[18] But what Upward seems to have found in Wordsworth was something far more personal. He found justification to take himself and his own disillusionment as his main subject, without fear of solipsism. Upward took Wordsworth's work as a demonstration of something of which he needed continual reassurance: that his own emotions had some necessary relation to material reality and to history. In this way, Wordsworth provided the link for Upward from politics back to imaginative literature. Though he wishes it were otherwise, Upward's true subject was never society but himself; Wordsworth showed him that spiritual autobiography is not necessarily an escape from reality, but can be a special way to approach reality.

Upward recently said that he found support in Wordsworth for 'rejecting the established style of my time and trying to write simply.'[19] Upward's plain style is utilitarian and earnest; yet it is flexible enough to range over a variety of experiences and moods without appearing to change registers, and this constancy makes it seem convincingly objective. When Upward describes a moment of vision, we do not doubt that he experienced it. But his style usually lacks elaborate artistry or metaphoric enrichment, and some critics dislike this. In his *Biographia Literaria* Coleridge deplored Wordsworth's 'matter-of-factness' which he regarded as essentially unpoetic.[20] Yet Wordsworth with his professed intention of writing poetry in 'the language really used by men'[21] transformed the very idea of poetry in his time, and his fidelity to reality (such as it was) is one key to his power. For Upward, literary change is a necessary part of political change, and it is clear that he cultivated an ordinary style both because it suited his anti-Romantic purpose of telling about his attempt to lead an ordinary life, and also because he wished to rebel against his Modernist literary predecessors; thus, near the end of the trilogy Sebrill urges himself not to fear his chosen style:

Don't let me be afraid of bleakness. There is a need for poetry to break with the over-richness of twentieth-century bourgeois modernism, to get rid of lit-

---

18 *Spiral*, 471.   19 ALS, 12 Dec. 1987, to K. B.   20 (1817), ch. 21.
21 Preface to the *Lyrical Ballads* (1800).

erary allusiveness, clotted imagery, deliberate ambiguities. A revolt against modernism is as necessary today as a revolt against eighteenth-century poetic conventions was in Wordsworth's time.[22]

Revolt plumbs the depths of Upward's character. He is the grandson of a dissenter—a Congregationalist with radical Calvinist sympathies—and the son of what we would now call an atheist. This helps to explain why he chose some of the literary models that he did. Moreover, there is a clear link between this religious inheritance and his Marxism. In his late story 'The Night Walk', the hero actually attends a Party meeting in what he recognizes as 'a small church, or more probably a Nonconformist chapel', a symbolic connection which Upward says is also a truly reported fact.[23] In *The Spiral Ascent* the most significant spots of time are charged with Sebrill's repeated recognition that he is and wishes to be different from those around him; they are moments of rebellion, expulsion, or differentiation. At school when Sebrill was the last boy in his year to be released from fagging and failed to find any real friends among his peers, 'the conviction came to me, as intensely as if it had been spoken to me in a vision, that I was not inferior to them but only different from them, and I knew I was glad to be different'.[24] He defies the school authorities, cheats on his exams, is deliberately slovenly in OTC until he is demoted, refuses when he is older to use his own fag (though he admits to having beaten one fag because 'I wanted to find out what it was like to beat someone'[25]), and speaks out for the abolition of the whole fagging system. These events hark back to an earlier episode with his father in which Sebrill first recognized that there was something 'odd about me' and that his father 'loved me for it'.[26] But Sebrill's sense of his difference is complicated by the knowledge that his being singled out means someone else is being overlooked. On that evening, while sitting alone with his parents by the fire, he had begun to weep for no apparent reason; then, when he was in bed in the room he shared with one of his brothers, his father had come to comfort him:

He bent his head down towards mine and he whispered to me, 'You are my eldest and my best boy'. My first feeling was of alarm lest Hugh might be awake too now and might overhear these whispered words. I loved him and I

---

[22] *Spiral*, 739.

[23] *The Night Walk and Other Stories* (London, 1987), 174; conversation with K. B., 19 July 1988.

[24] *Spiral*, 626.   [25] Ibid. 647.   [26] Ibid. 559.

sensed how they could hurt him if he heard them. I believe he was asleep, but even this afternoon more than fifty years later the thought that he might have heard them makes me uncomfortable, as does the thought of how they might affect him if I were to tell him of them at any time in future. My second feeling was of reassurance and gladness.[27]

It seems remarkable that *first* Sebrill felt fear that his brother might be hurt and only *afterwards* felt joy at being his father's chosen favourite, moreover, that over fifty years later this fear still disturbs him. Apparently this is how Upward recollects the experience from his own childhood, though it seems likely that he has unconsciously rearranged the sequence of emotions, and that his sense of guilt remains vivid after so many years precisely because he quickly suppressed, with the emotional puritanism also characteristic of his mature writing, the natural joy any child would feel at being the favourite. Throughout his life Upward's desire to be chosen, to be different, even his desire to be an artist, was undermined by his deep-seated suspicion that he had no right to think of himself as in any way better or more gifted than others, and moreover that he might harm them by thinking or acting as if he were. In a slightly different vein, the feeling that he was exceptional felt at times like a burden, 'I began to see myself as someone out of the ordinary, from whom much was expected; and this was to result many times in wretchedness for me when I grew older.'[28]

This conflict was perhaps born out of and certainly intensified by Upward's adolescent desire to defy his mother whose social snobbery caused him great unhappiness in childhood. If he felt at one with the radical values that set his paternal forebears apart from society, he resented her genteel aspirations. In a late story clearly about her, 'Her Day', Upward makes the understanding observation that 'She preferred to make her own fashions. She wanted to be different—and not only in the way she dressed—from the majority of the people she grew up among.'[29] His understanding is based on identification, for he, too, wished to be different; but she wished to be different by being better than those around her, and this apparently moved him to wish to be different by being, from the point of view of her values, worse. Sebrill recalls of his mother, 'her ruling concern had been to ensure that her own life and the lives of those she loved should be as unlike the lives of the poor as possible.' However understanding

[27] *Spiral.*   [28] Ibid. 560.
[29] *The London Magazine* (Nov. 1979); repr. in *The Night Walk*, 8.

Sebrill is in maturity of the fact that his mother may have been driven by fear of the true poverty she apparently glimpsed as a girl, in earlier years her snobbery enraged him. She feared 'that unless we were kept on the right path we might when we grew older slip further and further down toward the social abyss which since her first glimpses of it she had never been able to become wholly unaware of'.[30] Sebrill gravitated rebelliously towards this abyss, determined to be a misfit in the privileged world of public school and university into which his mother's ambition pushed him. Later he deliberately threw over acceptable jobs and became fascinated with the working classes, fulfilling his sense of duty to the poor and the socially downtrodden by joining the workers' party and marrying a working girl who was one of his comrades.

Eventually Sebrill's impulse to rebel carried him even further down the abyss of the ordinary; he was attracted as if fatally to the possibility of personal failure (in a later chapter Upward uses the word 'abyss' again to describe Sebrill's early fears about his poetic future, 'I had anxiety symptoms when I woke in the morning and I glimpsed an abyss of everlasting failure ahead of me'[31]), and he was in a sense determined to divest himself both of the achievements of his parents and grandparents, passed on to him by the capitalist system, and also of his own achievements. He wanted to reach the bottom of the abyss, to relinquish the things which in one part of himself he most desired, as if following his own *via negativa* or again expressing his mystical bent in a proletarian dark night of the soul. In *No Home But the Struggle*, Sebrill recollects on both sides of his family an aspiration towards self-cultivation. Books and travel and languages were treasured both by his parents and by his father's parents; but the right to these things had been earned by long years of work in trade by both sets of grandparents. They had succeeded in boosting their children, Sebrill's parents, into the middle class—Sebrill's father was a doctor; his mother trained briefly as a nurse, then tried acting, and afterwards travelled until her engagement. Still, the lives of his father and his father's brother had been circumscribed by financial dependence on the generation above them; their father had dictated to them their life work and his choices had not suited them well. Sebrill inherited both the aspiration to culture and the certainty that the freedom to fulfil this aspiration had to be earned by hard work, probably of some

[30] *Spiral*, 530.   [31] Ibid. 783.

unrelated kind, although he recalls that in childhood his father gave him sixpence for every poem he could recite. Broadly speaking, this is all true of Upward himself (he insists there is a distinction between his real self and his fictional self; still, it occasionally fades nearly away). On the one hand, Upward was born into more privileged circumstances than either of his parents and he was able to imagine a life devoted to art, but on the other hand he nevertheless needed— unlike Isherwood when they first left university—to earn a living. Apparently Upward, like his character Sebrill, chafed against this necessity because he wanted to be an artist, and yet he felt compelled towards it, partly because he genuinely admired the financial achievements of his paternal grandfather, and the greater freedom such achievements could buy, and partly because he so resented his mother's romanticism and her social ambitions for him. The friction between these contradictory impulses was soul-destroying; in the end, he pursued the utterly ordinary life his mother so feared for him, and which he himself also feared, with an almost self-destructive relish. Alan Sebrill's moment of deepest despair during his illness in *The Rotten Elements* comes after he decides he cannot be a poet or even a Party member, as if these identities are far too distinctive and the challenge of living up to them far too burdensome; he clings to the identity of, simply, schoolmaster, a profession toward which he has felt both repulsion and obligation. At the very moment that he fully accepts this life, anonymous and without ambition of any kind, his cure begins, 'He had succeeded in resigning himself to the prospect of living neither the poetic life nor the Party life, but the ordinary life, the schoolmaster's life.'[32] Almost immediately he begins to be able to write again—but not for publication—and to work again for political change—but not as a Party member.

Upward's rebelliousness formed the basis of his friendship with Isherwood, who was impressed by his behaviour at school. In *Lions and Shadows*, Isherwood described 'Chalmers' as having had a magnetic and inspiring effect upon him when they first met: 'Never in my life have I been so strongly and immediately attracted to any personality, before or since. Everything about him appealed to me. He was a natural anarchist, a born romantic revolutionary'.[33] Isherwood was also impressed by the cult of gloom in Upward's early poetry; the cult of gloom was the seed for the world of Mortmere, and the name

---

[32] *Spiral*, 474.   [33] *Lions*, 18–19.

(crudely inverting the French for dead mother) suggests the shared antagonism towards their mothers which drove both of them in adolescence and afterwards. Upward recently said that he wrote 'The Railway Accident' (the only Mortmere story he ever published) 'to amuse my homosexual literary friends'.[34] The story was written in 1928 when these friends were Auden and Isherwood—later there was others as well—who shared a distinctive sense of humour and offered Upward a special kind of literary challenge. Indeed, in creating Mortmere, Upward helped to shape that sense of humour—a kind of unleashed boyish hysteria akin to what Auden in his 1929 journal described as 'The Prep School atmosphere'[35]—which both Auden and Isherwood put to use, notably in *The Orators*, *The Dog Beneath the Skin*, and *Lions and Shadows*. Isherwood wrote to Upward in 1949, 'I never cease to be grateful to you for having helped me to acquire the play instinct early, with Mortmere,' and he went on to define the play instinct as 'the glee, the insane Mortmere-anarchic element in all experience, however ghastly.'[36] While Isherwood found this 'glee' immensely useful, Upward eventually expunged it from his writing altogether. He now says that he and Isherwood 'never regarded our Mortmere writing as anything more important than an imaginative game'; although it offered them, in his words, 'a free-discipline school in which we could uninhibitedly exercise our powers as writers'.[37]

In the 1920s and 1930s Upward, Isherwood, Auden, Spender, and a few others certainly generated a unique literary excitement, perhaps partly out of their desire to impress one another. Probably the enthusiasm of this group for the weird fantasy world he shared with Isherwood pushed Upward to play and perform closer to the realm of true madness than he might have chosen to himself. There was a genuine danger of his becoming enthralled by the admiration of these precocious and devouring talents (Isherwood and Auden borrowed substantially from Upward in the late 1920s and early 1930s), but Upward's instinct toward imaginative self-preservation had begun to emerge early, long before he was attracted to Marxism, with an impulse to tone down his writing and to restrain his melodramatic imagination. In *Lions and Shadows* Isherwood tells how Chalmers

---

[34] 'Remembering Mortmere', *London Magazine*, NS 27.11 (Feb. 1988), 55.
[35] The unpublished journal kept for a few months in 1929 is in the Berg; this passage is printed in *EA*, see 301.
[36] ALS, Upward Papers, British Library.   [37] 'Remembering Mortmere', 54.

developed a new theory of the novel based on his admiration for Forster's *Howards End*:

Our frightful mistake was that we believed in tragedy: the point is, tragedy's quite impossible nowadays . . . We ought to aim at being essentially comic writers . . . The whole of Forster's technique is based on the tea-table: instead of trying to screw all his scenes up to the highest possible pitch, he tones them down until they sound like mothers' meeting gossip . . . In fact, there's actually less emphasis laid on the big scenes than on the unimportant ones: that's what's so utterly terrific.[38]

Forster ever after remained a literary hero to Upward as well as to Isherwood, and indeed Forster appears as J. R. Sedgely in Upward's late story 'The Procession', reassuring the Upward character that he, unlike most critics, understands Upward's later plain style to be better than his earlier fantastic style, even though it is not as good as Sedgely had once hoped for from him.

Upward's attachment to his homosexual literary friends was undoubtedly genuine, especially in the case of Isherwood with whom he remained close until Isherwood's death; nevertheless, their attractiveness to him must have lain partly in their conventionally unacceptable sexuality and their own defiant attitudes. Choosing them offered yet another way to rebel against his mother's genteel aspirations. But Upward was not homosexual, and he proved to be a misfit even in this group in which he was, by legend, once regarded by the others as the supreme judge of literary merit and the most eccentric talent. Ultimately Upward dropped out of the literary life shared by his friends; the challenge of living up to his reputation even within this little group must have become as burdensome to him as living up to his father's or his mother's expectations. If it was Isherwood's homosexuality, his own inability to fit in, which in part made him attractive to Upward, it was also his homosexuality which helped eventually to divide them. *The Spiral Ascent* begins and ends with the decisive episode on the Isle of Wight in which Richard Marple (the character based on Isherwood) leaves Sebrill behind in order to pursue a boy he has fallen in love with (we learn in volume three that the lover is male but there are broad hints in volume one). Sebrill finds a lover of his own, and transfers some of his intense emotions onto her, but she too rejects him for someone else, precipitating the psychological crisis that leads to his giving up the poetic life and joining the Communist Party.

No other episode in the trilogy is described with such passionate intensity as this first one. The language is enriched by adolescent enthusiasm, grandiose to the point of absurdity, and frequently beautiful. The friendship between Marple and Sebrill generates, at least for Sebrill, the sheer excitement typically associated with erotic love. In Richard's company, Alan is perpetually 'in a state of elation'.[39] But this lover-like elation is sublimated into the realm of language, and Alan prefers their intellectual intercourse to any physical satisfaction. Like a pair of original Adams, the friends name for each other what they see, transforming the world with words:

> Memory or some not clearly perceived external object would suggest a poetically interesting word, and the word would make them look closely at an object whose own fascination would then be reflected back on the word, giving it more than doubled beauty and power. They walked in a rapture of imagery. And Alan thought that no other activity on earth—not even making love—could compare with this savouring of words.[40]

The dialogue in an abandoned version of this opening chapter makes even clearer than the published version that when Richard suddenly decides to leave the island where he has asked Alan to join him so that they can lead the literary life together, he is rejecting their shared imaginative world, 'almost as soon as I saw you in the motorcoach I knew that I could not return to our world again'. By 'our world', Richard says he means 'our being together and seeing everything as material for poetry'.[41] Upward wrote and rewrote the passage; manuscript fragments from the 1940s and 1950s suggest that this visionary time with Isherwood was a main focus of his struggle to write, as if his expulsion from the world they had shared was an expulsion from the realm of language itself. Like an inconstant muse, Isherwood encouraged him from abroad by letter, but Upward had to forge his new style alone.

The dramatic effect of Isherwood's sudden and relatively unfeeling rejection is conveyed by twin passages in *In the Thirties* in which Sebrill views himself in a mirror, first together with Marple and then alone after Marple has left. In the first passage, the pair are excited by their Romantic discovery that only the doomed are beautiful and

---

[39] *Spiral*, 10.   [40] Ibid. 11.   [41] British Library.

that their own fate as writers is to walk the earth, recording and celebrating the doomed like a pair of *poètes maudits*:

> They found themselves standing in front of the big gilt-framed mirror. On the mantelshelf to one side of it there was a vase of Cape gooseberries, and to the other side a vase of honesty; and in its pewter-coloured depths, like a view veiled by faint rain, part of the hallway appeared through the open door of the sitting-room. Above the lincrusta dado in the hallway an engraving of Holman Hunt's *Light of the World* was made visible by the dimly pinkish-golden glow of evening. High against the wallpaper a feathery head of pampas grass intruded, the umbrella-stand in which its stem was based being out of sight behind the door-jamb. They themselves, more vivid in the foreground, stood half-facing each other, at right-angles, both looking into the mirror. They were of much the same height, both rather short. Richard quoted Matthew Arnold's sonnet on Shakespeare:
>
> > '"All pains the immortal spirit must endure,
> > 'All weakness which impairs, all griefs which bow,
> > 'Find their sole speech in that victorious brow."'
>
> He spoke the lines half-ironically, guarding against seeming guilty of the naïve presumption of likening Alan and himself to Shakespeare, but in spite of, or because of, Richard's irony they were conscious as they looked at their reflected faces that there was suffering and victory in those brows too. They were conscious of belonging, however humbly, among the English poets. Awe came upon them as they continued to look at themselves. They saw not merely the two individual representatives but the ages-old and ever-living greatness which was here represented. They would be true to poetry, Alan told himself, no matter what miseries and humiliations they might have to undergo for it, no matter even what crimes they might perhaps have to commit for it.[42]

This is an extraordinary passage, at once melodramatic and utterly convincing because of its careful modulations in tone between the grandiloquent and the deflationary; it is excited, yet cautiously self-aware, too embarrassed to bear its own enthusiasm without qualification, yet unable to leave it unspoken. The accoutrements of *fin-de-siècle* poetic fantasy are all there, peppered with faint touches of comedy—the poets are 'both rather short'. The description of the setting is marvellously realistic, and almost certainly based upon actual fact, yet characteristically for Upward, many of the items described have pointed symbolic significance. The 'vase of honesty', for instance, suggests that there is some truth in the image in this fantastic mirror, even though the distant view of the hallway seems 'veiled by a faint rain' as by a mist of the imagination. The engraving of Hunt's Pre-Raphaelite painting of Christ (a widely-known picture of the Saviour carrying a lantern in a dim garden choked with weeds— sentimental, heavily stylized, and oppressively moralistic) also suggests the false illumination that can be loaned to a scene by the imagina- tion, and, more importantly, calls to mind what was in Upward's view an outmoded ideology that had failed to save any of the masses from their servitude and was now to be replaced by Marxism. In the pas- sage immediately following this one, Richard announces his departure.

The next time Alan sees himself in the mirror, without Marple's inspiring companionship, he has already decided that he has failed as a poet and that he must find a job, but as he views himself in the mirror his self-hatred becomes so intense that he is almost paralysed with fear. He cannot face the thought of returning to schoolmastering and prepares to kill himself:

he turned towards the mantel-piece. The large gilt-framed mirror above this, with white swans in green reeds painted on the two lower corners of the glass, showed him a face for which he could have no sympathy. It was the face, he thought, of a self-fancying spoilt darling, of the overvalued son from a bourgeois home who had been unreasonably expected and had himself expected to do something exceptional, to be different from the common crowd, to be a great poet, a genius, whereas the truth very probably was that he had no talent at all, that he was a pampered young or no longer quite so young shirker who considered himself too good for the kind of everyday job in which he might perhaps have been of some slight use to the community. Alan stood peering for more than a minute at his own image; and the detail of its features—the effeminate eyelashes and the long-lipped mouth— increased his dislike and his contempt for it.

An incipient auto-hypnotic dizziness caused him to stop peering. Then he became conscious of himself not merely as a mirror-image but as someone apart from the mirror. He himself, no longer the reflected object but now the living subject standing here in this room in front of this mantelpiece, was the shirker and the failure. Fear grew inside him. The image, though he still saw it, became as indefinite to him as if it had been visually blurred, and all his attention was held by the feeling of anguished helplessness which was steadily and uncontrollably developing in the very centre of his body. It was like despair made physical: it was like a translation into nervous agony of the thought that now he was wholly lost and abandoned and that his dearest hope in life was finished forever.[43]

[43] Ibid. 32.

The mirror itself suggests, according to the materialist rubric Upward espoused when he read *Materialism and Empirio-Criticism* and which he put forward in his 'Sketch for a Marxist Interpretation of Literature', the way literature reflects reality. Staring at his reflection the second time, Sebrill becomes conscious of himself as a real person; he is the material reality reflected in the mirror image, just as Upward himself is the material reality reflected in the character Alan Sebrill. However, this solitary, disillusioned Sebrill is no more nor less real than the manic, ambitious Sebrill who some days earlier in the very same room stared into the mirror with Richard Marple and saw an altogether different scene. Indeed, Upward's use of the mirror in these two passages shows that literature can reflect reality in more than one way, and still be true to life. The two reflections offered here are infused with two different kinds of emotion, and this is in part because they occur at two different moments in time. Despite Upward's ironic use of details such as Hunt's *Light of the World*, it is not necessarily the case that the first reflection is false and the second true; these reflections accurately describe two different emotional truths about one human being in one setting. Moreover, the difference in these emotional truths has consequences in the material world, since the precipitous change in mood leads Alan to join the Communist Party. Thus, the passages reveal the changes at work underneath the surface of material reality just as in his 'Sketch for a Marxist Interpretation of Literature' Upward had argued, good Marxist writing should do: '[modern writing] must view not merely the surface of life, not isolated aspects of life, but the fundamental forces at work beneath the surface.'[44]

Alan's two images in the mirror are, in a sense, the thesis and antithesis of an ongoing dialectic at work throughout the novel; their synthesis occurs in his decision to join the Communist Party and to be connected again with something outside his solitary self. But this is only a temporary poise in his evolution and, in turn, it becomes a new thesis which will breed a further antithesis—his eventual revolt from the Party—as his personal development spirals on, downward into the abyss of the materially ordinary and upward into the heights of self-understanding. Upward borrows the dialectic from Hegel just as Marx and Engels had done before him. In *Materialism and Empirio-Criticism* Lenin had observed that Marx and Engels had tried to see to it that the materialists should not 'throw away the valuable kernel of the idealist system—the Hegelian dialectics'.[45] Upward points crudely to the dialectical design of his work in his 'Author's Note' (in the rear free endpapers of the volume), which describes it as 'two interlinked dialectical triads', and the formal abstraction of his explanation there is characteristically calculated to downplay his achievement. Within the novel he more subtly reveals the working of the dialectic by combining it with what he learned from Wordsworth and from his other English literary models. The first two volumes, *In the Thirties* and *The Rotten Elements*, are arranged in chronological order, and though the narrative in them oscillates between changing perspectives—vision and disillusion, poetry and Marxism, exhilaration and despair—it achieves no reconciliation between them, no lasting synthesis. The third volume, *No Home But the Struggle*—in which Upward circles back, following the example of Wordsworth, to his childhood prehistory—reveals the earlier trajectory that first established the direction of his life, and reflects upon the meaning of the whole; only then does the work take on convincing meaning. The weight of emphasis in the earlier volumes lies upon the difficult necessities of earning a living and of immersing in the practical struggle to change the world; these leave little time for the creative life of the mind. By the start of the third volume, the revolution has not come to pass, and the only real change is in Sebrill's personal circumstances. Despite his disillusionment with the Party and with Stalin, he has not forsaken his Marxist principles, but their role in his life has become complex and undulating rather than doctrinaire. With the freedom of his retirement and his new literary methods, Sebrill looks inward, recovering from his memories an account of his own evolving political and artistic consciousness. This consciousness, as it is reflected in his writing, is a new synthesis, reconciling through self-understanding the conflicting forces that have shaped his life. Thus, as in the larger Hegelian dialectic, his own personal history proves to be a coming to consciousness of what he is. Upward's artistry is increasingly understated as the trilogy progresses, though it is no less in evidence. At the end of the final volume, when he again describes the youthful episode with Richard Marple on the Isle of Wight, the narrative is swiftly paced, matter-of-fact, and emotionally reticent, bravely displaying the controlled transformation of his style. This

---

[45] Lenin, *Materialism*, 205.

return to the novel's beginnings and to the crisis from which Sebrill first launched himself into a life committed to Marxism recalls again the fevered energy of his first conversion experience, and suggests that even now, in old age, he is once again preparing to renew the struggle. The spiralling return also highlights the central role in Sebrill's creative life of his friendship with Richard Marple. For Upward, the friendship with Isherwood was crucial to his artistic identity. Their letters attest to a continual, serious, and reciprocal exchange of ideas, work, and criticism. Isherwood's very existence, let alone his fond encouragement, persistently challenged Upward to carry on with his writing. Yet the pain suppressed by Sebrill when Marple leaves him on the Isle of Wight suggests what it cost Upward to recognize that their artistic aims were ultimately altogether different from one another, and that in his writing he was entirely alone. When Isherwood died, Upward remarked that he would probably stop writing. But this has proven not to be the case.

Appendix: Edward Upward and his Friendship with Auden

Edward Upward (1903–   ) first met W. H. Auden in a Soho restaurant in 1927, but the two had been corresponding about Auden's poetry since, probably, early 1926. Christopher Isherwood, who introduced them, had already begun to mythologize their literary prowess to one another and he later described their peculiarly hierarchical literary friendship (which extended downward in order of age from Upward, Isherwood, and Auden to include the still younger Stephen Spender) in *Lions and Shadows* (1938). In *Lions and Shadows*, Upward appears as 'Allen Chalmers', Auden as 'Hugh Weston', and Spender as 'Stephen Savage'.

Upward and Isherwood first met in the History Sixth at Repton and Isherwood followed Upward to Corpus Christi College, Cambridge where Upward read History and English. The two were inseparable at Cambridge and remained close lifelong friends. Upward wished to be a writer, but on leaving University needed to earn a living and so became a private tutor and subsequently a schoolmaster. In 1961, after twenty-nine years at his last post, at Alleyn's School, Dulwich (he became head of the English department and a housemaster there), he retired with his wife to a family house on the Isle of Wight where he had often spent childhood holidays.

In 1934, after a self-imposed two-year probationary period during which he attended cell meetings, Upward joined the Communist

Party of Great Britain. He was an active member until leaving it in 1948.

Upward's literary output tends to fall into three periods. His juvenilia, mostly Gothic in atmosphere, includes some technically proficient poetry and the notorious Mortmere stories written with Isherwood at Cambridge in the 1920s; much of Mortmere was imaginative talk between the two friends, never written down, and the surviving stories Upward has long since disavowed for their pornographic and sadistic tendencies. (He allowed a censored version of the latest one, 'The Railway Accident', written in 1928, to be published in 1949, but only under a pseudonym; Auden was especially enthusiastic about this story and several times read the unexpurgated version, now lost, to academic audiences.) During the 1930s, when he was becoming increasingly committed to Communism, Upward published a few pieces of short fiction in *New Country*, *New Writing*, and *Left Review*; his longest work from this second period is *Journey to the Border* (1938). Eventually in 1962, the three volumes of Upward's trilogy, *The Spiral Ascent*, began to appear. Upward calls his trilogy a novel, asserting that it is a work of imagination and not an autobiography or even a disguised autobiography; nevertheless, he also says that it is based on fact, and the experiences of the main character, Alan Sebrill, clearly reflect Upward's own life. The first volume, *In the Thirties* (1962), describes the unhappy failure of Sebrill's early literary ambitions, his decision to join the Communist Party, the start of his marriage, and the birth of the first of his two children. *The Rotten Elements* (1969) traces his falling out with the Party after the Second World War and his eventual departure with his wife from the Party ranks. In *No Home But the Struggle* (1977), Sebrill retires to the Isle of Wight, where, among other things, he becomes engrossed in recollections of his childhood and education. All three volumes deal tenaciously with the theme of the artist's struggle to write in the face of other apparently more pressing obligations. Upward's latest collection of short fiction, *The Night Walk and Other Stories*, appeared in 1987, and his more recent work in *The London Magazine*. The diaries which he began to write simultaneously with Isherwood in the 1920s number, so far, nearly seventy volumes, all unpublished, though Upward has drawn on them for his fiction.

At the beginning of their friendship Upward was for Auden essentially an extension, more remote and severe, of Isherwood's critical, literary-elder-brother persona. Auden was delighted to be praised by

Upward, and he borrowed from Mortmere a few specific details and a great deal of atmosphere for his juvenilia and early published work, especially *The Orators*. Many of the books Upward told Isherwood to read eventually found their way into Auden's hands, and shared names for special literary heroes (such as 'Emmy', 'Kathy', and 'Wilfred' for Emily Brontë, Katherine Mansfield, and Wilfred Owen) appear first in some of Upward's early letters. (Upward told Isherwood to read the work of Bronislaw Malinowski in the mid-1920s, and Auden soon did just that.) But Upward's most significant influence on Auden occurred during the early 1930s, when Auden became fascinated with Upward's resolve to become a Communist. When Auden visited him at Ottershaw College in the summer of 1932 (Upward taught there for a term before going to Alleyn's), Upward allowed Auden to read one of his diaries in which he described his growing affinity for Marxism. Auden was apparently putting himself imaginatively into Upward's shoes that August when he wrote 'A Communist to Others', once widely influential and now disparaged for its lack of authenticity. Later Auden echoed in 'Look, stranger, at this island now' and in 'August for the people and their favourite islands' Upward's prose poem 'The Island'. And, writing as a fellow schoolmaster, Auden dedicated to Upward the Ode 'What siren zooming is sounding our coming' (1930) included in *The Orators*.

Upward's political convictions have remained largely unchanged since the 1930s, even though he has long since left the Communist Party. Since the 1960s he has worked for CND. Politics ultimately came between Upward and Auden, starting around the time that Auden departed for America in 1939. Like so many of his contemporaries, Upward was disillusioned when Auden abandoned his perceived role as poet of the young British Left. Later Upward resented deeply Auden's growing liberalism, in particular his support for Kennedy and afterwards for the Vietnam War. After Auden's death, Upward came to regret the distance that had grown up between them, but as he suggests in his late stories 'At the Ferry Inn' and 'The Poet Who Died', his regret was really only nostalgia for their idealistic youth and for the promise that he still feels Auden failed to fulfil. Despite his fond admiration for Auden, the political and moral differences between them were real.

Interviews, Dialogues, and Conversations with W. H. Auden: A Bibliography

EDWARD MENDELSON

THIS is a list of published reports of words that Auden spoke in private and public conversation, on the lecture platform, and at the radio or television microphone. It includes all varieties of Auden's reported speech, ranging from conventional journalistic interviews to conversations vaguely remembered fifty years later. It replaces the corresponding section in *W. H. Auden: A Bibliography 1924–1969*, 2nd edn. (Charlottesville, Va., 1972), compiled by B. C. Bloomfield and Edward Mendelson.

The first of the four sections of this list includes interviews with Auden together with news stories about him and reviews of his books that include reports of his conversation.

The second section includes transcripts and reports of lectures, poetry readings, broadcasts and broadcast interviews, public dialogues, and debates; announcements of forthcoming talks are not included. The list includes transcriptions of Auden's lectures and broadcasts, but does not include texts that were printed in *The Listener* and elsewhere from his typescripts. These are included in section C of the 1972 *Bibliography* and in the supplement published in *Auden Studies 1*. If a published transcript of a broadcast was based on a surviving typed transcript, the typed transcript is mentioned in the notes. A more detailed list of broadcasts and transcripts is projected for a future volume of *Auden Studies*. There seems to be no basis for the report in 'London Day by Day', *Daily Telegraph*, 19 August 1982, p. 12, that Auden appeared in *Cover to Cover*, a brief film made by the National Book League for the first demonstration broadcasts of television in Britain, on 27 August 1936.

The third section of this list includes news stories, essays, and books that include quotations from Auden but are not primarily about him; the items listed in this section would have been published even if Auden had not been available to provide a quotation.

The fourth and largest section includes Auden's conversation as recalled in memoirs and biographical studies, or quoted or described in published letters. It also includes reports of Auden's attitudes and beliefs when those reports are evidently based on conversations with him, and fictional accounts of characters based more or less directly on Auden by authors who knew him. Some of these accounts, like that in Nicholas Blake's *A Question of Proof*, sound the clear note of authenticity; others are clearly imaginary, but apparently have some basis in fact that may be worth recording here. Plays and novels by authors who never met Auden are excluded, as are statements transmitted posthumously from the beyond.

I have omitted accounts of Auden that merely note his attendance at a dinner or a lecture or his presence at a university or city, but that do not report anything he said. Unless the British and American editions of books with quotations or other reports have different titles or paginations, I have listed only the first edition. In quoting a few trivial or relatively inaccessible items in the notes, I have tried to spare researchers some time that would otherwise be wasted hunting for the originals. It seems likely that the familiar quotations in some items may have been lifted without acknowledgement from earlier ones.

A couplet sometimes attributed to Auden in news stories and reminiscences ('I think that I would rather like | To be the saddle of a bike') was in fact written by one of his friends, probably John Betjeman or Louis MacNeice; see *Letters from Iceland* (1937), p. 113. Auden was mistakenly cited as the author of the statement on Marianne Moore issued by Yale University when she received the Bollingen Prize; the statement appears in the Yale University News Bureau press release 250 (12 January 1951), p. 1, and was quoted in *Newsweek*, 39. 4 (28 January 1952), 65, in *Yale Alumni Magazine*, 15. 5 (February 1952), 21, and elsewhere.

References to *The Times* and *Sunday Times* are to the newspapers printed in London.

Readers will, I hope, treat this list as a preliminary draft of work in progress. It is inevitably incomplete. Stephen Spender mentions in *World within World* (p. 299) an interview that seems otherwise unknown. The University of Wyoming Library has a fire-damaged three-page typescript of an interview with Joy Da[vidman?] titled 'When Poet Meets Poet', prepared in around March 1939; its appearance in print, if it ever occurred, has not been traced. I have located one item **(I18)** only in the form of a press syndicate's dispatch to its subscribers, but not in a newspaper; it is conceivable but unlikely that it was never published.

I have undoubtedly omitted many reports in college and local newspapers of Auden's readings and lectures, and I have seen some items only in the form of unidentified or inadequately dated press cuttings. Some entries omit page numbers; I have seen these items only in the form of cuttings, and hope to print further details when an expanded version of this list appears in a future edition of the Auden *Bibliography*. Further items for that edition will include material from the present volume of *Auden Studies*.

As in the bibliographical supplement in the first volume of *Auden Studies*, I have used a simplified transcription of title-pages and have listed imprints in conventional style (place: publisher, date). As in the normal practice of descriptive bibliography, capitalization of titles has been reduced to the level of prose.

A section of addenda includes material that I had overlooked when this list was first prepared, and some items that appeared while this volume was in press.

Among the many friends who helped to locate items on this list, those who deserve special thanks include B. C. Bloomfield, Nicholas Jenkins, Richard Davenport-Hines, Christopher Phipps, Katherine Bucknell, Audrey Goodman, Michael J. Durkan, and Jonathan Galassi. The compiler will be grateful for additions and corrections, which may be sent to him in care of the Department of English, 602 Philosophy Hall, Columbia University, New York, New York 10027.

INTERVIEWS WITH AUDEN AND NEWS STORIES ABOUT HIM

I1 John Hayward. London letter. *Sun*, New York, 12 Oct. 1935, p. 13.
Indirect quotations of Auden's views on the Group Theatre.

I2 R. B. Marriott. W. H. Auden: 'Dramatists should go to the music-hall.' *Era*, London, 5 Feb. 1936, p. 20.

I3 'Quis'. Mr Auden og fyrirætlanir hans. *Sunnudagsblað vísis* (supplement to *Vísir*), Reykjavík, 26. 175 (28 June 1936), 5.

I4 King honours Auden. *News chronicle*, London, 24 Nov. 1937, p. 1.

An early edition had a longer version of the story, with the same quotations, on the same page, under the title 'King honours poet'. Quoted in Julian Symons, *The thirties: a dream revolved* (London: Cresset, 1960), p. 61.

I5 [Unidentified newspaper interview, Nov. 1937.]
Briefly quoted in **I650**.

I6 Ying ming chi che chien hsien kuei lai [Famous British correspondents back from the front]. *Ta kung pao*, Hankow, 22 Apr. 1938, p. 3.
An interview by Ma Tong-na with Auden and Isherwood, followed by an account of Auden's remarks on modern British poetry.

I7 May Cameron. Author! Author! . . . England's white-haired literary boys, W. H. Auden and Christopher Isherwood, talk of China and themselves. *New York post*, 9 July 1938, p. 11.

I8 An interview with W. H. Auden. *Granta*, Cambridge, 47. 1090 (23 Nov. 1938), 124.
A comic account of an interview that scarcely occurred.

I9 Young British poet to study our ways. *New York times*, 12 Mar. 1939, p. 24.
Printed in the City Edition only; not in the microfilm edition.

I10 Noted British authors to speak on modern trends in British writing. *Daily worker*, New York, 5 Apr. 1939, p. 9.
Indirect report; Auden plans to stay in America for more than a year.

I11 Jacqui Quadow. Auden turns campus poetry-conscious as he comments on life and writings. *Phoenix*, Swarthmore College, 59. 21 (9 Apr. 1940), 1.

I12 Arthur Zeiger. Wystan Hugh Auden. M.A. diss., Columbia University, 1941.
Interview quoted on pp. 60, 62, 67, and 72.

I13 William G. King. Music and musicians. *Sun*, New York, 22 Mar. 1941, p. 23.
Benjamin Britten comments: 'Auden and I were fascinated by the [Paul] Bunyan legend because we considered Bunyan not only as an American but as a figure symbolic of all frontier life.'

I14 Guggenheim award given W. H. Auden. *Michigan daily*, 7 Apr. 1942, pp. 1–2.

I15 Dick Lyman. Rumors, awe surround Auden's arrival here. *Phoenix*, Swarthmore College, 62. 2 (20 Oct. 1942), 1.

I16 Paul Seabury. Auden, would-be mine operator favors ungodly but intelligent. *Phoenix*, Swarthmore College, 63. 3 (14 Dec. 1943), 3.

I17 W. H. Auden to turn actor. *New York times*, 16 Apr. 1945, p. 19.
Auden will play the silent walk-on role of the monk in the Swarthmore College production of *The ascent of F6*. Auden changed the ending of the play from tragedy to 'optimistic satire'.

I18 Kent Stoddard. Time, space, science add up to poetry prize. [Syndicated by Associated Press Newsfeatures, *ca*. May 1945.]
This interview was prepared for release on the occasion of Auden's acceptance of the American Academy of Arts and Letters award of merit, which was scheduled for 18 May 1945, but did not occur because he was in Europe at the time. The interview exists as a mock-up distributed to subscribing editors, but no publication of it in a newspaper has been traced.

I19 Eleanor Follansbee Von Erffa. Auden at Swarthmore. *National Theatre Conference bulletin*, 7. 4 (Nov. 1945), 27–32.
Comments on the Swarthmore production of *The ascent of F6*.

I20 [Robert Fitzgerald.] Eclogue, 1947. *Time*, 50. 3 (21 July 1947), 98–100.
Review of *The age of anxiety* with quotations from an interview.

I21 Maurice Cranston. Poet's retreat. *John o'London's weekly*, 67. 1329 (6 Feb. 1948), 49–50.
Quoted without acknowledgement in a note on Auden's visit to London, 'John Bouverie's journal. The poet's return', *News chronicle*, 6 Apr. 1948, p. 2. Auden's travel plans were also reported in 'Shy poet', *Evening standard*, 19 Apr. 1948.

I22 [Frank Hadley.] Famous poet on holiday in Lake District. *West Cumberland times*, Cockermouth, 25 Aug. 1948, p. 4.
Auden is probably the source of the report that ' "Paid on Both Sides" used a setting, "Coldbarrow Farm", Horse and Farrier Inn and district generally reminiscent of the country around Threlkeld'. Hadley also reported anonymously that Auden was visiting his father: 'Poet re-visits Threlkeld', *Lancashire daily post*, 24 Aug. 1948, p. 1.

I23 Oskar Jancke. Begegnung mit W. H. Auden. *Deutsche Zeitung und Wirtschafts Zeitung*, Stuttgart, 5. 55 (12 July 1950), 11.
Indirect quotations.

I24 P. Lal. Auden the man. *Statesman*, Calcutta, 2 Sept. 1951, p. 10.

I25 M[aurice] D[olbier]. Interviewing a poet at the breakfast table. *Providence journal*, Providence, RI, 20 Jan. 1952, section 6, p. 8.

126 Notre carnet. *Preuves*, 2. 14 (Apr. 1952), 65.

Brief remarks on the role of American universities.

127 Claude Cézan. Le poète W. H. Auden nous présente l'œuvre du XXe siècle. *Les nouvelles littéraires*, 17 Apr. 1952, p. 1.

Brief remarks on translation, opera, and other subjects.

128 Paul V. Beckley. Librettists' readings to herald Stravinsky's 'Rake's progress'. *New York herald tribune*, 26 Jan. 1953, p. 17.

129 The Londoner's diary. Author of the rake. Becoming a professor. *Evening standard*, London, 13 Feb. 1953, p. 4.

Indirect quotations from a brief interview in New York on the opera and on the $5,000 pay for his Smith College appointment.

130 Henry Hewes. Broadway postscript: 'Rake's' progress. *Saturday review*, 36. 7 (14 Feb. 1953), 43–4.

131 Auden to pick best play end. *Sophian*, Smith College, 1. 47 (28 Apr. 1953), 1.

Two brief quotations specifying the new ending he asked students to compose for *The dog beneath the skin*.

132 Michael Davidson. The poet works to a timetable. [Unidentified newspaper, perhaps *Evening standard* or *Daily herald*, probably late Dec. 1953 or Jan. 1954.]

133 Edith T. Aney. British poetry of social protest in the 1930's: the problem of belief in poetry [*sic*] of W. H. Auden, C. Day Lewis, 'Hugh MacDiarmid,' Louis MacNeice, and Stephen Spender. Ph.D., diss., University of Pennsylvania, 1954.

Direct and indirect quotations on biographical matters, from an interview, 1952, *passim*.

134 Elizabeth Sewall. The tale of the quest for Auden. *Cambridge review*, 85. 1829 (13 Feb. 1954), 296.

Trivial report of a momentary meeting.

135 Poets do better, one of them says. *Los Angeles times*, 16 Mar. 1954, pp. 1, 3.

136 Michele Regine. Il poeta inglese Auden prende alloggio a Forio. *Il giornale*, Napoli, 9 July 1954, p. 4.

Auden is probably the source of the report that Auden and Kallman propose to write a script for a film on Mozart—perhaps an erroneous account of the project for the televised translation of *The magic flute*.

137 N[ikos] Spanias. O poiētēs W. H. Auden. *Kypriaka grammata*, Nicosia, 19. 323 (Nov. 1954), 420–2.

I38 Ettore Settanni. Intervista ad Ischia con il poeta Auden. *Il giornale*, Napoli, 10 Oct. 1955, p. 9.

I39 Sidney Fields. Only human. *New York mirror*, 29 Jan. 1956, p. 35.
Biographical interview.

I40 Will Lissner. Poet, judge assist a samaritan. *New York times*, 3 Feb. 1956, pp. 1, 49.
Auden gives Dorothy Day money to pay a fine. Also reported as 'The saint & the poet', *Time*, 67. 11 (12 Mar. 1956), 89–90. See also I479.

I41 A. C. M. How Prof. Auden may stimulate Oxford writing. *Oxford Mail*, 1 June 1956, p. 8.
Extensive comments on Oxford and writing.

I42 The Londoner's diary. Auden's first lecture. *Evening standard*, 11 June 1956, p. 4.
Returning to Christ Church makes him feel 'just like a new boy at a public school'.

I43 'Atticus'. The initial shove. *Sunday times*, 24 June 1956, p. 3.
Auden identifies Robert Medley as the person who first encouraged him to write poetry.

I44 [Ettore] Settanni. Auden a Ischia. *Il giornale*, Napoli, 17 July 1956, p. 3.

I45 Cecilia Mangini. Poesia senza oscurità. *Il punto*, Roma, 2 Nov. 1957, p. 16.

I46 Gabriel Pomerand. W. H. Auden: 'Il n'y a plus d'écrivains en France depuis 1789'. *Arts*, Paris, 679 (16–22 July 1958), 4.

I47 Franz Hitzenberger. Amerikas bedeutendster Lyriker trat Weinhebers Nachfolge an. *Neues Österreich*, 19 Oct. 1958, pp. 5–6.

I48 'John London'. Peasant poet. *News chronicle*, 21 Oct. 1958, p. 3.
He has 'real peace' in his new house in Kirchstetten.

I49 M. S. Handler. Austria restful, W. H. Auden finds. *New York times*, 2 Nov. 1958, section 1, p. 133.

I50 Alberico Sala. Notizie bibliografiche e informative [untitled interview]. *Inventario*, Milano, 14. 1–6 (Jan.–Dec. 1959), 344–6.

I51 Piero Nardi. Intervista con Guido Piovene e Wystan Auden ospiti della Fondazione Giorgio Cini. *L'Italia che scrive*, 42. 1 (Jan. 1959), 1–3.

I52 Betty Bridgman. W. H. Auden says 'no'. *Christian Science monitor*, 7 Jan. 1959, p. [8].

I53 Paul Hume. Ft. Myer GI takes over star's role of Stravinsky opera on brief notice. *Washington post*, 13 Feb. 1959, pp. A1, C7.

Includes excerpts from a discussion by Auden and Kallman on *The rake's progress*.

I54 Auden, Barzun, and Trilling form board. *New York times*, 1 Apr. 1959, p. 33.

One sentence on the attraction to readers of the Mid-Century Book Club.

I55 Professor's denial. *Sunday times*, 10 May 1959, p. 31.

Auden 'furious' at 'absolutely false' reports that he is writing lyrics for a musical based on Isherwood's *Goodbye to Berlin*.

I56 Wieland Schmied. Ein Ort für Dichter: Besuch bei W. H. Auden in Kirchstetten. *Die Presse*, Wien, 5 July 1959, p. 17.

I57 Auden im Wienerwald: ein Altar aus Sandwiches. *Die Wochen-Presse*, Wien, 14. 28 (11 July 1959), 10.

I58 Jan Koprowsky. Z Audenem o Polsce, Austri i literaturze. *Odgłosy*, Łódź, 2. 43 (25 Oct. 1959), 8.

I59 George Stillman. A personal interview with W. H. Auden. *Trace*, 35 (Aug.–Sept. 1959), 18–20.

I60 Jan Koprowsky. Spotkanie z W. H. Audenem. *Życie literackie*, 10. 12 (426), (20 Mar. 1960), 10.

A revised version appears in Koprowsky's *Z południa i północy* (Katowice: Śląsk, 1963) as 'U Wystana Hugha Audena', pp. 143–8.

I61 William A. McWhirter. Auden sits in on Intime rehearsal. *Daily Princetonian*, 20 Apr. 1960, p. 1.

Brief remarks on staged version of *The age of anxiety*.

I62 William B. Macht. Influx of actors, critics will view 'Age of anxiety'. *Daily Princetonian*, 28 Apr. 1960, pp. 1, 3.

I63 'Difficult' poetry? *Listener*, 63. 1623 (5 May 1960), 787–8.

Excerpt from a BBC Television interview with Philip Burton, broadcast 24 Apr. 1960.

I64 Kenneth Allsop. W. H. Auden on the economics of poetry. *Daily mail*, London, 15 June 1960, p. 8.

I65 Jack McPhaul. Poet Auden holds a rare press conference here. *Chicago sun-times*, 19 Nov. 1960, section 2, p. 7.

I66 'Atticus'. Mainly about people. *Sunday times*, 11 June 1961, p. 15.

Brief interview.

I67 Alberto Arbasino. Un poeta al Grand Hotel. *Il mondo*, Roma, 13. 29 (18 July 1961), 7.

Auden at the première of *Elegy for young lovers*. Reprinted as 'W. H. Auden' in his *Sessanta posizioni* (Milano: Feltrinelli, 1971), pp. 34–9.

I68 Robert Phelps. A bird of passage. *Harper's bazaar*, New York, 96th year, 3016 (Mar. 1963), 140, 203–4.

I69 Londoner's diary. Auden musical? *Evening standard*, 18 Sept. 1963, p. 6.

Two sentences on the proposal that he write lyrics for *Man of La Mancha*.

I70 S. M. L. Aronson. It must be the poet. *Yale daily news*, 11 Dec. 1963, p. 3.

I71 B. C. Bloomfield, *W. H. Auden, a bibliography: the early years through 1955*. Charlottesville: University Press of Virginia, 1964.

The notes include information offered by Auden in an interview with the compiler, *passim*. Also in the second edition: B. C. Bloomfield and Edward Mendelson, *W. H. Auden, a bibliography, 1924–1969* (Charlottesville: University Press of Virginia, 1972).

I72 Joel Ohlsson. Möte met Auden. *Lundagård*, Lund, 44. 9 (1964), 5.

I73 The editor's window. *Yale alumni magazine*, 27. 5 (Feb. 1964), 5.

Remark on a ten-day visit: 'Nobody tried to make me *laugh*.'

I74 Skáldið Auden í Íslandsvíking í annað sinn. *Vísir*, 13 Apr. 1964, pp. 1, 5.

I75 M[atthias Johannesen?] Spjall við Auden. *Morgunblaðið*, Reykjavík, 14 Apr. 1964, pp. 12, 17.

I76 Tomislav Sabljak. Susret s W. H. Audenem: zapravo, davno smo se već sreli. *Telegram*, Zagreb, 5. 225 (14 Aug. 1964), 3, 8.

I77 Tomislav Sbaljak. Portret pjesnika W. H. Audena. *Republika*, Zagreb, 20. 11 (Nov. 1964), 477–8.

Brief account of Auden's visit to Zagreb, Aug. 1964.

I78 Lars Gustafsson. Hotel Royal: Budapest kl ½ 8 f.m.: frukost med mr Auden. *Expressen*, Stockholm, 26 Nov. 1964, p. 4.

I79 Klaus Geitel. Ein Gedicht kann viele Jahre kosten: Gespräch mit W. H. Auden—der Dichter als Gast der Ford Foundation in Berlin. *Die Welt*, Hamburg, 26 Nov. 1964, p. 7.

Extensive dialogue. A few lines are translated into English in the column 'Life & letters today', *Encounter*, 24. 3 (Mar. 1965), 95.

I80 John G. Blair. *The poetic art of W. H. Auden*. Princeton: Princeton University Press, 1965.

Indirect quotations from an interview, pp. 124, 178.

181 Cornelia Jacobsen. Ein halbes Jahr zu Gast in Berlin. *Die Zeit*, Hamburg, 23 Apr. 1965, p. 22.

182 C. S. The poet who preaches love. *Glasgow herald*, 28 Aug. 1965, p. 6.

183 London day by day. Poets as performers. New York conformist. *Daily telegraph*, 30 Aug. 1965, p. 6.
Auden is a registered Democrat, the 'only New York intellectual who supports President Johnson on Vietnam'; if he were in England he would be a Conservative.

184 Londoner's diary. An Auden hymn. *Evening standard*, 2 Nov. 1965, p. 6.
Indirect report that Dean C. A. Simpson asked Auden to write a hymn for the Festival of St. Frideswide, an October event at Christ Church, and that Auden said he would consider it.

185 Christopher Burstall. Portrait gallery. *Sunday times*, 21 Nov. 1965, magazine, pp. 22–4.

186 Lea Gibbs Park. Poet of perspectives: the style of W. H. Auden. Ph.D. diss., Northwestern University, 1966.
Interview quoted on pp. 206, 229, 363, and 377.

187 Breon Mitchell. W. H. Auden and Christopher Isherwood: the 'German influence'. *Oxford German studies*, 1 (1966), 163–72.
Based partly on conversations with Auden on the plays, Mar. 1965.

188 [John Plotz.] Interview with W. H. Auden. *Island*, Cambridge, Mass., 2 (Spring 1966), 2–7.

189 F. E. Worte, die nach Musik verlangen: Gespräch mit dem Dichter und Übersetzer W. H. Auden. *Die Presse*, Wien, 23 June 1966, p. 6.

190 Auden on poetry: a conversation with Stanley Kunitz. *Atlantic*, 218. 2 (Aug. 1966), 94–102.

191 Stephen Wakelam and Heather Dubrow. Modern writers have no place here—Auden. *Varsity*, Cambridge, 59. 3 (22 Oct. 1966), 10.

192 Peter Stadlen. Beyond the reach of words. *Daily telegraph*, London, 29 Oct. 1966, p. 11.
Extensive reported opinions on opera.

193 Jeremy Campbell. In the house where Trotsky lived, W. H. Auden re-writes the Ring . . . *Evening standard*, London, 14 Dec. 1966, p. 7.
Auden in fact never had any plans to rewrite Wagner's Ring cycle.

I94 Polly Platt. W. H. Auden. *American scholar*, 36. 2 (Spring 1967), 266–70.

I95 'Mandrake'. Of drugs and drivel. *Sunday telegraph*, 29 Oct. 1967, p. 5.

I96 Philip Hodson. W. H. Auden interviewed on the occasion of his poetry reading at the Union. *Isis*, Oxford, 8 Nov. 1967, p. 14.

I97 Paul Hirschhorn. 'And in the quiet oblivion of this water, let them stay'. *Penumbra*, New York, 1, 3–4 (1968), 37–40.
An evidently unreliable report of an interview.

I98 Raymond A. Sokolov. Auden at sixty. *Newsweek*, 71. 5 (29 Jan. 1968), 77–8.

I99 David Pryce-Jones. The rebel who got away. *Daily telegraph*, 9 Aug. 1968, magazine, pp. 20–2.
Reprinted in briefer form as 'Conversation with W. H. Auden', *Holiday*, 45. 6 (June 1969), 56, 66–7.

I100 Jean Campbell. Moon madness and the poet. *Evening standard*, 1 Jan. 1969, p. 11.

I101 Terry Coleman. Summer gathering of the poets. *Guardian*, London, 10 July 1969, p. 4.
Interview at the Poetry International festival.

I102 Byron Rogers. Poet's lament for bored youth. *Times*, 11 July 1969, p. 2.

I103 Londoner's diary. The charm of Auden. Reticent. Science. *Evening standard*, 12 July 1969, p. 6.

I104 Susan Barnes. This island now by W. H. Auden: Britain today through the eyes of its most famous living poet. *Sun*, London, 12 July 1969, p. 3.

I105 Richard Holmes. The whole point of poetry. *Times*, 19 July 1969, p. 21.
At the Poetry International Festival.

I106 The Times diary. *Times*, 21 July 1969, p. 21.
Indirect quotation of his refusal to speak on the BBC on the moral, historical, and philosophical implications of the moon landing.

I107 Jean Campbell. Lonely Auden: will Oxford give him refuge? *Evening standard*, 10 Dec. 1969, p. 19.
Partly prompted by the appearance of I109. Among other remarks, 'He told me this week that he is "putting out feelers" at Christ Church,

Oxford, in the hope that his old college will invite him to spend his declining years in a set of rooms there.' A further report, probably not based on direct conversations, appears in: Simon Kavanagh, 'Expatriate Auden returning home', *New York post*, 9 Jan. 1970, p. 15; this is attributed to the *London express*, but cannot be found in the microfilm text of the *Daily express*.

I108 Craft interview—W. H. Auden. *New York quarterly*, 1 (Winter 1970), 7–13.

Unsigned interview by Mary Jane Fortunato and William Packard. Reprinted in *The craft of poetry, interviews from* The New York quarterly, William Packard, editor (Garden City, NY: Doubleday, 1974), pp. 1–9. An excerpt appears as 'Auden on his craft', *Intellectual digest*, 2. 10 (June 1972), 74–5.

I109 Jon Bradshaw. Holding to schedule with W. H. Auden. *Esquire*, 73. 1 (Jan. 1970), 137–9, 26, 28 [*sic*].

See letters to the editor, ibid., Apr. 1970, p. 24. A rearranged and somewhat longer version of the interview appeared as 'Oh Wystan!', *Harper's bazaar*, London, Feb. 1970, pp. 46–51. The *Esquire* version also appeared as 'W. H. Auden and his graffiti' [title from contents page], *Observer*, 7 Nov. 1971, magazine, pp. 35–6, 39–41, 43, 45. For Auden's comments on this interview, as reported by Isherwood, see Philip Oakes, 'Here on a visit', *Sunday times*, 15 Feb. 1970, p. 52.

I110 Auden angry at report of plan to return. *Daily telegraph*, 13 Jan. 1970, p. 17.

Auden 'absolutely furious' at reports like those listed in I107.

I111 Webster Schott. Autumn for the 'age of anxiety'. *Life*, 68. 3 (30 Jan. 1970), 52, 52A–B, 53–4.

Reprinted in *Life [Atlantic]*, Amsterdam, 48. 3 (16 Feb. 1970), 52–6.

I112 Arthur H. Lubow. W. H. Auden: 'Can sixty make sense to sixteen-plus?' *Harvard crimson*, 12 Mar. 1970, pp. 3–4.

I113 Susan Bellos. Auden's gloomy view of history. *Jerusalem post*, 10 Apr. 1970, p. 4.

I114 Mosheh Dor. "Al Awschvits i efshar likhtov shirim' [Impossible to write poems about Auschwitz]. *Ma'ariv*, Tel-Aviv, 10 Apr. 1970, p. 13.

I115 Roy Perrott. Auden. *Observer*, 28 June 1970, p. 25.

Reprinted as 'W. H. Auden: the poet as punctual man', *Washington post*, 19 July 1970, section B, p. 5.

I116 Charles Osborne. A rhyme of poets. *Sunday times*, 5 July 1970, p. 27.

Auden at the Poetry International festival.

I117 Auden w swoim domu. *Życie literackie*, 20. 33 (968), (16 Aug. 1970), 15.

I118 W[ill] K[eller]. City without walls. *Merian*, Hamburg, 23. 9 ([Sept.] 1970), 42–3.

In German.

I119 Stacy Waddy. Horse-drawn into Auden's Eden. *Guardian*, 4 Sept. 1970, p. 10.

Reprinted as 'Auden's kind of Eden', *Manchester guardian weekly*, 103. 10 (12 Sept. 1970), 14.

I120 William Foster. Auden the poetic exile. *Scotsman*, Edinburgh, 28 Nov. 1970, week-end Scotsman, p. 1.

I121 Edd D. Wheeler. W. H. Auden and his American experience. Ph.D. diss., Emory University, 1971.

Interview (19 Mar. 1970) quoted, p. 64; indirectly quoted, pp. 61, 99–100, 134.

I122 Interview with W. H. Auden. *Concern*, Nyack, NY, 6. 1 (Winter 1971), 9–14.

Conducted by Arkadi Nebolsine, Serge Schmemann, Irene Fokatis, and James Couchell.

I123 Judson Hand. New York through the eyes of a poet. *New York daily news*, 13 Jan. 1971, p. 46.

I124 Michael Ballantyne. Untidy, like the rest of us. *Montreal star*, 6 Mar. 1971, p. 25.

Detailed report of a reading at McGill University.

I125 Marin Knelman. W. H. Auden as campus minstrel: a great poet can be crabby too. *Globe and mail*, Toronto, 6 Mar. 1971, p. 24.

I126 Peterborough. London day by day. Poets of the world. *Daily telegraph*, 9 July 1971, p. 14.

Auden at Poetry International, made 'sure that the timing of his contribution was strictly kept'.

I127 Sydney Edwards. Breaking the bread with Mr. Auden. *Evening standard*, 9 July 1971, p. 21.

I128 Judith Cook. W. H. Auden—the hungry quest. *Birmingham post*, 10 July 1971, p. 6.

I129 Charles Mitchelmore. W. H. Auden: interlude near the Vienna woods. *Women's wear daily*, 13 July 1971, pp. 1, 26.

I130 Alan Levy. In the autumn of the age of anxiety. *New York times*, 8 Aug. 1971, section 6 (magazine), pp. 10–11, 29, 31, 34, 36, 42–3.

Reprinted in *New York times biographical edition*, 2 (8 Aug. 1971), 2751–6. Revised and expanded in Levy's *W. H. Auden: in the autumn of the age of anxiety* (Sag Harbor, NY: Permanent Press, 1983). The original interview was reported briefly by Jeremy Campbell, 'A wrong number for Auden', *Evening standard*, 18 Aug. 1971, p. 11. See also **I180**.

I131 Vistan Khju Odn: 'Počesten sum i obvrzan pak da dojdam.' *Nova Makedonija*, Skopje, 29 Aug. 1971, p. 7.

Interview at a poetry festival in Struga.

I132 Nicholas de Jongh. Auden—strongest survivor of them all. *Guardian*, 9 Oct. 1971, p. 1.

I133 Bernard Weinraub. Auden: 'a difference in memories'. *New York times*, 19 Oct. 1971, p. 52.

A longer version of this interview, with additional quotations, appeared as 'W. H. Auden: "We're all contemporaries"', *International herald tribune*, Paris, 20 Oct. 1971, p. 16; and this longer version was syndicated by the New York Times News Service. The first version is reprinted in *New York times biographical edition*, 2 (19 Oct. 1971), 2729, and was widely syndicated (for example, in *Cincinnati enquirer*, 15 June 1972, p. 30).

I134 Poet says drugs ruin creativity and distort time. *Evening bulletin*, Philadelphia, 18 Nov. 1971, Suburban West News, p. 29C.

Brief report on a talk at Swarthmore College; see next item.

I135 Betty McElrey. Famed poet Auden urges authenticity, plays game of life seeking 'good art'. *Phoenix*, Swarthmore College, 19 Nov. 1971, p. 2.

I136 Israel Shenker. W. H. Auden plans to move back home to England. *New York times*, 7 Feb. 1972, p. 28.

Reprinted the next day in many newspapers that subscribed to the New York Times New Service. A shorter version appeared as 'Another institution leaves New York City: W. H. Auden', *International herald tribune*, Paris, 8 Feb. 1972, p. 14. Adapted without acknowledgement to the original as 'Leaving the muggers', *Evening standard*, 7 Feb. 1973.

I137 Mabel Elliott. Auden to leave America and live in Oxford college. *Daily telegraph*, 8 Feb. 1972, p. 15.

I138 Philip Howard. Mr. Auden returning to live at Oxford. *Times*, 8 Feb. 1972, p. 1.

I139 Unexpected place for best martini. *Daily telegraph*, 10 Feb. 1972, p. 16.

Auden found it in Ashby de la Zouch, and assumed that an American military base had once been nearby.

I140 W. H. Auden 65 ára: vonast til þess að heimsækja Ísland. *Morgunblaðið*, 24 Feb. 1972, p. 2.

I141 Christopher Bone. W. H. Auden in the 1930's: the problems of individual commitment to political action. *Albion*, 4. 1 (Spring 1972), 3–11.

Includes a very brief account of Auden's trip to Spain, from an interview on 30 Mar. 1968.

I142 Daniel Halpern. Interview with W. H. Auden. *Antaeus*, 5 (Spring 1972), 135–49.

I143 Auden on opera, detective writers, wit, politics, the camera, drugs, poets, and poetry. *Swarthmore College bulletin*, 69. 6 (May 1972), 2–3, 5–6, 10.

'This excerpt was taken from a tape recording made last November, when W. H. Auden visited the classroom of Professor Brendan Kennelly.'

I144 Martha Duffy. Poet Auden joins the artistic migration. *Life*, 72. 17 (5 May 1972), 89.

I145 Nicholas de Jongh. Auden to keep US ties. *Guardian*, 21 June 1972, p. 1.

Will not change his citizenship if invited to be Poet Laureate; the headline in early editions was 'Auden rejects change'. Quoted in 'Sayings of the week', *Observer*, 25 June 1972.

I146 Penny Symon. Mr. Auden 'cross' at laureate rumours. *Times*, 22 June 1972, p. 2.

Reported as 'W. H. Auden: kein Hofdichter', *Die Presse*, Wien, 26 June 1972, p. 5.

I147 Michael Andre. A talk with W. H. Auden. *Unmuzzled ox*, New York, 1. 3 (Summer 1972), 5–11.

Reappears as 'W. H. Auden: intermezzo' in Andre's dissertation, 'Levertov, Creeley, Wright, Auden, Ginsberg, Corso, Dickey: essays and interviews with contemporary American poets' (Ph.D. diss., Columbia University, 1974), pp. 126–36.

I148 Philip Toynbee. Mellow fruitfulness. *Sunday times*, 8 Oct. 1972, p. 38.

On free verse: '*kein spass*'.

I149 W. H. Auden talking to Lynda Lee-Potter. *Daily mail*, 14 Oct. 1972, p. 7.

Briefly quoted in 'Notes on people', *New York times*, 18 Oct. 1972, p. 38.

I150 David Bell. W. H. Auden comes home. *Oxford mail*, 16 Oct. 1972.

Brief comment.

I151 Keith Nurse. W. H. Auden returns to Oxford. *Daily telegraph*, 17 Oct. 1972, p. 17.

Brief comment.

I152 Mr. Auden comes to Oxford. *Times*, 17 Oct. 1972, p. 16.

Brief comment.

I153 Fred Coleman. Auden says 'intrigue' preceded his return. *Daily American*, Rome, 19 Oct. 1972.

An Associated Press dispatch from London; probably also printed in other newspapers.

I154 Return of the exile poet. *Oxford times*, 20 Oct. 1972.

Brief comment.

I155 'Atticus' [Allan Hall]. Auden shuffles back. *Sunday times*, 29 Oct. 1972, p. 32.

I156 W. P. Nicolet. Auden's The fall of Rome. *Explicator*, 31. 3 (Nov. 1972), item 22.

Auden confirmed the author's interpretation during a recent reading tour.

I157 Don Chapman. The poetic life—out of a suitcase. *Oxford mail*, 1 Nov. 1972.

I158 Tim Devlin. A poet out to cause a bit of bother. *Times*, 4 Nov. 1972, p. 14.

I159 Peter Mortimer. Old wedding-cake face. *The journal, Newcastle*, 18 Dec. 1972, p. 8.

I160 Man cleared of theft from Oxford poet. *Oxford times*, 12 Jan. 1973, p. 12.

Brief report of Auden's testimony at the trial. For further reports see: 'Man thought Auden a "soft touch", court told', *Daily telegraph*, 5 Jan. 1973; and 'Poet says: I was robbed', *Sun*, London, 5 Jan. 1973, p. 7.

I161 Sharon Griffiths. Auden: New Yorker in an Oxford fog. *Radio times*, 192. 2568 (25 Jan. 1973), 12.

Remarks on Oxford, in an article that previews Auden's BBC appearance on 28 Jan. 1973.

I162 Oxford 'hell' says Auden. *Daily telegraph*, 30 Jan. 1973, p. 17.
The first of many reports of Auden's replies and explanations in telephone interviews after a remark about Oxford in a letter to Michael Newman was quoted without his consent in Newman's 'In praise of East Fifth', *New York times*, 27 Jan. 1973, p. 29. Auden's further comments appear in: Mel Juffe, 'Auden glares at limelight', *New York post*, 31 Jan. 1973, p. 3. Based on these sources, the incident was also reported in 'Notes on people', *New York times*, 31 Jan. 1973, p. 47; 'Sayings of the week', *Observer*, 4 Feb. 1973, p. 9; 'Newsmakers', *Newsweek*, 81. 7 (12 Feb. 1973), 44; and 'People', *Time*, 101. 7 (13 Feb. 1973), 35.

I163 Remembering and forgetting—W. H. Auden talks to Richard Crossman about poetry. *Listener*, 89. 2291 (22 Feb. 1973), 238–40.
Adapted from a BBC Television interview, 28 Jan. 1973. 'Londoner's diary', *Evening standard*, 29 Jan. 1973, p. 6, quotes Auden's correction of his statement in the broadcast that he had not altered his poem 'Hell is neither here nor there'.

I164 John Dugdale. Beneath the skin. *Isis*, Oxford, 11 Mar. 1973, p. 23.
Brief interview on an Oxford production of *The dog beneath the skin*.

I165 Albany at large. Baht 'at. *Sunday telegraph*, 29 Apr. 1973, p. 2.
Auden refused to read a lesson at the inaugural service at the parish church of St. Margaret, Ilkley, because the vicar insisted on using the New English Bible text.

I166 Theft. *Cherwell*, Oxford, 146. 1 (3 May 1973), p. 1.
Remarks on the theft of his wallet.

I167 Alex Rentoul. Fraud: you may be the victim. *Isis*, Oxford, 4 May 1973, p. 7.
Auden on the theft of his wallet, and other matters.

I168 Londoner's diary. The strange way W. H. Auden takes a bath. *Evening standard*, 26 June 1973, p. 20.
No hot water at the Spenders.

I169 Shyam Bhatia. An afternoon with Auden. *Statesman*, Calcutta and Delhi, 5 Aug. 1973, magazine, p. i.

I170 Timothy Foote. Auden: the sage of anxiety. *Time*, 102. 15 (8 Oct. 1973), 113–14.
Includes quotations from unpublished interviews that Foote conducted in 1963 in preparation for a projected *Time* cover story about Auden; the interviews were also used by Humphrey Carpenter in his *W. H. Auden: a biography* (I650).

I171 W. H. Auden. The art of poetry XVI [interview with Michael Newman]. *Paris review*, 57 (Spring 1974), 32–69.

Interview given in Autumn 1972. Reprinted in *Writers at work: the* Paris review *interviews, fourth series*, edited by George Plimpton (New York: Viking, 1976), pp. 243–69; and in *Poets at work: the* Paris review *interviews*, edited by George Plimpton (New York: Viking, 1989), pp. 283–306. For an exchange on this interview, see 'Interviewing Auden', letters by Newman and Jonathan Wilson, *Commentary*, 63. 5 (May 1977), 10.

I172 Ileana Čura. Povodom godišnice smrti pesnika Vistan Hju Odna (1907–1973). *Književna kritika*, Beograd, 5. 4 (July–Aug. 1974), 98–106.

Includes an interview with Auden in Yugoslavia, 1971.

I173 Elizabeth Sussex. *The rise and fall of British documentary: the story of the film movement founded by John Grierson*. Berkeley: University of California Press, 1975.

Recollections of the G.P.O. Film Unit, pp. 65–7, 72, 79, 194.

I174 Walter Kerr. An unpublished interview (1953). *Harvard advocate*, 108. 2–3 ([1975]), 32–5.

I175 Marvin Cohen. An interview with W. H. Auden. *Arts in society*, 12. 3 (Fall–Winter 1975), 365–7.

I176 Donrae Hogsett. Auden remembered. *Syracuse guide*, WONO-FM, Syracuse, NY, 2 (Oct. 1975), 21–2.

An interview given in 1972.

I177 Suresh Raichura and Amritjit Singh. A conversation with W. H. Auden. *Southwest review*, 60. 1 (Winter 1975), 27–36.

Transcribed from an interview conducted on 28 Mar. 1972; a typescript is in the Berg Collection.

I178 William B. Wahl. *Poetic drama interviews: Robert Speaght, E. Martin Browne & W. H. Auden*. Salzburg: Institüt für englische Sprache und Literatur, Universität Salzburg, 1976. (Salzburg Studies in English Literature, Poetic Drama & Poetic Theory, 24.)

'My impressions of W. H. Auden: his last interview', pp. 93–107; the interview was unproductive, and the interviewer lost his notes before writing his report.

I179 James K. Lyon. *Bertolt Brecht in America*. Princeton: Princeton University Press, 1980.

Brief remark from an interview, *ca.* 1970, about his collaboration with Brecht, p. 238.

I180 Alan Levy. Auden as interviewee. *W. H. Auden 1907–1973: Ergebnisse eines Symposions*, Redaktion: Michael O'Sullivan. [Wien:] Niederösterreich-Gesellschaft für Kunst und Kultur, [1988], pp. 125–34.

Account of four interviews in 1971. See also I130.

I181 Glenn Loney. Elegy for a bacchic rake. *Opera monthly*, 4. 11 (Mar. 1992), 10–16.

Interview conducted in 1970. The interviewer's notes are in the Berg Collection.

REPORTED SPEECHES, LECTURES, READINGS, BROADCASTS, DIALOGUES, AND PERFORMANCES

I182 School notes. *St. Edmund's School chronicle*, 7. 11 (June 1921), 175.

'A note from Mrs Auden gives us some welcome news of W. H. Auden (1915–1920). He has just won the top Scholarship at Holt. He has also been acting and took the part of Miss Ashford in "The Private Secretary." This was in a house play, and his acting was such that he has been chosen for a part in the School play which comes off in July.' Quoted in I534.

I183 House plays. *Gresham*, Gresham's School, Holt, 9. 5 (11 June 1921), 81–2.

Auden showed 'distinct promise' in a house production of *The private secretary*, p. 82.

I184 Debating society. *Gresham*, 9. 5 (11 June 1921), 87–8.

On 19 Mar. 1921 Auden took part in a debate on 'That in the opinion of this House we are no better than our forefathers.' He 'questioned the personal cleanliness of our Norse Ancestors. Their "heaven" probably meant a place of deep drinking', p. 87.

I185 Much ado about nothing. *Gresham*, 9. 6 (23 July 1921), 100–3.

Auden played the role of Ursula: 'Hero and her waiting maid Ursula were charming; the wool-winding scene was attractive and it went well. Ursula made a happy contrast to Beatrice', p. 101.

I186 The taming of the shrew. *Gresham*, 9. 12 (29 July 1922), 171–2.

'Auden struggled nobly against overwhelming odds to give Katharina her rightful dominant position in the play, but was completely swamped by Petruchio's all-pervading personality from the moment he appeared. To do justice to the character of Katharina is an extremely trying task for any mere male, and Auden was "far from assisted" by a poor wig and clothes that can only be described as shocking. Under so many adverse circumstances, however, it reflected the greatest credit on him that he contrived to infuse considerable dignity into his passionate outbursts, and moreover by his spirited performance showed that determination can overcome almost insurmountable difficulties.'

I187 Society of Arts. *Gresham*, 10. 4 (31 Mar. 1923), 56–7.

Auden read a paper on 'Folk Lore': 'The lecturer first showed how many ancient tales, customs, and beliefs were based upon historical facts. Their study, therefore, threw considerable light upon the life of the common people of the past, and formed an important adjunct to the more usual activities of the archaeologist. To show this the lecturer pointed out the extraordinary way in which tales may be found to be common to races of the most diverse character.' With W. H. M. Roberts, he arranged a concert of modern music for the Society of Arts, and, with Roberts, performed at the piano Delius's 'A song before sunrise' and 'On hearing the first cuckoo in Spring'.

I188 Natural History Society. *Gresham*, 11. 4 (4 Apr. 1925), 68–70.

Auden 'during the last two terms' read a paper on 'Enzyme action', p. 69.

I189 C.H.T. The tempest. *Gresham*, 11. 6 (25 July 1925), 99–101.

Auden played the role of Caliban, 4 July 1925. 'And why did Caliban come in first munching? . . . However it was a happy thought, at his second entrance, to bring him on with the Elves. And later on, in spite of difficulties of voice, the actor gave us enthralling action; when he got—what Shakespeare gave him—the bottle, and lumbered about right brutishly.' A review in the *Times* by T.B.H. is reprinted on pp. 100–1: 'Auden should be given a further word of praise for his grasp of "Caliban" apart from the roystering scenes,' p. 101 (but this does not appear in the note on the performance in the final edition of the *Times*, 9 July 1925, p. 11).

I190 Poetry and film. *Janus*, [2] (May 1936), 11–12.

Authorized report, in the third person, of a lecture to the North London Film Society. Reprinted in Auden and Isherwood's *Plays and other dramatic writings by W. H. Auden 1927–1938* (Princeton: Princeton University Press, 1988), pp. 511–13.

I191 Star man's diary. Poets in China. *Star*, London, 7 Nov. 1938, p. 4.

Brief indirect report of a lecture on China by Auden and Isherwood for the Group Theatre.

I192 When democracy is a 'sham'. *Birmingham post*, 24 Oct. 1938, p. 13.

Report of Auden's speech at a conference on 'The schools and the state' held by the English Section of the New Education Fellowship, at High Leigh, Hoddesdon, 22–3 Oct. 1938. The full text, apparently printed from

Auden's manuscript, appears as 'Democracy's reply to the challenge of dictators' (the title of the session in which Auden spoke), *New era in home and school*, 20. 1 (Jan. 1939), 5–8.

I193 A[lexander] N[eil] S[kinner]. Spain. *Salopian*, Shrewsbury School, 58. 2 (19 Nov. 1938), 37–8.

Report of 'Spain', a lecture to the 1918 Society at the school, 30 Oct. 1938.

I194 Auden gives optimistic faith. *Daily tar heel*, University of North Carolina, 5 Apr. 1939, pp. 1, 4.

Report of a lecture at the Human Relations Institute at the University, 4 Apr. 1939. Also reported briefly in 'Scores our moves to curb "have-nots"' (the title refers to a different speaker), *New York times*, 5 Apr. 1939, p. 10. See also **I741**.

I195 British poet talks to literary group. *Daily Princetonian*, 27 Apr. 1939, p. 1.

Brief report of a talk to a student group on culture and education.

I196 Auden relates nature of man and poet's aim. *College news*, Bryn Mawr College, 25. 22 (10 May 1939), 1–2.

Detailed report of a lecture on the poet's position in modern society.

I197 The outlook for 'poetic drama'. *France-Grande Bretagne*, 22. 188 (July–Aug. 1939), 226–34.

Report of a lecture to the Association France-Grande Bretagne, at the Sorbonne, 8 Dec. 1938. An extensively emended text appears in Auden and Isherwood's *Plays and other dramatic writings by W. H. Auden 1927–1938* (Princeton: Princeton University Press, 1988), pp. 513–22.

I198 *Writers teach writing*. New York: League of American Writers, 1940.

'The largest class the school ever had was a course in poetry readings conducted by W. H. Auden which drew an attendance upwards of 30', p. 5.

I199 Hervie Haufler. Auden offers 'paradoxical' poet's view. *Michigan daily*, 13 Jan. 1940, p. 1.

Report of a talk, 'A sense of one's age'. Further comment appears in: 'Morty-Q', 'Of all things . . .' [column], ibid., 14 Jan. 1940, p. 4.

I200 Daniel Lionel. Poet's idea of half truths. *Brooklyn daily eagle*, 11 Feb. 1940, section C, p. 9.

Report of the first in Auden's lecture series at the New School for Social Research.

I201 Auden gives Turnbull lectures. *The Johns Hopkins news-letter*, Johns Hopkins University, 44. 27 (6 Feb. 1940), 1.

Accounts of two lectures, 'Poetry and the old world' and 'America is where you find it'.

I202 Bids Smith class seek 'open society'. *New York times*, 18 June 1940, p. 26.

Report of the Smith College commencement address; published in full from Auden's typescript as 'Romantic or free?', *Smith alumnae quarterly*, 31. 4 (Aug. 1940), 353–8.

I203 W. H. Auden discusses mimesis and allegory in last poet's reading. *Wellesley College news*, 31 Oct. 1940, p. 3.

Brief report of a lecture, 'Mimesis and allegory'.

I204 Auden presents second Spencer Trask lecture and gets literary third degree from The Club. *Daily Princetonian*, 8 Nov. 1940, p. 1.

Brief report of lecture whose full text was included in *The intent of the critic*, edited by Donald A. Stauffer (Princeton: Princeton University Press, 1941), and of a discussion with students afterwards.

I205 W. H. Auden here for a week's visit; will give first speech at 8 tonight. *Daily Collegian*, State College, Pennsylvania, 18 Feb. 1941, p. 1.

Brief quotation from a recent radio interview, apparently at Swarthmore College.

I206 Auden attracts capacity crowd. *Daily Collegian*, 19 Feb. 1941, p. 1.

Report of Auden's lecture on 'English poetry of the thirties'.

I207 Professor's duty told. *Michigan daily*, 15 Mar. 1942, p. 2.

Report of Auden's informal talk at the Language and Literature section of the Michigan Academy of Science, Arts, and Letters.

I208 Campus comment. *Phoenix*, Swarthmore College, 62. 2 (20 Oct. 1942), 4.

Auden in class.

I209 Auden addresses Phi Beta banquet on self-realization. *Phoenix*, Swarthmore College, 42. 12 (19 Jan. 1943), 1.

Report of a lecture, 'Vocation and society'.

I210 Auden emphasizes independent study and specialization. *Phoenix*, Swarthmore College, 42. 16 (2 Mar. 1943), 4.

Report of a discussion, 'The role of education in a democratic society'.

I211 April Oursler. Purpose of poetry explained by Auden. *College news*, Bryn Mawr College, 14 Oct. 1943, pp. 1, 4.

I212 Auden explains real function of all ritual. *Phoenix*, Swarthmore College, 44. 3 (1 Apr. 1944), 1.

Report of a lecture, 'Ritual'. The same page contains an April Fool spoof in the form of a news story announcing Auden's appointment as Dean of Men at Swarthmore and his purported program.

I213 Personality types viewed by Auden in last Collection. *Phoenix*, Swarthmore College, 45. 13 (13 Feb. 1945), 3.

Report of a lecture, 'The world of flesh and the devil' [*sic*]. (Collection is the title given to a series of lectures at Swarthmore.)

I214 *The humanistic tradition in the century ahead*, Princeton University bicentennial conferences, series 1, conference 6. Princeton: Princeton University, 1946.

A summary account of the conference, 16–18 Oct. 1946, with a summary of Auden's talk, pp. 18–20; Auden's name is not mentioned. Auden apparently prepared a different summary of his talk that was distributed by him at the conference in the form of a three-page mimeographed leaflet titled *W. H. Auden . . . 'The effect of democratic and totalitarian thought upon the humanistic tradition'*.

I215 Books—authors. *New York times*, 27 Sept. 1946, p. 21.

'Mr. Auden has announced that in his course [at the New School for Social Research], which runs through both semesters, he proposes to read all Shakespeare's plays in chronological order.'

I216 Capacity crowd hears W. H. Auden, poet, speak. *Barnard bulletin*, Barnard College, 51. 25 (25 Nov. 1946), 1.

Brief report of Auden's lecture, 'False faiths and revealed religions', in the Fifth Annual Columbia Conference on Religion.

I217 Bernadine Kielty. Authors between books. *Book-of-the-Month Club news*, Dec. 1946, p. 29.

Auden's joke at the start of a lecture. Adapted in *The Little, Brown book of anecdotes*, Clifton Fadiman, general editor (Boston: Little, Brown, 1985), p. 27.

I218 Winnie Sorg. Auden says art impossible under modern dictatorship. *Wellesley College news*, 9 Dec. 1947, p. 3.

Interview on poetry, war, and politics. A brief report of a reading appears in an unsigned adjacent story: 'W. H. Auden reads works showing wit and maturity'.

I219 W. H. Auden gives Bergen Lecture. *Yale daily news*, 17 Feb. 1948, pp. 1–2.

Report of 'Don Quixote or the ironic hero.'

I220 *The dictionary of humorous quotations*, edited by Evan Esar. Garden City, NY: Doubleday, 1949.

'A professor is one who talks in someone else's sleep', p. 20. Probably quoted from an unidentified report of a lecture.

I221 W. H. Auden depicts role of modern poet. *Ram*, Fordham College, New York, 17 Feb. 1950, p. 1.

Report of 'Nature, history, and poetry'; illustrated with a photo of Christopher Isherwood, captioned 'W. H. Auden'.

I222 Barnard students hear Auden, poet, discuss literature. *Columbia spectator*, 8 Mar. 1950, p. 1.

I223 *Transcript of a speech by W. H. Auden, under the auspices of the Cooper Foundation and the Department of English, at Swarthmore College on Mar. 9, 1950.* [Swarthmore, Pennsylvania, 1950.]

A 10-page mimeographed transcript. Also reported in I224.

I224 W. H. Auden introduces his theory of poetry. *Phoenix*, Swarthmore College, 70. 8 (15 Mar. 1950), 1, 3.

Report of 'Nature, history, and poetry'.

I225 Merger of science and religion urged. *New York times*, 20 Apr. 1950, p. 31.

Three sentences quoted from Auden's address 'The witness of the layman', read in his absence at a convocation at the Yale Divinity School. The title of the article refers to another speaker's talk.

I226 'Cultural freedom not totally bereft of politics': foreign delegates' views on totalitarian threat. *Times of India*, Bombay, 27 Mar. 1951, pp. 1, 7.

Further brief quotations appear in 'Men, matters and memories—by Ariel', ibid., 1 Apr. 1951, p. 6.

I227 Auden outlines role of layman in community. *New York herald tribune*, 22 Oct. 1951, p. 12.

Six paragraphs from Auden's sermon at the Protestant Episcopal Church of the Epiphany, New York. Reported as 'Body & soul', *Time*, 58. 18 (29 Oct. 1951), 57. A further report appears in Geoffrey Grigson, 'The poet in the pulpit', *Sunday times*, 28 Oct. 1951, p. 7.

I228 Parnaso. *Il mondo*, Roma, 4. 18 (3 May 1952), 7.

Brief quotation from a Congress for Cultural Freedom meeting in Paris. A different, indirect quotation appears in: Hellmut Jaesrich, 'Brief aus Paris: Töne und Theorien', *Der Monat*, 4. 86 (July 1952), 345–52 (Auden on p. 349).

I229 Notes on *The rake*. *Opera news*, 17. 19 (9 Mar. 1953), 24.

Detailed report of a lecture by Auden and Kallman, 28 Jan. 1953. Reprinted in Auden and Kallman's *Libretti and other dramatic writings by*

W. H. Auden 1939–1973 (Princeton: Princeton University Press, 1993), pp. 616–17.

I230 Auden defines comic themes. *Sophian*, Smith College, 1. 43 (14 Apr. 1953), 1–2.

Report of a lecture.

I231 Symposium debates age-old topic, stimulating discussion, no solution. *Sophian*. 1, 47 (28 Apr. 1953), 1, 3.

Report of a symposium at Smith College on art and morals, 23–4 Apr. 1953. A 30-page typed transcript of a panel discussion, 24 Apr. 1953, is in the Smith College Archives. Briefly reported in *Poetry*, 83. 1 (Oct. 1953), 55–6.

I232 W. H. Auden visits San Francisco. *San Francisco chronicle*, 8 Oct. 1954, p. 10.

Report of a press conference.

I233 George H. Ford. *Dickens and his readers*. Princeton: Princeton University Press, 1955.

One-sentence report of a lecture, 'Dingley Dell and the Fleet' delivered in 1951, p. 13 (reference note on p. 270).

I234 Push-button age is cramping poet's style, W. H. Auden says. *St. Louis post-dispatch*, 17 Oct. 1955, section B, p. 3.

Report of a lecture in a Washington University symposium 'The writer and his public'; briefly quoted in 'Push-button poetry', *Newsweek*, 46. 18 (31 Oct. 1955), 52.

I235 *Minutes of a meeting of the Commission on Literature, Department of Worship and the Arts, National Council of Churches . . . New York, November 21, 1955.*

A five-page mimeographed leaflet with paraphrases of Auden's remarks on projects for critical essays, censorship, and other subjects. The Commission was established, and Auden named as a member, on 11 Jan. 1954; no minutes of other meetings have been located, and it is possible that no other meetings occurred.

I236 [Advertisement for George Allen & Unwin.] *Spectator*, 195. 6649 (2 Dec. 1955), 771.

Excerpt from a review of *Return of the king*, by J. R. R. Tolkien, broadcast by BBC Radio 3, 16 Nov. 1955: 'If someone dislikes it, I shall never trust their literary judgment about anything again.' Also in similar advertisements: *Times literary supplement*, 16 Dec. 1955, p. 763; and *New statesman and nation*, 50. 1293 (17 Dec. 1955), 837. Quoted in *The letters of J. R. R. Tolkien*, selected and edited by Humphrey Carpenter, with the assistance of Christopher Tolkien (London: George Allen & Unwin, 1981), p. 229. A mimeographed transcript is in the BBC Written Archives Centre.

I237 *Ezra Pound at 70.* Norfolk, Conn.: New Directions, 1956.

'There are very few living poets, even if they are not conscious of having been influenced by Pound, who could say, "My work would be exactly the same if Mr. Pound had never lived."' Brief excerpt from a contribution to a broadcast on Pound on WYBC, New Haven, 5 Dec. 1955, p. 4. A mimeographed transcript of the broadcast is in the Yale University Library.

I238 Novel by O'Hara wins book prize. *New York times*, 8 Feb. 1956, p. 24.

Report of the National Book Awards ceremony, with quotations from Auden's acceptance speech. See also, 'O'Hara, Auden and Kubly win Book Awards', *New York herald tribune*, 8 Feb. 1956, p. 14. Questions and answers at a press conference are quoted in: John K. Hutchens, 'Authors, critics, speeches, prizes', *New York herald tribune*, 12 Feb. 1956, section 6 (book review), pp. 2, 4; and 'The 7th National Book Awards', *Publishers weekly*, 169. 7 (18 Feb. 1956), 1013 (excerpt from Auden's speech on 1016–17).

I239 W. H. Auden on Dostoyevsky: a broadcast to Russia. *Manchester guardian*, 17 Feb. 1956, p. 10.

Transcript of a Radio Liberation broadcast, 9 Feb. 1956. Marie C. Stopes wrote a letter criticizing Auden's grammar, 'Poet's English', ibid., 5 Mar. 1956, p. 8.

I240 Making, knowing and judging. *Oxford magazine*, 74. 24 (14 June 1956), 496.

Brief report of Auden's inaugural lecture as Professor of Poetry.

I241 The education of a poet. *Times literary supplement*, 15 June 1956, p. 361.

Report of Auden's inaugural lecture.

I242 John Thompson. Auden at the Sheldonian. *Truth*, London, 156. 4160 (15 June 1956), 690.

I243 'Atticus'. Audible Auden. *Sunday times*, 17 June 1956, p. 3.

Report of Auden's inaugural lecture. The lecture was also quoted in 'Sayings of the week', *Observer*, 17 June 1956, p. 7.

I244 George A. Auden. W. H. Auden [letter to the editor]. *Observer*, 23 Dec. 1956, p. 8.

Reports that Auden and the Chinese ambassador spoke (in 1938) at the Birmingham Town Hall on the plight of the four Christian universities in China.

I245 W. H. Auden on secular and religious poetry. *Glasgow herald*, 25 Feb. 1957, p. 8.

Report of a sermon delivered at Edinburgh. Also reported as 'Poet's sermon in St. Giles': Professor Auden talks on literature', *Scotsman*, 25 Feb. 1957, p. 8. A garbled report of a dinner, attended by Auden, of the Associated Societies of Edinburgh was published as 'Men only but Marga went', *Bulletin*, Glasgow, 27 Feb. 1957.

I246 Bennet M. Berger. Sociology and the intellectuals: an analysis of a stereotype. *Antioch review*, 27. 3 (Fall 1957), 275–90.

Auden at an unidentified conference at the Museum of Modern Art on 'The role of the intellectual in modern society', a few years earlier, pp. 281–2.

I247 'Age of anxiety' blamed on diminished identity. *Washington post*, 28 Jan. 1958, p. A9.

Report of a lecture and discussion at the Washington School of Psychiatry in the series 'Character in literature and psychoanalysis'.

I248 Modern world and poetry. *Glasgow herald*, 6 May 1958, p. 5.

Report of the W. P. Ker lecture, 'The hero in modern poetry'. Also reported as 'Contemporary hero in poetry: Professor Auden on revolt against the crowd', *Times*, 6 May 1958, p. 6.

I249 K. W. Grandsen. The spoken word: Auden on Byron. *Listener*, 59. 1521 (22 May 1958), 876.

Review of Auden's Oxford lecture on *Don Juan*, 12 May 1958, which was broadcast two days later.

I250 Cricket Stanton. Auden explores Christian art in first of Mars lectures. *Daily Northwestern*, Northwestern University, 29 Jan. 1959, p. 1.

Report of 'The things that are Caesar's'.

I251 Cricket Stanton and Mark Haggard. Auden probes 'Pickwick papers'. *Daily Northwestern*, 30 Jan. 1959, p. 1.

Report of 'Dingley Dell and the Fleet'.

I252 Editorial. *Fortune*, 61. 1 (Jan. 1960), 83–4.

Paraphrases Auden's comment on why he no longer reads newspapers, from 'Culture in conflict', a discussion with Jacques Barzun, Lionel Trilling, and David Suskind, broadcast in *Open end*, WNTA Television, New York, 8 Nov. 1959. The broadcast is described in more general terms in Kenneth Tynan, 'Culture in trouble', in his *Curtains: selections from the drama criticism and related writings* (New York: Atheneum, 1961), pp. 375–6. A brief allusion to this broadcast ('Auden haggling with Professor

Trilling over who was oldest') appears in Gore Vidal, 'Writers in the public eye,' *Times literary supplement*, 25 Nov. 1965, pp. 1042–3 (Auden on p. 1042); reprinted as 'Writers and the world' in his *Homage to Daniel Shays: collected essays 1952–1972* (New York: Random House, 1972), pp. 210–18 (Auden on p. 212); and his *United States: essays 1952–1992* (New York: Random House, 1993), pp. 41–5 (Auden on p. 42). The same broadcast is quoted in I823, p. 16.

I253 Helen Bevington. *When found, make a verse of.* New York: Simon & Schuster, 1961.
Brief account of a talk in New York, 1939, p. 46.

I254 John Ardagh. Socrates in the Cadena. *Observer*, 5 Feb. 1961, p. 21.
General account of Auden's Oxford lectures.

I255 Max Bluestone. The iconographic sources of Auden's 'Musée des Beaux Arts'. *Modern language notes*, 39. 4 (April 1961), 331–6.
Brief quotation on the atomization of time, from 'Culture in conflict', a discussion with Jacques Barzun, Lionel Trilling, and David Suskind, first broadcast in *Open end*, WNTA Television, New York, 8 Nov. 1959 (see I252), but cited here from a 1960 re-broadcast by WGBH Television, Boston, p. 332.

I256 W. H. Auden at evening of poetry reading. *Rockefeller Institute quarterly*, 6. 1 (Jan.–Mar. 1962), 8.
Brief report of a reading and talk at the Institute, 30 Jan. 1962.

I257 Overflow crowd hears 'powerful poet' Auden give intimate reading. *Yale daily news*, 13 Mar. 1962, p. 1.
Includes quoted comment on 'Hammerfest'.

I258 Auden tells SUIowans—poet's work isn't his own. *Daily Iowan*, University of Iowa, 14 Mar. 1963, p. 1.
Report of a talk, 'The poet and his poems'.

I259 Philip A. McCombs. Poet W. H. Auden, professors discuss humans and worlds. *Yale daily news*, 17 Dec. 1963, pp. 1, 3.
Report of a panel discussion, 'Contemporary man: the world ill-lost'.

I260 Poets honour three past masters. *Times*, 11 May 1964, p. 14.
At the Poetry Society, 9 May 1964, Auden introduces 'Elegy for J.F.K.' with a comment on the international style; partly quoted in 'Sayings of the week', *Observer*, 17 May 1964, p. 11, and in 'Ideas and men', *New York times*, 24 May 1964, section 4, p. 11; fully quoted in 'The annual luncheon', *Poetry review*, 55. 2 (Summer 1964), 123.

I261 Robie Macaulay. Poets meet in Berlin. *Congress news*, Congress for Cultural Freedom, Paris, Winter 1964–5, pp. 1–2.

Brief account of Auden's remarks at the International Conference of Poets in Berlin, held on 22–4 Sept. 1964.

I262 A. Alvarez. *Under pressure. The writer in society: Eastern Europe and the U.S.A.* Harmondsworth: Penguin, 1965.

Excerpts from a BBC conversation with Alvarez and others broadcast 3 June 1964, pp. 160, 165–6.

I263 S[ean] D[ay]-L[ewis]. No pomp or pretence in W. H. Auden. *Daily telegraph*, 29 Nov. 1965, p. 14.

Review, with quotations, of 'Poet of disenchantment: W. H. Auden', a BBC-1 Television film, broadcast 28 Nov. 1965. Another, unsigned, review also includes quotations: 'Face to face with W. H. Auden', *Times*, 29 Nov. 1965, p. 14. A mimeographed transcript is in the BBC Written Archives Centre. See also **I280** and **I436**.

I264 W. H. Auden and Denys Munby. Work and labour. *Frontier*, 9. 3 (Autumn 1966), 173–7.

A reported version, by John Wilkins, of the first session of a conference on 'The new morality?' organized by the University Teachers Group at St. Anne's College, Oxford, 16 Apr. 1966. A version edited from a recording appeared as: W. H. Auden, Denys Munby, 'Work and fruitful effort', *Breakthrough*, 15 ([Oct.] 1966), 6–10.

I265 R. U. K. 'Leben ohne Wort ist fade . . .' *Kurier*, Wien, 10 Oct. 1966, p. 10.

Report of a reading, quoting Auden's remark on Josef Weinheber.

I266 Où sont les vierges . . . ? Corrupting the neutrons. *Guardian*, 19 Oct. 1966, p. 8.

Report of Auden's sermon at Westminster Abbey.

I267 Auden at Villanova. *Delaware County daily times*, Chester, Pennsylvania, 7 Feb. 1967, p. 11.

On fairy stories, poetry, and fame.

I268 Gail Stockholm. Poet W. H. Auden reads from his work. *Chicago tribune*, 14 Feb. 1967, section 2, p. 1.

Brief remarks.

I269 Literary myths as bearers of religious meaning: a conversation. *ARC directions*, [3] (Spring 1967), 1–2, 6.

Excerpts taken 'with a minimum of editing' from a discussion by Auden and others at a meeting of Fellows of the Foundation for the Arts, Religion and Culture, in New York.

I270 A dialogue with his audience. *Barat review*, 2. 2 (June 1967), 80–2.

Excerpts from a seminar at Barat College, 14 Feb. 1967.

I271 Terry Coleman. Poetry International at the Queen Elizabeth Hall. *Guardian*, 13 July 1967, p. 5.

Auden explained that the odd lines in 'The cave of making' ended in dactyls.

I272 Georgene Bivens. Famed poet offers views on drugs, love, poetry . . . and what have you? *Carlisle sentinel*, Carlisle, Penn., 6 Mar. 1968.

Auden at Dickinson College. A clipping from an unidentified newspaper in the Swarthmore College Library includes further quotations from the same event; the story is headed 'Auden is cited at Dickinson, reads poetry'. Further quotations appear in: Paul B. Beers, 'Reporter at large', *Harrisburg evening news*, 8 Mar. 1968. An untitled one-page news release from the college's News Office, dated 6 Mar. 1968, included quotations from an informal discussion with students.

I273 R. Y. Pelgrift and Tom Kleh. Auden delights overflow crowd. *Daily Princetonian*, 7 Mar. 1968, p. 1.

Comments from a reading.

I274 Auden's awe at Solihull gas works. *Solihull news*, 2 Nov. 1968, p. 18.

'During a reading of his poetry this week in Great St. Mary's Church, Cambridge, Auden, in his poem on reaching the age of 60, referred to the time as a small boy when he had gazed in awe at Solihull Gasworks. He later explained that he had lived in Solihull from 1908 to 1913 and had often been taken to the gasworks as the air down there was reputed to be very healthy.'

I275 Pendennis goes to Sweden to meet the 'superminds'. Are we going to survive? *Observer*, 21 Sept. 1969, p. 44.

Report of Auden and others at the Nobel Foundation's symposium, 'The place of value in a world of facts'. A highly fictionalized version of the symposium appears in I473.

I276 Riveted by Auden. *Evening standard*, 30 Oct. 1969, p. 16.

One sentence quoted from a poetry reading.

I277 Amanda Cross [pseudonym of Carolyn Heilbrun]. *Poetic justice*. New York: Alfred A. Knopf, 1970.

Detective novel with an account of a reading, pp. 163–4.

I278 *Columbia University, University Seminar on the Nature of Man, Minutes, Date: Jan. 15, 1970 . . . Speaker: W. H. Auden.* [New York, 1970].

The 26-page minutes of the seminar, with excerpts from Auden's address about the Nobel Symposium 'The place of value in a world of facts', pp. 2–9, and further comments, pp. 10–17. Partially reprinted as 'They had forgotten how to laugh and how to pray', *Columbia forum*, 13. 4 (Winter 1970), 46–8; and excerpted as 'Forgotten laughter, forgotten prayer', *New York times*, 2 Feb. 1971, p. 37 [early editions, p. 35].

I279 Poet praises value of prayer, carnival. *Christian advocate*, Nashville, 14. 7 (2 Apr. 1970), 23.

Auden at a meeting of the Society for the Arts, Religion, and Contemporary Culture in New York.

I280 John Whitehead. Well, would you know more? *London magazine*, n.s. 10. 2 (May 1970), 97–100.

Brief quotation from 'Poet of disenchantment: W. H. Auden', a BBC-1 Television film, 28 Nov. 1965, p. 100. See also I263.

I281 McCandlish Phillips. Auden and the physicians: a tonic mixture. *New York times*, 16 Dec. 1970, p. 49.

Report of a visit to the Downstate Medical Center, New York. Also reported briefly, with an indirect quotation converted into a direct quotation, in 'People', *Time*, 96. 26 (28 Dec. 1970), 22. One remark, 'Political history is far too criminal a subject to be a fit thing to teach children', was reprinted in many newspapers (e.g., 'Timely quotes', *Plainview daily herald*, Plainview, Texas, 5 Jan. 1971, p. 8).

I282 [Untitled report of a reading.] *Yale daily news*, 13 Jan. 1971, p. 1.

I283 Mary Holland. On the road with Orwell. *Observer*, 17 Jan. 1971, p. 23.

Quotations from Auden's remarks included in a BBC-1 *Omnibus* television broadcast on Orwell, 10 Jan. 1971. Also quoted in: Karl Miller, 'Opinion', *The review*, 27–8 (Autumn–Winter 1971–2), 41, 51.

I284 Microphone hinders Auden's reading. *Globe and mail*, Toronto, 12 Feb. 1971, p. 13.

One sentence on the bad microphone.

I285 Auden blends sarcasm, satire in poetry reading. *Daily Collegian*, University Park, Pennsylvania, 16 Feb. 1971, p. 3.

Report of a reading on 13 Feb. 1971.

I286 Poet captivates an audience. *Providence evening bulletin*, 4 Mar. 1971, p. 25.

Brief comments on poems.

I287 Hugh Hebert. Big Spender. *Guardian*, 23 Nov. 1971, p. 10.

Vague report of a discussion between Spender and Auden at the Institute of Contemporary Arts, London, Oct. 1971.

I288 Bob Adams. A great poet and a great performer. *Bryn Mawr–Haverford College news*, 20 Nov. 1971, p. 8.

Report of a reading at Haverford College; the 'great performer' was another poet at a different reading.

I289 Peter Porter. I and we. *New statesman*, 82. 2124 (3 Dec. 1971), 800.

Broadcasting review, with quotations from Auden's BBC Radio 3 discussion with Hans Keller on music, broadcast 20 Nov. 1971. Keller recalls his conversation with Auden before the broadcast in 'The words and the music', *Sunday times*, 1 Feb. 1981, p. 43.

I290 Theatre and the visual arts: a panel discussion. *Theatre and the visual arts*, ed. Robert O'Driscoll and Lorna Reynolds. Shannon: Irish University Press, for University College, Galway, 1972 (Yeats Studies, series 2), pp. 127–38.

A transcript of a discussion among Auden, Marshall McLuhan, Buckminster Fuller, Jack MacGowran, and A. N. Jeffares, at the University of Toronto, 10 Feb. 1971. A slightly different version of the transcript, with an introduction that quotes from Auden's letters to O'Driscoll, was published as 'Marshall McLuhan/W. H. Auden: duel or duet?', edited by Robert O'Driscoll, *Canadian forum*, 61. 709 (May 1981), 5–7, 17. Reports of the discussion were published as follows: DuBarry Campau, 'The Irish take apart the visual arts', *Toronto telegram*, 11 Feb. 1971, p. 57; Don Rubin, 'Poet W. H. Auden a delight at seminar in Irish studies', *Toronto star*, 11 Feb. 1971, p. 26; Alan H. Cowle, 'Master minds and McLuhan', *Irish press*, Dublin, 12 Feb. 1971, p. 6; 'Brennan Hall panel truck has flat tyre and broken muffler', *Varsity*, University of Toronto, 12 Feb. 1971, p. 13; and Marie Tido, 'Jottings on a recent panel discussion', *Varsity*, 26 Feb. 1971, p. 7.

I291 Melvin Maddocks. Auden in transit—metre running. *Christian Science monitor*, 20 Mar. 1972, p. 9.

General report of a reading at Boston College.

I292 Art and the dead. *Listener*, 88. 2274 (26 Oct. 1972), 538.

Extensive quotations from Michael Parkinson's interview with Auden and Sir John Gielgud, broadcast by BBC-1 Television, 7 Oct. 1972. Also reported by James Kirkup, 'News and views', *Eigo seinen (The rising generation)*, 118. 10 (Jan. 1973), 574–5.

I293 Kenneth Rose. Albany at large. Signing off. *Sunday telegraph*, 26 Nov. 1972, p. 2.

Brief report of a reading.

I294 A colloquium on Tennyson. *Listener*, 89. 2293 (8 Mar. 1973), 302–5.

Comment by Auden in a broadcast discussion, 'Tennyson, 80 years on', BBC Radio 3, 8 Dec. 1972.

I295 W. H. Auden, poet of the 'thirties . *Sunday telegraph*, 30 Sept. 1973, p. 7.

Reports that the last poem Auden read at his reading in Vienna on the night of his death was his clerihew on Kant.

I296 Poets on poetry—Auden and others. *Listener*, 90. 2328 (8 Nov. 1973), 629.

Quotations from an interview with Patrick Garland on BBC-1 Television, broadcast 5 Nov. 1973.

I297 William Carlos Williams. Man orchid. *Massachusetts review*, 14. 1 (Winter 1973), 77–117.

Auden reading in New York, Apr. 1940, p. 85. Williams's account (in his portion of a work written in collaboration with Fred Miller and Lydia Carlin) is quoted, with additional notes by Williams, in Paul Mariani, *William Carlos Williams: a new world naked* (New York: McGraw-Hill, 1981), pp. 436–7; Auden is also briefly reported at a party, 1947, p. 536. Williams mentions the 1940 reading in *The autobiography of William Carlos Williams* (New York: Random House, 1951), p. 310.

I298 Charles Causley. Letter from Jericho. *Collected poems 1951–1975*. London: Macmillan, 1975.

Poem about Auden's reading at Edinburgh, probably in 1965, pp. 269–71.

I299 Robert Fulford. Auden recalled: never, but never meet your heroes. *Toronto star*, 23 July 1977, section H, p. 3.

Report of Auden's interview with Fulford broadcast on CBC Television, 24 May 1971.

I300 T. E. B. Howarth. *Cambridge between two wars*. London: Collins, 1978.

Auden read 'remarkably salacious extracts from the Mortmere saga' on a visit, 15 Nov. 1936, p. 165. See also **I754**.

I301 Marvin Bell. Auden twice. *Seattle review*, 4. 2 (Fall 1981), 75–9.

One sentence from Auden's reading at Cornell College, Iowa, probably in the late 1960s. Reprinted in his *Old snow just melting: essays and interviews* (Ann Arbor: University of Michigan Press, 1983), pp. 5–10.

I302 Bernard Knox. W. H. Auden. *Grand Street*, 1. 2 (Winter 1982), 18–27.

Auden enthusiastically recited Kipling's 'The gods of the copybook headings' at a reading in New York in 1939, p. 22. Reprinted in his *Essays ancient and modern* (Baltimore: The Johns Hopkins University Press, 1990), pp. 216–23.

I303 Stanley Burnshaw. *Robert Frost himself.* New York: George Braziller, 1986.

Brief account of Auden, Burnshaw, and Thomas Johnson reading and commenting on Frost's poems in a broadcast on WNDT Television, New York, 29 Jan. 1963, pp. 191–2.

I304 E. M. Halliday. *John Berryman and the thirties: a memoir.* Amherst: University of Massachusetts Press, 1987.

Remark at a reading at the Keynote Club in New York (misremembered as at Columbia University), 1939, p. 170.

I305 I. A. Richards. *Selected letters of I. A. Richards, CH*, edited by John Constable. Oxford: Clarendon Press, 1990.

Report of a lecture at Harvard, 16 Nov. 1939, p. 105.

I306 W. H. Auden and Chester Kallman. *Libretti and other dramatic writings by W. H. Auden 1939–1973*, edited by Edward Mendelson. Princeton: Princeton University Press, 1993.

Transcript of an extempore BBC Third Programme talk on *The rake's progress*, broadcast 28 Aug. 1953, pp. 621–6. Quotations from a BBC Third Programme discussion among Auden, Kallman, and Hans Werner Henze about *Elegy for young lovers*, broadcast 13 July 1961, p. 647.

REPORTED REMARKS

I307 The field-day in the Devil's Punch Bowl. *St. Edmund's School chronicle*, 7. 3 (June 1917), 51–5.

Report of the drill of the St. Edmund's School Rifle Club, in which one group of forces was led by Corpl. Auden (junior), whose tactical advice is reported indirectly.

I308 School notes. *St. Edmund's School chronicle*, 7. 6 (Nov. 1919), 91.

At a variety entertainment for the school on 25 October 1919, 'Robinson, Fagge and Sant performed with much grace in a country dance which would have been excellent if the accompanist, Auden, had not taken the bit between his teeth and bolted; however, he recovered later and played his next accompaniment with much skill. Auden also recited, likewise Tutton.' Quoted in I534.

I309 School notes. *St. Edmund's School chronicle*, 7. 8 (June 1920), 114.

Report of a performance by an enlarged choir of Liza Lehmann's *Fairy cantata*: 'A word of praise must be given to Auden, to whom fell the arduous task of leading the choir, and to whom in great part the success of the "attack" was due.' Quoted in I534.

I310 [Harold Llewellyn Smith.] S.E.S.L.S. *St. Edmund's School chronicle*, 7. 8 (June 1920), 119.

Report of the St. Edmund's School Literary Society, which had been planned simultaneously by Rosamira Bulley and by Auden and Harold Llewellyn Smith. 'The object is almost solely the reading of Shakespeare's works, and last term we read at any rate part of the "Merchant of Venice", while this term we are doing "A Midsummer-Night's Dream"'. Further recollections of the Society appear in I367 and I534.

I311 J[ames] Iliff. Thought. *Badger*, Downs School, 1. 2 (Autumn 1933), 22.

Prose piece by a 10-year-old pupil: 'Mr Auden told me to take a pencil-sharpener in my hand and think about it for five minutes.'

I312 Nancy Johnstone. *Hotel in flight*. London: Faber & Faber, 1937.

Brief report of Auden at Casa Johnstone, in Tossa de Mar, Spain, 1937. The jacket copy ends: 'And W. H. Auden, just back from Spain and Tossa, says none of these adventures are exaggerated.'

I313 'Slingsby' [Peter Fleming]. All round man. *Night and day*, 1. 18 (28 Oct. 1937), 6.

Brief report of meeting Auden 'a long time ago' and being asked by him 'if we didn't think Peter Pan the most immoral play ever written.' Reprinted (on a page of excerpts from a later number of the magazine) in *Night and day*, ed. Christopher Hawtree (London: Chatto & Windus, 1985), p. 238.

I314 Louis MacNeice. *I crossed the Minch*. London: Longmans, Green, 1938.

Briefly quoted on going North, pp. 18–19.

I315 Louis MacNeice. *Modern poetry: a personal essay*. London: Oxford University Press, 1938.

Indirect reports of Auden's opinions, pp. 86–9, 191.

I316 F. Tillman Durdin. Japanese in dire straits. *New York times*, 16 Apr. 1938, pp. 1, 6.

Indirect quotation from Shanghai about a Chinese railroad, p. 6.

I317 We shall soon talk in *** says Jeffrey Farnol. *News chronicle*, London, 5 Dec. 1938, p. 3.

One of a series of articles about authors' responses to the classics, with Auden's remarks on a list of authors prepared by the newspaper.

I318 *The little man* [advertising flyer]. Cincinnati: The little man, 1939.
An advertisement for the Summer 1939 issue of the *Little man* magazine; Auden is quoted as saying of one 'experiment in coordination of type and picture': 'I can't read it'. The remark may be an invention of the editors.

I319 G. E. G[rigson]. Remarks on painting and Mr. Auden. *New verse*, n.s. 1. 1 (Jan. 1939), 17–19.
Indirectly quoted on his preference for the painting of William Coldstream.

I320 Noonday & night. *Time*, 34. 18 (30 Oct. 1939), 66.
Two sentences about nationalism, in a survey of European writers on the war.

I321 Louis MacNeice. American letter. *Horizon*, 1. 7 (July 1940), pp. 462, 464.
Quoted indirectly about America. Reprinted in *Selected prose of Louis MacNeice*, edited by Alan Heuser (Oxford: Clarendon Press, 1990), pp. 74–7.

I322 Benjamin Appel. The exiled writers. *Saturday review of literature*, New York, 22. 26 (19 Oct. 1940), 5.

I323 Anna Maria Armi. *Poems*. New York: Random House, 1941.
'Her translations of the Petrarchan sonnets are considered by Mr. Auden and Mr. [Mark] Van Doren the best renderings so far' (from the dust-jacket).

I324 The Londoner's diary. *Evening standard*, 9 July 1941, p. 2.
Interview with Erika Mann, with an indirect report of Auden's attitudes: 'even though he tries to pretend he is uninterested in the war, she told me he jumped for joy when the Bismarck was sunk.'

I325 Louis MacNeice. Traveller's return. *Horizon*, 3. 14 (Feb. 1941), 110–17.
Quoted indirectly about America. Reprinted in *Selected prose of Louis MacNeice*, edited by Alan Heuser (Oxford: Clarendon Press, 1990), pp. 83–91.

I326 Famous English Jesuit scholar to give lecture on scepticism. *Michigan daily*, 5 Dec. 1941, p. 1.
On Father Martin d'Arcy: 'the most brilliant theologian in England'.

I327 Klaus Mann. *The turning point: twenty-five years in this century.* New York: L. B. Fischer, 1942.

Diary of Auden's remarks in a radio broadcast, 19 Mar. 1941, pp. 341–3. A 9-page duplicated transcript of the broadcast is in the Yale University Library. Expanded, with additional material about Auden, as *Der Wendepunkt: ein Lebensbericht* (Frankfurt: S. Fischer, 1952), pp. 333–4, 446–7.

I328 Tom O'Hara. Quotable poets find no merit in Pound award. *New York herald tribune*, 21 Feb. 1949, p. 19.

When asked the origin of the name of the Bollingen Prize Auden said 'You know, I really don't know.' The headline refers to other poets.

I329 Harvey Breit. Talk with Dr. Niebuhr. *New York times*, 8 May 1949, section 7 (book review), p. 22.

Reinhold Niebuhr briefly describes Auden's conversation and theology.

I330 Speaking of pictures. A high-fashion man portrays highbrows. *Life*, 27. 15 (10 Oct. 1949), 17.

Auden on a photograph by George Platt Lynes in which he poses holding the lid of a metal dustbin: 'a rather unusual shot'.

I331 Week of anxiety. *Newsweek*, 35. 10 (6 Mar. 1950), 78.

On Jerome Robbins's ballet based on Leonard Bernstein's symphony *The age of anxiety*: 'it really has nothing to do with me. Any connections with my book are rather distant.'

I332 British still hunt diplomats in vain. *New York times*, 10 June 1951, p. 14.

Briefly quoted on Burgess and MacLean in a Reuters dispatch from Rome; a similar dispatch appeared as 'Message from Mr. Burgess', *Manchester guardian*, 11 June 1951, p. 5.

I333 Don Seamen. Burgess knew atom spy. *Daily express*, London, 13 June 1951, p. 1.

On Burgess and MacLean.

I334 James Burnham. Parakeets and parchesi: an Indian memorandum. *Partisan review*, 18. 5 (Sept.–Oct. 1951), 557–68.

Auden's remark on an Indian dancer, at the time of his attendance at a meeting of the Congress for Cultural Freedom, p. 568.

I335 Stravinsky's opera in English has premiere in Venice tonight. *New York herald tribune*, 11 Sept. 1951, p. 22.

On Stravinsky's English pronunciation: 'But after all, he doesn't have to sing it.'

I336 Eugenio Montale. Sulla scia di Stravinsky. *Corriere della sera*, Milano, 19 Sept. 1951, p. 3.

Brief remark on the division of the churches. Reprinted in Montale's *Fuori di casa* (Milano–Napoli: Riccardo Ricciardi, 1969), pp. 331–7; translated by

Jonathan Galassi in Montale's *The second life of art* (New York: Ecco, 1982), pp. 245–50.

I337 Combined opera-tion. *Sunday times*, 10 Feb. 1952, p. 8.
Brief report of Igor Stravinsky's account of his preliminary discussions with Auden on *Delia*.

I338 Nigel Dennis. The double life of Henry Green. *Life*, 23. 5 (4 Aug. 1952), 85.
'W. H. Auden has declared him to be "the best English novelist alive."'

I339 John Mollson. Stravinsky's new opera has U.S. premiere. *New York herald tribune*, 15 Feb. 1953, p. 34.
Auden and Kallman were satisfied with the German and Italian translations, but not the French. 'Auden said he was perfectly pleased to have his words "the servants of Mr. Stravinsky's music. They have their moment of glory, the moment in which they suggest a certain melody; once that is over . . . they must efface themselves and cease to care what happens to them."'

I340 Winthrop Sargeant. Firebird's progress. *Life*, 34. 12 (23 Mar. 1953), 151–2, 154, 157–60.
Auden quotes Stravinsky on Stravinsky's habits, p. 158.

I341 Diana Trilling. The other night at Columbia: a report from the academy. *Partisan review*, 26. 2 (Spring 1959), 214–30.
Auden tells Trilling 'I'm ashamed of you' when she says she was moved by a poetry reading by beat poets, p. 222. Reprinted in her *Claremont essays* (New York: Harcourt, Brace & World, 1964), pp. 153–73 (Auden on p. 163). Trilling says of the same occasion, 'Auden was there and spoke condescendingly of Ginsberg', in Lis Harris, 'Di and Li', *New Yorker*, 69. 29 (13 Sept. 1993), 90–9 (Auden on p. 98).

I342 Philip Day. A pride of poets. *Sunday times*, 26 June 1960, p. 6.
Report of a party celebrating the publication of *Homage to Clio*; Auden is reported to be working on his two final Oxford lectures.

I343 T. S. Eliot deplores modern-verse study. *New York times*, 30 Dec. 1960, pp. 1, 9.
'Mr. Auden said, "I entirely agree. The poets read in school should well be dead."', p. 9.

I344 Glyndebourne to hear Henze opera with Auden libretto next summer. *New York times*, 15 Jan. 1961, section 2, p. 9.
Brief quotations on *Elegy for young lovers*.

I345 Lincoln Kirstein. The new Augustan age. *Nation*, 198. 5 (4 Feb. 1961), 106–8.

Comment on the music at the presidential inauguration of John F. Kennedy. Reprinted in Kirstein's *By with to & from: a Lincoln Kirstein reader*, edited by Nicholas Jenkins (New York: Farrar, Straus & Giroux, 1991), pp. 332–37.

I346 Louis MacNeice. That chair of poetry. *New statesman*, 61. 1561 (10 Feb. 1961), 210, 212.

Auden described the institution of the Oxford Professor of Poetry as 'comically absurd'.

I347 The 'desert' blooms. *Newsweek*, 47. 12 (20 Mar. 1961), 94, 96.

Comment on the climate for writers in America.

I348 Grim problems of Bowery and its derelicts complicate City's new clean-up drive. *New York times*, 20 Nov. 1961, p. 36.

'"One sees bums around, but they don't annoy us. I'm terrified," he continued. "All this tearing up of old neighborhoods! Leave the Bowery as it is!"'

I349 Stravinsky at 80: some say the greatest. *Newsweek*, 49. 21 (21 May 1962), 53, 55.

Indirect quotation on Stravinsky's change of mind about *The rake's progress*, p. 55.

I350 Bernard Taper. *Balanchine*. New York: Harper & Row, 1963.

Indirect quotation on Balanchine as a genius, p. 8; quotation on Lincoln Kirstein, p. 220. Also in the English edition (London: Collins, 1964), pp. 15 and 186. The third revised edition, *Balanchine: a biography* (New York: Times Books, 1984), omits the indirect quotation in the first edition, replaces it with a different quotation on Balanchine, pp. 4–5, and reprints the quotation on Lincoln Kirstein, p. 204. The indirect quotation on Balanchine as a genius also appears in the first part of an earlier version of the book, published as 'Choreographer—I', *New Yorker*, 36. 9 (16 Apr. 1960), 49–131 (Auden on p. 84).

I351 Book revelatory of Hammarskjold. *New York times*, 12 Jan. 1964, p. 7.

Reports that Auden and Leif Sjöberg meet several times a week to work on the translation of *Markings*, and that Auden has revised one quarter of the final version.

I352 Gisele Freund and V. B. Carleton. *James Joyce in Paris: his final years*. New York: Harcourt, Brace & World, 1965.

Five words on Joyce, p. 93.

I353 T. S. Eliot's rites to be tomorrow. *New York times*, 6 Jan. 1965, p. 39.

Brief tribute to Eliot; from a Reuters dispatch from Berlin probably also published elsewhere.

I354 The telltale hearth. *Time*, 85. 25 (18 June 1965), 74, 75, 75A–B, 76, 78.

Auden praises Phyllis McGinley, p. 74.

I355 Thomas Meehan. Public writer no. 1? *New York times*, 12 Dec. 1965, section 6 (magazine), pp. 44–5, 130–6.

Quoted on not knowing Bob Dylan's work, p. 136.

I356 Mitteilungen. *Josef Weinheber-Gesellschaft*, Wien, 1966–7, p. 55.

Brief remarks on Weinheber.

I357 The elvish mode. *New Yorker*, 41. 48 (15 Jan. 1966), 24.

Account of a meeting of the New York Tolkien Society.

I358 Trial in Moscow scored in West. *New York times*, 15 Feb. 1966, p. 8.

Auden on the trial of the dissident writers Sinyavsky and Daniel: 'This is a very shocking thing.' He also signed an appeal.

I359 Susan Jeanne Moore. W. H. Auden: the emergence of a distinctive voice. Senior thesis, Mount Holyoke College, 1967. [Not seen.]

Indirect quotation on 'Nones', p. 86; cited in Richard Johnson, *Man's place* (Ithaca, NY: Cornell University Press, 1973), p. 197.

I360 Random House gets choice literary job. *New York times*, 12 Dec. 1967, p. 52.

Auden says 'Mene, mene, tekel, upharsin' at a drawing to choose the publisher of the *National literary anthology*.

I361 The Times diary. Heavyweights move in. *Times*, 17 Oct. 1968, p. 12.

Auden and others work to nominate Roy Fuller for Oxford Professor of Poetry.

I362 William H. Honan. Le mot juste for the moon. *Esquire*, 72. 1 (July 1969), 140–1.

Auden's suggestion for the first words to be spoken on the moon, and comments on the journey.

I363 Dinner meeting of the Institute, Feb. 5, 1969: Poetry reading . . . *Proceedings of the American Academy of Arts and Letters and the National Institute of Arts and Letters*, 2nd series, no. 20 (1970), 40.

Interjection ('Rubbish!') against William Meredith's remark that using hendecasyllabics was 'a terribly pig-headed thing to do with a poem'.

I364 Brendan Lehane. Isherwood plays a guessing game. *Daily telegraph*, 7 Aug. 1970, magazine, pp. 18–20.

Two brief remarks on Isherwood.

I365 Jean Campbell. New York, we love you. *Evening standard*, 14 Jan. 1971, p. 15.

Brief comment on New York City.

I366 Charles Simmons. The last word: Malcolm de Chazal. *New York times*, 10 Oct. 1971, section 7 (book review), p. 55.

Brief comment on Chazal.

I367 [John Willett.] Commentary. *Times literary supplement*, 5 Nov. 1971, p. 1390.

Report of a fiftieth-anniversary meeting of the St. Edmund's School Literary Society. Also described in **I534**.

I368 Otto Friedrich. *Before the deluge: a portrait of Berlin in the 1920's*. New York: Harper & Row, 1972.

Reminiscences of Berlin, pp. 304, 322.

I369 Paul Horgan. *Encounters with Stravinsky: a personal record*. New York: Farrar, Straus & Giroux, 1972.

Horgan gets Auden's agreement to serve on the Honorary Committee for a Stravinsky festival at the Santa Fe Opera, 1962, p. 208.

I370 N. J. Loftis. *Black anima*. New York: Liveright, 1973.

Loftis's poems have 'been highly praised by, among others, W. H. Auden' (back cover).

I371 Daily Mail diary. In line for the post . . . the bard with the most. *Daily mail*, 14 Mar. 1973, p. 13.

One sentence in support of Spender for Oxford Professor of Poetry.

I372 Leo Clancy. Playground poets meet Auden. *Daily mail*, 15 Mar. 1973, p. 3.

Early editions include one sentence from Auden's remarks awarding prizes to youthful poets; later editions omit the quotation and revise the article as 'Playground poets come to town'. Reported, with further remarks by Auden as 'Cheltenham girl poet praised by W. H. Auden', *Gloucestershire echo*, Cheltenham, 15 Mar. 1973, p. 1. ('Paying tribute to the high standard of entries, Mr. Auden said: "Of all of them I think I liked little Angharad [Wynne-Jones]'s best. She showed remarkable imagination and surprising talent for one so young"'.)

1373 Anthony Holden. Electing the muse of Oxford. *Sunday times*, 6 May 1973, p. 20.

Auden was 'disgusted with [Roy] Fuller for funking it', that is, for not reading the Creweian Oration in Latin.

1374 Anthony Holden. Chairing the bard. *New statesman*, 85. 2201 (25 May 1973), 765–6.

On elections to the chair of poetry at Oxford, with two remarks by Auden. One of these remarks was picked up in 'John Wain gets chair in poetry from Oxford', *New York times*, 27 May 1973, section 1, p. 37.

REMEMBERED CONVERSATIONS

1375 Nicholas Blake [C. Day-Lewis]. *A question of proof.* London: Collins, The Crime Club, 1935.

Auden fictionalized as Nigel Strangeways, *passim*. (In the second Strangeways novel, *Thou shell of death*, 1936, the resemblance to Auden almost disappears, and is completely absent in later novels in the series.)

1376 [Louis MacNeice.] Hetty to Nancy. *Letters from Iceland*, by W. H. Auden and Louis MacNeice (London: Faber & Faber, 1937), pp. 156–99.

Spoof account of a visit to Iceland, with Auden fictionalized as Maisie. In the same book, the speaker Craven in MacNeice's poem 'Eclogue from Iceland', pp. 124–35, is loosely based on Auden.

1377 Christopher Isherwood. Some notes on Auden's early poetry. *New verse*, 26–7 (Nov. 1937), 4–9.

Reprinted, with introductory comments, in his *Exhumations* (London: Methuen, 1966), pp. 17–22, and in various later collections of essays on Auden. Also reprinted, with a postscript, as 'Some notes on the early poetry' in *W. H. Auden, a tribute*, edited by Stephen Spender (London: Weidenfeld & Nicolson, 1975), pp. 74–9.

1378 Stephen Spender. Oxford to Communism. *New verse*, 26–7 (Nov. 1937), 9–10.

Conversations at Oxford and after.

1379 Louis MacNeice. Letter to W. H. Auden. *New verse*, 26–7 (Nov. 1937), 11–13.

Auden is 'someone who does not like flowers in his room'. Reprinted in *Selected literary criticism of Louis MacNeice*, edited by Alan Heuser (Oxford: Clarendon Press, 1987), pp. 83–6.

1380 Christopher Isherwood. *Lions and shadows: an education in the* *twenties*. London: Hogarth Press, 1938.

Auden represented as Hugh Weston, *passim*.

I381 Laura Riding. *Collected Poems*. London: Cassell, 1938.

'W. H. Auden . . . has told me that I am "the only living philosophical poet"', p. xxi. Possibly quoted from a letter.

I382 Edward Upward. *Journey to the border*. London: Hogarth Press, 1938.

Auden fictionalized as Gregory Mavors.

I383 Erika and Klaus Mann. *Escape to life*. Boston: Houghton Mifflin, 1939.

At the Downs School Auden taught the boys 'how to write and speak English'; his plans to come to America, p. 9. In the German edition based on the original manuscript, *Escape to life: deutsche Kultur im Exil* (München: Spangenberg, 1991), p. 21.

I384 Louis MacNeice. Not tabloided in slogans. *Common sense*, 9. 4 (Apr. 1940), 24–5.

Review of *Another time* with comments on Auden's views on poetry and politics. Reprinted in *Selected literary criticism of Louis MacNeice*, edited by Alan Heuser (Oxford: Clarendon Press, 1987), pp. 114–16.

I385 Bennett Cerf. Trade winds. *Saturday review*, New York, 25. 37 (12 Sept. 1942), 20.

Auden and Isherwood see *Hellzapoppin* on their first night in New York in 1939.

I386 Antony Bourne. Where shall John go? II—U.S.A. *Horizon*, 9. 49 (Jan. 1944), 13–23.

Very indirect, perhaps hearsay, account of Auden in New York, p. 16.

I387 James Stern. *The hidden damage*. New York: Harcourt, Brace, 1947.

Account of the work in Germany in 1945 by the Strategic Bombing Survey 'team' headed by Auden, who appears in the book as Mervyn, *passim*.

I388 Cyril Connolly. Introduction. *Horizon*, 93–4 (Oct. 1947), 1–11.

Indirect quotations of Auden in New York. Reprinted as 'American injection' in Connolly's *Ideas and places* (London: Weidenfeld & Nicolson, 1953), pp. 166–82.

I389 Nevill Coghill. Sweeney agonistes (an anecdote or two). *T. S. Eliot: a symposium . . .* , edited by Richard March and Tambimuttu (London: Editions Poetry London, 1948), pp. 82–7.

Auden discovers Eliot, 1926, p. 82.

I390 Stephen Spender. The life of literature: I. *Partisan review*, 15. 11 (Nov. 1948), 1194–1211.

Conversations quoted, pp. 1204–11. Not the same as Spender's account in *World within world*.

I391 Stephen Spender. W. H. Auden at Oxford. *World review*, n.s. 6 (Aug. 1949), 45–9.

Slightly different from the account in *World within world*.

I392 Howard Griffin. Conversation on Cornelia Street: dialogue with W. H. Auden. *Accent*, 10. 1 (Autumn 1949), 51–8.

Reprinted in I653.

I393 James I. C. Boyd. [Reminiscences of the Downs School.] *Badger*, Downs School, 24 (Spring 1950), 36–7.

'Lighter moments came when . . . W. H. Auden, then taking English, would have a preliminary view of photos for his contest. This was for the best set of views of the staff, taken when teaching the boys. Unfortunately somebody spilled the beans in the Common Room and many were the cameras confiscated. The contest was abandoned.'

I394 Stephen Spender. *World within world*. London: Hamish Hamilton, 1951.

Conversations quoted, *passim*. Spender's indirect report of Auden's Harvard lecture on *Don Quixote* was repeated without acknowledgement in later newspaper reports, including: 'Pendennis', 'Table talk: Anglo-American', *Observer*, 31 Aug. 1952, p. 5; 'Time for poetry', *Evening news*, London, 10 Feb. 1956.

I395 Howard Griffin. A dialogue with W. H. Auden. *Hudson review*, 3. 4 (Winter 1951), 575–91.

Reprinted in I653.

I396 Rupert Doone. The theatre of ideas. *Theatre newsletter*, 6. 131 (29 Sept. 1951), 5.

Vague report of conversations in the 1930s about the theatre.

I397 Ronald Duncan. An answer to Auden. *Opera*, London, 2. 12 (Nov. 1951), 630–2.

A reply to Auden's essay 'Some reflections on opera as a medium', with a brief account of a conversation with Auden about the essay.

I398 Howard Griffin. Conversation on Cornelia Street, IV: a dialogue with W. H. Auden. *Accent*, 12. 1 (Winter 1952), 49–61.

Reprinted in I653.

I399 Howard Griffin. Snobbery and sainthood: a dialogue with W. H. Auden. *Avon book of modern writing*, [1] (1953), 125–43.
Reprinted in **I653**.

I400 Howard Griffin. Conversation on Cornelia Street, V: a dialogue with W. H. Auden. *Accent*, 13. 1 (Winter 1953), 42–7.
Reprinted in **I653**.

I401 Howard Griffin. A dialogue with W. H. Auden. *Partisan review*, 20. 1 (Jan.–Feb. 1953), 74–85.
Reprinted in **I653**.

I402 Robert Craft. *The rake's progress* in Venice. Boston University, College of Music, Music Festival [program], 17 May 1953, pp. [9–10].
'We were in the dining car when we passed through Verona, and an earnest American voice said, "Didn't Shakespeare live here?" to which Auden replied, "But surely it was Bacon."'

I403 Stephen Spender. W. H. Auden and his poetry. *Atlantic*, 192. 1 (July 1953), 74–9.
Indirect quotations from Oxford and after. Reprinted in *Auden: a collection of critical essays*, edited by Monroe K. Spears (Englewood Cliffs, NJ: Prentice-Hall, 1964), pp. 26–38.

I404 Christopher Isherwood. The head of a leader. *Encounter*, 1. 1 (Oct. 1953), 29–33.
Isherwood told Ernst Toller in 1939, 'A friend of mine [Auden] calls them [skyscrapers] The Fallen Angels', p. 32.

I405 Howard Griffin. Conversation on Cornelia Street: a dialog with W. H. Auden. *Poetry*, 83. 2 (Nov. 1953), 96–106.
The longer text of the original typescript is printed in **I653**.

I406 Arthur Koestler. *The invisible writing: being the second volume of* Arrow in the blue. London: Collins, 1954.
Indirectly quoted on a recollection of Valencia, p. 336.

I407 Gerald Hamilton. The importance of not being Norris. *Punch*, 227. 5958 (17 Nov. 1954), 639.
Auden reads his 'Ode to the New Year' in Brussels, 1938. Also reported in Hamilton's *Mr. Norris and I* (London: Allan Wingate, 1956), p. 131; his *Desert drums*, second edition (Washington: Guild Press, 1966), p. 85; and his *The way it was with me* (London: Leslie Frewin, 1969), p. 56. The reading is also recalled and quoted in Claud Cockburn, *I, Claud . . .* (Harmondsworth: Penguin, 1967), p. 188.

1408 John Malcolm Brinnin. *Dylan Thomas in America: an intimate journal.* Boston: Little, Brown, 1955.

Indirect quotation of Auden's warning about Thomas's drunkenness, p. 18. In the British edition (London: Dent, 1956), pp. 13–14.

1409 Frank McEachran. The unspoken word. *Grasshopper,* Gresham's School, Holt, 1955, pp. 35–7.

Indirect, slightly exaggerated report of Auden at Gresham's, partly based on stories told to McEachran by John Pudney.

1410 Conversation: a dialog between W. H. Auden and Howard Griffin. *Semi-colon,* 1. 4 ([1955]), 1–2.

Reprinted in **1653**.

1411 Stephen Spender. It began at Oxford. *New York times,* 13 Mar. 1955, section 7 (book review), pp. 4–5.

Brief report of Auden's views.

1412 Tom Driberg's column. *Reynolds news,* 12 Feb. 1956, p. 4.

Indirect report of Auden's reminder that Driberg had introduced Eliot's work to Auden.

1413 [Stephen Spender.] The dog beneath the gown. *New statesman and nation,* 51. 1317 (9 June 1956), 656–7.

Biographical sketch; reprinted in *New statesman profiles* (London: Phoenix House, 1957), pp. 211–16.

1414 William Carlos Williams. *The selected letters of William Carlos Williams,* edited with an introduction by John C. Thirlwell. New York: McDowell, Obolensky, 1957.

Williams reports in 1952 that Auden offered his house in Ischia for use the following year, p. 313.

1415 John Pollock. *The last boat.* London: Anthony Blond, 1958.

Novel, with Auden caricatured as H. P. Corfield.

1416 C. Day Lewis. *The buried day.* London: Chatto & Windus, 1960.

Indirect quotations, pp. 176–9.

1417 John Lehmann. *I am my brother.* London: Longmans, Green, 1960.

Indirect report of publication plans, 1938, pp. 14–15, and fuller report of a visit to England, 1945, pp. 289–91; the second report is reprinted in his *In my own time* (Boston: Little, Brown, An Atlantic Monthly Press Book, 1969), pp. 388–90.

1418 Jessica Mitford. *Hons and rebels.* London: Victor Gollancz, 1960.

Mitford and Esmond Romilly encounter Auden and Isherwood at the apartment of an artist-collecting heiress, 1939, pp. 180–1. See also **1715**.

I419 John Pudney. *Home & away: an autobiographical gambit*. London: Michael Joseph, 1960.

Auden at Gresham's School, pp. 45–8, and writing 'Hadrian's Wall', pp. 97–8. Excerpted as 'Auden as a schoolboy', *Guardian*, 21 May 1960, p. 6.

I420 Igor Stravinsky and Robert Craft. *Memories and commentaries*. Garden City, NY: Doubleday, 1960.

Planning and writing *The rake's progress*, pp. 144–54. In the British edition (London: Faber & Faber, 1960), pp. 254–66.

I421 Ragnar Jóhannesson. Í fylgd með Auden. *Andvari*, Reykjavík, n.f. 2. 3 (Winter 1960), 245–58.

Auden in Iceland, 1936; indirect quotations.

I422 John Betjeman. [Tribute to Edmund Blunden.] *Edmund Blunden, sixty-five*. Hong Kong: [University of Hong Kong English Society,] November 1961.

Auden praises Blunden, 1926, pp. 24, 27. Quoted in Thomas Mallon, *Edmund Blunden* (Boston: Twayne, 1983), p. 105; and in Barry Webb, *Edmund Blunden: a biography* (New Haven, Conn.: Yale University Press, 1990), p. 189.

I423 Louis MacNeice. When I was twenty-one: 1928. *Saturday book*, 21 (1961), 230–9.

Brief remarks. Reprinted in *Selected prose of Louis MacNeice*, edited by Alan Heuser (Oxford: Clarendon Press, 1990), pp. 222–35.

I424 Michael Davidson. *The world, the flesh and myself*. London: Arthur Barker, 1962.

Brief remarks, pp. 126–30.

I425 Christopher Isherwood. *Down there on a visit*. New York: Simon and Schuster, 1962.

Auden fictionalized as Hugh Weston; briefly quoted on his return from Belgium, 1938, p. 183.

I426 Thomas Mann. *Briefe 1937–1947*. Frankfurt am Main: S. Fischer, 1963.

Brief report of a visit from Auden, Dec. 1941, p. 231. Translated in *Letters of Thomas Mann 1889–1955*, selected and translated from the German by Richard and Clara Winston (New York: Alfred A. Knopf, 1971), p. 386.

I427 Igor Stravinsky and Robert Craft. *Dialogues and a diary*. Garden City, NY: Doubleday, 1963.

Conversations, 1951, 1959, and 1962, pp. 108, 110–12, 114, 129, 201–3, 268–9.

1428 Basil Wright. Britten and documentary. *Musical times*, 104, 1449 (Nov. 1963), 779–80.
Brief account of Auden's collaboration with Britten.

1429 Chester Kallman. Looking and thinking back. [Libretto booklet with recording of] *Stravinsky conducts* The rake's progress (New York: Columbia Records, 1964), pp. 33–4.
Discussions while writing the libretto.

1430 A conversation with Claud Cockburn. *Review*, Oxford, 11–12 ([1964]), 51–3.
Indirect quotation from Auden in Spain.

1431 J.F.K., ultimate sacrilege, and Stravinsky [interview with Igor Stravinsky]. *New York times*, 6 Dec. 1964, section 2, p. 15.
Reports his conversations with Auden on 'Elegy for J.F.K.'; reprinted in **1438**.

1432 Hugh D. Ford. *A poet's war: British poets and the Spanish Civil War*. Philadelphia: University of Pennsylvania Press, 1965.
Indirect report of Charles Duff's recollections of Auden in Spain, p. 288.

1433 Louis MacNeice. *The strings are false: an unfinished autobiography*. London: Faber & Faber, 1965.
Miscellaneous comments, 1928–40, indirectly reported, pp. 28–9, 113–14, 155, and 232.

1434 Kenneth Rexroth. [Reported comment.] W. H. Auden. *The platonic blow*. New York: Fuck You Press, 1965.
'Wystan told me that he learned more about writing poetry from writing "The Platonic Blow" than from anything he had ever written' (cover page).

1435 Lady's man moves on. *Observer*, 24 Jan. 1965, p. 22.
Brief interview with Rex Harrison, who recalls auditioning for *Man of La Mancha* before Auden was replaced as lyricist: 'Auden actually sang his lyrics. Extraordinary experience.'

1436 Stuart Hood. The box at the opera. *Spectator*, 215. 7171 (3 Dec. 1965), 741.
Remark on opera, recalled from Ischia; also includes a review of 'Poet of disenchantment: W. H. Auden', a BBC-1 Television film, broadcast 28 Nov. 1965. See also **1263**.

1437 Harold Nicolson. *Diaries and letters 1930–1939*, edited by Nigel Nicolson. London: Collins, 1966.
Indirectly quoted from a visit, 1933, p. 153; a second visit is reported in 1937, p. 310.

I438 Igor Stravinsky and Robert Craft. *Themes and episodes*. New York: Alfred A. Knopf, 1966.

Conversations about 'Elegy for J. F. K.', pp. 57–9 (reprinted from **I431**); other conversations, 1964 and 1966, pp. 305–12, 348–52; see also pp. 96–7), 246.

I439 Klaus Geitel. Henzes Bekenntnis zur Tradition [interview with Hans Werner Henze]. *Die Welt*, Hamburg, 13 July 1966, p. 9.

Henze recalls conversations with Auden on *The bassarids.* Reprinted as 'Tradition und Kulturerbe' in Henze's *Schriften und Gespräche 1955–1979* (Berlin: Henschelverlag, 1981), pp. 104–7, and translated by Peter Labanyi as 'Tradition and cultural heritage' in Henze's *Music and politics* (London: Faber & Faber, 1982), pp. 143–6.

I440 Eberhard Bethge. *Dietrich Bonhoeffer: Theologe, Christ, Zeitgenosse*. München: Chr. Kaiser, 1967.

Reports that Auden talked with Bonhoeffer in mid-June 1939, p. 739, note 162.

I441 E. R. Dodds. Background to a poet: memories of Birmingham, 1924–36. *Shenandoah*, 18. 2 (Winter 1967), 6–11.

Slightly revised in his *Missing persons: an autobiography* (Oxford: Clarendon Press, 1977), pp. 119–23.

I442 Naomi Mitchison. Young Auden. *Shenandoah*, 18. 2 (Winter 1967), 12–15.

I443 Bonamy Dobrée. W. H. Auden. *Shenandoah*, 18. 2 (Winter 1967), 18–22.

Brief remarks.

I444 John Betjeman. Five [one of five comments on Auden]. *Shenandoah*, 18. 2 (Winter 1967), 47.

Brief remark. Reprinted in *Shenandoah: an anthology*, James Boatwright, editor (Wainscott, NY: Pushcart Press, 1985), p. 21.

I445 Lincoln Kirstein. Siegfriedslage. *Shenandoah*, 18. 2 (Winter 1967), 51–5.

Versified account of Auden in Germany, 1945. Reprinted in *For W. H. Auden, February 21, 1972*, edited by Peter H. Salus and Paul B. Taylor (New York: Random House, 1972), pp. 50–5, and, with a postscript, in *W. H. Auden, a tribute*, edited by Stephen Spender (London: Weidenfeld & Nicolson, 1975), pp. 128–33. Also reprinted in *Shenandoah: an anthology*, James Boatwright, editor (Wainscott, NY: Pushcart Press, 1985), pp. 25–9; and in Kirstein's *Rhymes of a PFC*, revised edition (Boston:

David R. Godine, 1981), pp. 180–5, and in his *The poems of Lincoln Kirstein* (New York: Atheneum, 1987), pp. 246–50.

I446 Carlo Izzo. 'Good-bye to the Mezzogiorno.' *Shenandoah*, 18. 2 (Winter 1967), 80–2.

Auden asks Izzo to translate it.

I447 Paul Kont. Prima l'arte, dopo la technica. *Die Zukunft*, Wien, [22.] 6 (late Mar. 1967), 24–7.

Indirectly quoted conversation on 'For the time being', which Kont was setting to music as *Inzwischen*.

I448 Evan Esar. *20,000 quips and quotes*. Garden City, NY: Doubleday, 1968.

'A real book is not one that we read, but one that reads us', p. 87.

I449 *Brian Howard, portrait of a failure*, edited by Marie-Jaqueline Lancaster. London: Anthony Blond, 1968.

Howard's reports of conversations with Auden, pp. 373, 397, 525.

I450 Dom Moraes. *My son's father: an autobiography*. London: Secker & Warburg, 1968.

Auden during his term as Professor of Poetry at Oxford, pp. 190–2, 205–6. Partly excerpted as 'Allen Ginsberg kissed the carpet', *Daily telegraph*, 27 Sept. 1968, colour magazine, and as 'Somewhere else with Allen and Gregory', *Horizon*, New York, 11. 1 (Winter 1969), 66–7.

I451 Willa Muir. *Belonging: a memoir*. London: Hogarth Press, 1968.

Auden and Edwin Muir debate religion, 1949–50, p. 255.

I452 *Selected letters of Theodore Roethke*, edited by Ralph J. Mills, Jr. Seattle: University of Washington Press, 1968.

Roethke's quotations from Auden's conversation, pp. 128–9, 194, and 202; indirect quotations, pp. 90, 115, 135, 176, 191, 231, and 255.

I453 Denis de Rougemont. *Journal d'une époque 1926–1946*. Paris: Gallimard, 1968.

Conversation at Middagh Street, around Mar. 1941, p. 470.

I454 Alan Seager. *The glass house: the life of Theodore Roethke*. New York: McGraw-Hill, 1968.

Auden on Roethke, pp. 67, 149, 182, 208; indirect quotations, pp. 115, 211, 214, and 227.

I455 Aldous Huxley. *Letters of Aldous Huxley*, edited by Grover Smith. London: Chatto & Windus, 1969.

Huxley reports that Auden and Isherwood are interested in revamping a stage adaptation of *Lady Chatterley's lover*, 1940, pp. 456–7. Possibly Auden never heard of this project, which may have been mooted by Isherwood and Huxley on his behalf.

1456 Storm Jameson. *Journey from the north: autobiography of Storm Jameson, volume 1*. London: Collins & Harvill Press, 1969.
Auden 'scarcely spoke' at a meeting of the Writers' Committee of the Anti-War Council, in a shabby flat near Buckingham Palace, Oct. 1934, pp. 306–7.

1457 Igor Stravinsky and Robert Craft. *Retrospectives and conclusions*. New York: Alfred A. Knopf, 1969.
Conversations, 1948, 1951, 1952, 1953, pp. 145–9, 160–5, 173–6, 178–9, and 248.

1458 An interview with John Berryman. *Harvard advocate*, 103. 1 (Spring 1969), 4–9.
At a meeting of the National Institute of Arts and Letters, 'Auden got up and said, "We in England feel . . .", but then he suddenly remembered it was the *American* Institute of Arts and Letters!' (p. 9). Reprinted, attributed to Robert B. Shaw, in *Antaeus*, 8 (Winter 1973), 7–19 (Auden quoted on p. 19).

1459 Allen Ginsberg. *Indian journals, March 1962–May 1963: notebooks, diary, blank pages, writings*. San Francisco: Dave Haselwood Books, City Lights Books, 1970.
Vague recollection of Auden on Ischia praising William Carlos Williams, p. 190.

1460 Allen Ginsberg. *Notes after an evening with William Carlos Williams*. Brooklyn, NY: Portents, 1970. (Portents, 17)
Williams told Ginsberg that when he visited Auden they had nothing to say except formalities. Paraphrased in: Louis Simpson, *A revolution in taste* (New York: Macmillan, 1978), p. 62.

1461 Louis Kronenberger. *No whippings, no gold watches*. Boston: Little, Brown, 1970.
Auden as host to a dinner party during his professorship at Oxford, pp. 212–16.

1462 Charles A. Lindbergh. *The wartime journals of Charles A. Lindbergh*. New York: Harcourt Brace Jovanovich, 1970.
Auden visits on 8 Dec. 1940, p. 424. An impression of Auden, based on this visit, appears in Anne Morrow Lindbergh, *War within and without* (New York: Harcourt Brace Jovanovich, 1980), pp. 153–4.

I463 Edith Sitwell. *Selected letters 1919–1964*, edited by John Lehmann and Derek Parker. London: Macmillan, 1970.

Auden's report of his tormenting admirers, 1952, p. 182.

I464 Igor Stravinsky [pseudonym of Robert Craft]. A maker of libretti. *Harper's magazine*, 240. 1439 (Apr. 1970), 112–24.

Brief remarks. Reprinted as 'The maker of libretti' in Stravinsky's *Themes and conclusions* (London: Faber & Faber, 1973), pp. 284–90.

I465 Joel Roache. *Richard Eberhart: the progress of an American poet.* New York: Oxford University Press, 1971.

Auden at St. Mark's School, 1939, pp. 103–6. Eberhart's memories are also in his poem 'To Auden on his fiftieth', in his *The quarry: new poems* (New York: Oxford University Press, 1964), pp. 32–4; and his *Collected poems 1930–1976* (New York: Oxford University Press, 1976), 238–9; and later collections.

I466 Robert Craft. Pages from a chronicle. *New York review of books*, 16. 3 (25 Feb. 1971), 20–1, 24–30.

Auden at the Stravinskys', 2 Dec. 1970. Reprinted in **I469**, pp. 395–6.

I467 Robert Craft. Stravinsky: end of a chronicle. *New York review of books*, 16. 21 (1 July 1971), 4–6, 8–14.

Auden at the Stravinskys', 30 Mar. 1971. Reprinted in **I469**, pp. 405–6.

I468 Paul Bowles. *Without stopping.* New York: G. P. Putnam's Sons, 1972.

Auden at home on Middagh Street, Brooklyn, *ca.* 1940, pp. 233–4; see also pp. 240–2.

I469 Robert Craft. *Stravinsky: chronicle of a friendship, 1948–1971.* New York: Alfred A. Knopf, 1972.

Auden in conversation with the Stravinskys, *passim.* Partly adapted from earlier books by Stravinsky and Craft and essays by Craft listed above.

I470 Scott Donaldson. *Poet in America: Winfield Townley Scott.* Austin: University of Texas Press, 1972.

A remark at a meeting with Scott, p. 249.

I471 *Grand opera, the story of the world's leading opera houses and per-sonalities*, edited by Anthony Gishford, introduced by Benjamin Britten. London: Weidenfeld & Nicolson, 1972.

Anthony Gishford's essay, 'Glyndebourne', reports that John Christie told Auden he shouldn't have written *Elegy for young lovers*, 1961, p. 190. Also told with inauthentic variations in Wilfrid Blunt, *John Christie of Glyndebourne* (London: Bles, 1968), p. 285, and repeated in Ethan Mordden, *Opera anecdotes* (New York: Oxford University Press, 1985), p. 244.

I472 Charles S. Holmes. *The clocks of Columbus: the literary career of James Thurber*. New York: Atheneum, 1972.

Auden demonstrates to Edmund Wilson his knowledge of Thurber minutiae, p. 289.

I473 Arthur Koestler. *The call-girls: a tragi-comedy*. London: Hutchinson, 1972.

Auden fictionalized as Sir Evelyn Blood (whose words are probably almost entirely invented), pp. 70–5, 98–102, 117–18, 122–5, 128, 137, 149, 151, 167–8, 177–8.

I474 Robin Maugham. *Escape from the shadows*. London: Hodder & Stoughton, 1972.

Auden on Ischia, pp. 202–3; in the American edition (New York: McGraw-Hill, 1973), pp. 192–4.

I475 Nevill Coghill. Thanks before going, for Wystan. *For W. H. Auden, February 21, 1972*, edited by Peter H. Salus and Paul B. Taylor (New York: Random House, 1972), pp. 33–44.

Auden at Oxford, 1925–8 and 1956–60.

I476 Louis Kronenberger. Stray notes for a memoir. *For W. H. Auden, February 21, 1972*, edited by Peter H. Salus and Paul B. Taylor (New York: Random House, 1972), pp. 56–61.

Brief remarks. Adapted as 'A friendship revised' in *W. H. Auden, a tribute*, edited by Stephen Spender (London: Weidenfeld & Nicolson, 1975), pp. 155–60.

I477 John Gruen. Love, life, work: Stephen Spender, an interview. *Vogue*, New York, 160. 9 (15 Nov. 1972), 55, 126, 135.

Brief remarks.

I478 Louise Bogan. *What the woman lived: selected letters of Louise Bogan*, edited and with an introduction by Ruth Limmer. New York: Harcourt Brace Jovanovich, 1973.

Auden in conversation, 1941, pp. 213 and 221; see also pp. 225, 226, 243, 260. 276, 317, 350, 359.

I479 William D. Miller. *A harsh and dreadful love: Dorothy Day and the Catholic Worker movement*. New York: Liveright, 1973.

Auden helps Dorothy Day in 1956, p. 251. See also **I40**.

I480 Stephen Spender. *W. H. Auden: a memorial address . . . delivered at Christ Church Cathedral, Oxford, on 27 October 1973*. London: Privately printed for Faber & Faber, 1973.

Miscellaneous remarks quoted. Partly reprinted as 'W. H. Auden (1907–1973)', *New York review of books*, 20. 19 (29 Nov. 1973), 3–4;

reprinted as 'Valediction' in *W. H. Auden, a tribute*, edited by Stephen Spender (London: Weidenfeld & Nicolson, 1975), pp. 244–8, and in I615.

I481 Colin Wilson. *Tree by Tolkien*. London: Covent Garden Press, INCA Books, 1973.

Remark on Tolkien, p. 1. The American edition (Santa Barbara: Capra Press, 1974), reprints the remark, p. 7, with an additional report, p. 43, not in the British edition.

I482 Nicolas Nabokov. 'Love's labour's lost' and its music. [Program booklet.] Opéra national/Théâtre royal de la monnaie, Bruxelles, 7 and 9 Feb. 1973.

Conversations on the libretto. Similar to I557.

I483 Harold Norse. An interview [with Winston Leyland]. *Gay sunshine*, San Francisco, 18 (June–July 1973), 1–8.

Brief remarks, p. 2. Reprinted as 'Winston Leyland interviews Harold Norse', *Gay sunshine interviews*, vol. 1, edited by Winston Leyland (San Francisco: Gay Sunshine Press, 1978), 207–37 (Auden on pp. 212–15).

I484 Lynn Rosellini. 'Always a nice word'. *Newsday*, New York, 30 Sept. 1973, pp. 6, 27.

Obituary notice with recollections by local shopkeepers.

I485 W. H. Auden. *Bookseller*, 3537 (6 Oct. 1973), 2183–4.

Anonymous obituary, including a reminiscence by Charles Monteith.

I486 Giacinto Spagnoletti. Ricordo di W. H. Auden: nessuno risponde per tutti. *La fiera letteraria*, 49. 41 (14 Oct. 1973), 26.

Auden at the Premio Internazionale di Poesia, Taormina, Christmas 1956.

I487 Michael Moynihan. Brother Bernard remembers W. H. *Sunday times*, 28 Oct. 1973, p. 3.

Brief remarks on his relation to his family.

I488 Edward Upward. Remembering the earlier Auden. *Adam international review*, 379–84 (1973–4), 17–22.

Further recollections in a letter by Mary Sandbach, ibid., 385–90 (1974–5), 104.

I489 G. S. Fraser. Glimpses of the poet. *Adam international review*, 379–84 (1973–4), 23–6.

Brief remarks.

I490 Edward Mendelson. Auden in New York: 1939–1941. *Adam international review*, 379–84 (1973–4), 27–33.

Auden told Kallman he rejected *The prolific and the devourer* because of its mandarin aphoristic style.

I491 David Pryce-Jones. 'Earthly paradise' (a Newdigate poem). *Adam international review*, 379–84 (1973–4), 39–43.

Auden at Oxford, 1960, and Kirchstetten, 1970.

I492 Robert Medley. W. H. Auden 1907–1973. *Gresham*, Gresham's School, Holt, 35. 3 (1973–4), 151–3.

I493 Anthony Hecht. W. H. Auden. *American PEN*, 5. 4 (Fall 1973), 14–15.

Indirect quotations of Auden in Ischia.

I494 Poet's view. *Birmingham evening mail*, 1 Oct. 1973.

'When W. H. Auden received an honorary Doctor of Letters at Birmingham University in 1967, changes in the city where he spent many boyhood years impressed him greatly.

'He told his hosts that he had never seen a city so changed.

'Although passing no judgements, he said "It is even more striking than New York."'

I495 W. A. [*sic*] Auden dies; poet taught at Swarthmore. *Delaware County daily times*, Chester, Pennsylvania, 1 Oct. 1973, p. 12.

Includes reminiscences of Auden's teaching.

I496 Catharine O. Foster. W. H. Auden remembered. *Bennington banner*, Bennington, Vermont, 4 Oct. 1973, p. 4.

At Bennington, 1946.

I497 Roy Fuller. W. H. Auden, 1907 to 1973. *Listener*, 90. 2323 (4 Oct. 1973), 439.

Brief remarks at a party and before a reading. A slightly longer version was distributed as a five-page leaflet, titled 'Wystan Hugh Auden', by the Poem-of-the-Month Club, London, in 1973.

I498 Stephen Spender. W. H. Auden 1907–1973. *New statesman*, 86. 2220 (5 Oct. 1973), 478.

General account of Auden's attitudes, followed by brief accounts by Charles Monteith (p. 479) and William Coldstream (p. 479). Spender's tribute is reprinted in *Partisan review*, 40. 3 (1973), 546–8; not the same as **I501**. Coldstream's is reprinted as 'A portrait' in *W. H. Auden, a tribute*, edited by Stephen Spender (London: Weidenfeld & Nicolson, 1975), pp. 58–9.

I499 Golo Mann. . . . und unabhängig zum Erstaunen: Erinnerungen an dem Dichter W. H. Auden. *Süddeutsche Zeitung*, 6–7 Oct. 1973, pp. 111–12.

Recollections, mostly from 1940. Translated as 'W. H. Auden, a memoir', *Encounter*, 42. 1 (Jan. 1974), 7–11; reprinted as 'A memoir' in *W. H.*

Auden, a tribute, edited by Stephen Spender (London: Weidenfeld & Nicolson, 1975), pp. 98–103.

I500 Peter L. Simpson. Concinnity and elegance of 'the greatest poet'. *St. Louis post-dispatch*, 7 Oct. 1973, p. 4B.
Brief recollection of Auden's visit to the author's home during a reading tour.

I501 Stephen Spender. W. H. Auden 1907–1973: an appreciation. *Washington post*, 7 Oct. 1973, pp. C1, C3.
Summary of Auden's attitudes.

I502 G. K. Maclachlen. Auden's poetry [letter to the editor]. *Daily telegraph*, 10 Oct. 1973, p. 18.
Reminiscence of Auden at Helensburgh, 1930, where he taught students French, how to stick stamps on the ceiling with a penny, and not to stand too close to a gas fire while wearing an academic gown.

I503 Amita Malik. Date with Auden. *Statesman*, Calcutta and Delhi, 14 Oct. 1973, pp. 11, 13.
Auden in India, 1951; reported without quotations.

I504 Janet Adam Smith. Auden and the 'Listener'. *Listener*, 90. 2325 (18 Oct. 1973), 532, 534.
In 1932, when F. R. Leavis complained in a review that some names in *The orators* 'come from a boy's romantic map', Auden said: 'They don't, you know. They're in Shetland.'

I505 George Christian Anderson. Remembers Auden. *Swarthmorean*, 19 Oct. 1973, p. 4.
Letter to the editor with brief recollections from Swarthmore and Oxford.

I506 W. G. Dent. In memory of W. H. Auden. *Weekly leaflet of Christ Church in Cambridge*, Cambridge, Mass., 42. 6 (21 Oct. 1973), 1–4.
Brief report of occasional meetings.

I507 Francis Hope. Meeting point. *New statesman*, 86. 224 (2 Nov. 1973), 645.
Auden, asked at a dinner party, affirms that animals have souls.

I508 Carman Moore. W. H. Auden. *Village voice*, New York, 18. 45 (8 Nov. 1973), 37.
Obituary with vague account of a visit to Kirchstetten, 1966.

I509 Richard Eberhart. W. H. Auden: a memoir. *Dartmouth*, Dartmouth College, 28 Nov. 1973, p. 2.

Auden at St. Mark's School, 1939, and later. Reprinted with minor changes as 'A tribute to W. H. Auden', *Poetry Society of America bulletin*, 63 (Dec. 1973), 13–15; in *Harvard advocate*, 108. 2–3 ([1975]), 30–1; and, as 'Remarks on Auden', in Eberhart's *Of poetry and poets* (Urbana: University of Illinois Press, 1979), pp. 202–4.

I510 Memories of Adrian Stokes—presented by Eric Rhodes. *Listener*, 90. 2333 (13 Dec. 1973), 812.

Brief comment on Stokes, *ca.* 1935, recalled by Andrew Forge.

I511 Anaïs Nin. *The diary of Anaïs Nin 1947–1955*, edited and with a preface by Gunther Stuhlmann. New York: Harcourt Brace Jovanovich, 1974.

Remark after a reading by Nin, 1954, p. 164.

I512 E. L. Stahl. The 'Faust' translation: a personal account. *Time was away: the world of Louis MacNeice*, edited by Terence Brown and Alec Reid. Dublin: Dolmen Press, 1974, pp. 67–85.

Around 1948–9 Auden turned down an invitation from the BBC to translate *Faust*, p. 67. Perhaps refers to an exchange by letter.

I513 Harry Watt. *Don't look at the camera*. London: Paul Elek, 1974.

Recollections of the making of *Night mail*, pp. 79–97.

I514 Jacques Barzun, Hannah Arendt, and William Meredith. Recollections of W. H. Auden. *Proceedings of the American Academy of Arts and Letters and the National Institute of Arts and Letters*, 2nd series, no. 24 (1974), 69–86.

I515 Stephen Spender. Commemorative tributes of the American Academy of Arts and Letters: W. H. Auden, 1907–1973. *Proceedings of the American Academy of Arts and Letters and the National Institute of Arts and Letters*, 2nd series, no. 24 (1974), 97–101.

Brief indirect quotations. Reprinted as 'Wystan Hugh Auden, 1907–1973' in *Harvard advocate*, 108. 2–3 ([1975]), 60–1.

I516 Norman Pittenger. Wystan Auden as a witness for the Christian faith. *Modern churchman*, n.s. 17. 2 (Jan. 1974), 90–2.

Remarks and conversations. See also Pittenger's 'A poet's expression of faith', *British weekly*, 4 Jan. 1974, section B, p. 8.

I517 Henry Mitchell. In celebration of Auden, homage from Stephen Spender. *Washington post*, 6 Jan. 1974, section H, pp. 1–2.

Spender recalls Auden.

I518 Daniel Halpern. A conversation with Christopher Isherwood. *Antaeus*, 13–14 (Spring–Summer 1974), 366–88.
Report of Auden's religious attitudes, p. 380.

I519 Christopher Isherwood. The art of fiction XLIX [interview with W. I. Scobie]. *Paris Review*, 57 (Spring 1974), 138–82.
On their plays and California, pp. 169–71. Reprinted in *Writers at work: the* Paris review *interviews, fourth series*, edited by George Plimpton (New York: Viking, 1976), pp. 209–42 (Auden remarks on pp. 233–4).

I520 James Kirkup. When poets die: William Plomer and W. H. Auden as I knew them. *Eigo seinen (The rising generation)*, 120. 1 (Apr. 1974), 20–1.

I521 Julian Symons. Whatever happened to the great detective? *Times*, 27 July 1974, p. 13.
Indirect report of Auden's taste for novels by Harry Kemelman.

I522 Alfred Läutner [pseudonym of Charles Osborne?]. The nine lives of *Poetry International. New review*, 1. 5 (Aug. 1974), 35–42.
Auden's remarks at the annual festivals.

I523 Maurice Feild. Wystan Auden—1907–1973. *Badger*, Downs School, 47 (Autumn 1974), 33–4.
Auden at the Downs School.

I524 Michael Yates. Wystan Auden 1907–1973. *Badger*, Downs School, 47 (Autumn 1974), 34.
Auden at the Downs School.

I525 John Button [interviewed by Steven Abbott and Thom Willenbecher]. Remembering Auden. *Fag rag*, Boston, 10 (Fall 1974), 14–19.
Miscellaneous conversations.

I526 Made things: an interview with Richard Howard. *Ohio review*, 16. 1 (Fall 1974), 43–58.
Quotes Auden's attitudes towards literary criticism, pp. 53–4; the same conversation is dramatized in **I568**.

I527 Richard Howard. Again for Hephaistos, the last time. *Ohio review*, 16. 1 (Fall 1974), 59–61.
Memorial poem for Auden with quotations. Reprinted in his *Fellow feelings* (New York: Atheneum, 1976), pp. 10–12.

I528 James Fenton. Advice to poets. *New statesman*, 88. 2270 (20 Sept. 1974), 380–1.
Remarks on influences.

I529 Stella Musulin. [Review of] W. H. Auden, *Gedichte—Poems. Literatur und Kritik*, 88 (Oct. 1974), 496–8.
Remarks on translations of his work.

I530 Peter Heyworth. The opera that Auden inspired. *Observer*, 6 Oct. 1974, magazine, pp. 55, 57–9, 61.
Interview with Hans Werner Henze about *The bassarids*. Reports of remarks and letters.

I531 Donna McDonald. Spender on Auden. *Descant*, Toronto, 10 (early Winter 1974), 34–7.
Interview with reminiscences.

I532 Frank MacShane. Encounters with Auden. *Columbia forum*, n.s. 3. 1 (Winter 1974), 39–41.
Partly reprinted as 'Auden's requiem', *Commonweal*, 100. 5 (5 Apr. 1974), 98.

I533 John Auden. A brother's viewpoint. *W. H. Auden, a tribute*, edited by Stephen Spender (London: Weidenfeld & Nicolson, 1975), pp. 25–30.

I534 Rosamira Bulley. A prep school reminiscence. *W. H. Auden, a tribute*, edited by Stephen Spender (London: Weidenfeld & Nicolson, 1975), pp. 31–4.

I535 Harold Llewellyn Smith. At St Edmund's 1915–1920. *W. H. Auden, a tribute*, edited by Stephen Spender (London: Weidenfeld & Nicolson, 1975), pp. 34–6.

I536 Robert Medley. Gresham's School, Holt. *W. H. Auden, a tribute*, edited by Stephen Spender (London: Weidenfeld & Nicolson, 1975), pp. 37–43.

I537 Sir John Betjeman. Oxford. *W. H. Auden, a tribute*, edited by Stephen Spender (London: Weidenfeld & Nicolson, 1975), pp. 43–5.

I538 Gabriel Carritt. A friend of the family. *W. H. Auden, a tribute*, edited by Stephen Spender (London: Weidenfeld & Nicolson, 1975), pp. 45–8, 57–9.
Written in collaboration with Rex Warner.

I539 Michael Yates. Iceland 1936. *W. H. Auden, a tribute*, edited by Stephen Spender (London: Weidenfeld & Nicolson, 1975), pp. 59–68.

I540 Cyril Connolly. Some memories. *W. H. Auden, a tribute*, edited by Stephen Spender (London: Weidenfeld & Nicolson, 1975), pp. 68–73.

I541 Anne Fremantle. Reality and religion. *W. H. Auden, a tribute*, edited by Stephen Spender (London: Weidenfeld & Nicolson, 1975), pp. 79–80, 89–92.

I542 Basil Boothby. An unofficial visitor. *W. H. Auden, a tribute*, edited by Stephen Spender (London: Weidenfeld & Nicolson, 1975), pp. 93–7.

I543 Ursula Niebuhr. Memories of the 1940s. *W. H. Auden, a tribute*, edited by Stephen Spender (London: Weidenfeld & Nicolson, 1975), pp. 104–18.

I544 Maurice Mandelbaum. Swarthmore. *W. H. Auden, a tribute*, edited by Stephen Spender (London: Weidenfeld & Nicolson, 1975), pp. 119–23.

I545 James Stern. The indispensable presence. *W. H. Auden, a tribute*, edited by Stephen Spender (London: Weidenfeld & Nicolson, 1975), pp. 123–7.

I546 Nicolas Nabokov. Excerpts from memories. *W. H. Auden, a tribute*, edited by Stephen Spender (London: Weidenfeld & Nicolson, 1975), pp. 133–6, 145–8.

I547 Robert Craft. The poet and the rake. *W. H. Auden, a tribute*, edited by Stephen Spender (London: Weidenfeld & Nicolson, 1975), pp. 149–55.

I548 Orlan Fox. Friday nights. *W. H. Auden, a tribute*, edited by Stephen Spender (London: Weidenfeld & Nicolson, 1975), pp. 173–81.

I549 Oliver Sacks. Dear Mr A . . . . *W. H. Auden, a tribute*, edited by Stephen Spender (London: Weidenfeld & Nicolson, 1975), pp. 187–95.

I550 David Luke. Homing to Oxford. *W. H. Auden, a tribute*, edited by Stephen Spender (London: Weidenfeld & Nicolson, 1975), pp. 202–8, 217.

I551 Charles Rosen. Public and private. *W. H. Auden, a tribute*, edited by Stephen Spender (London: Weidenfeld & Nicolson, 1975), pp. 218–19.

I552 Chester Kallman. The dome of the rock. *W. H. Auden, a tribute*, edited by Stephen Spender (London: Weidenfeld & Nicolson, 1975), pp. 226–8.

I553 Joan Simpson Burns. *The awkward embrace: the creative artist and the institution in America*. New York: Alfred A Knopf, 1975.
Remarks on the audience for his poems, recalled by W. McNeil Lowry, p. 457.

I554 Virginia Spencer Carr. *The lonely hunter: a biography of Carson McCullers*. Garden City, NY: Doubleday, 1975.
Auden at Middagh Street, partly described from a conversation with Carr, pp. 120–6 and *passim*.

I555 Willard R. Espy. *An almanac of words at play*. New York: Clarkson N. Potter, 1975.
Remarks on hearing that a friend wrote poetry, and to the effect that he would always wear carpet slippers when he became famous, pp. 246–7. Both are adapted in *The Little, Brown book of anecdotes*, Clifton Fadiman, general editor (Boston: Little, Brown, 1985), p. 27.

I556 Klaus Mann. *Briefe und Antworten*, Band I: 1937–1949, herausgegeben von Martin Gregor-Dellin. München: Spangenberg, 1975.
Indirect reflections on a conversation with Auden, Nov. 1939, pp. 89–90; see also p. 145. Golo Mann's 'Nachwort' reports another remark, p. 322. The same letters appear in: Klaus Mann, *Briefe* (Berlin: Aufbau, 1988), pp. 361, 408.

I557 Nicolas Nabokov. *Bagázh: memoirs of a Russian cosmopolitan*. New York: Atheneum, 1975.
Conversations, 1943–5, 1963, and 1969–73, pp. 218–31. (Nabokov's statement on p. 246 that Auden prepared the translations from Dante's *Vita nuova* that Nabokov used when setting sonnets from the work is incorrect. Nabokov used Rossetti's translation, although Auden may perhaps have chosen it for him.) See also Nabokov's conversation with Naomi Bliven and Bruce Bliven, Jr., 'Nabokov & the musical psyche', *Intellectual digest*, 3. 8 (Apr. 1973), 76–9.

I558 Sylvia Plath. *Letters home: correspondence 1950–1963*, selected and edited with a commentary by Aurelia Schober Plath. New York: Harper & Row, 1975.
Auden at Smith College, 1953, pp. 107–8, 110. A similar account appears in *The journals of Sylvia Plath*, foreword by Ted Hughes (New York: Dial

Press, 1982), pp. 77–8. Auden's advice to work on her verbs is reported in Linda Wagner-Martin, *Sylvia Plath: a biography* (New York: Simon & Schuster, 1987), p. 96. The further detail that at Smith Auden 'dismissed her poems as too glib' appears in: Anne Stevenson, *Bitter fame: a life of Sylvia Plath* (Boston: Houghton Mifflin, 1989), p. 43.

I559 Louis Simpson. *Three on the tower: the lives and works of Ezra Pound, T. S. Eliot and William Carlos Williams.* New York: William Morrow, 1975.

Auden disappears from a Poetry Society of America dinner at which Ezra Pound is denounced by Robert Hillyer, probably 1949, p. 84.

I560 Stephen Spender. *Eliot.* London: Fontana/Collins, 1975.

Auden asks Eliot why he likes playing patience, p. 240; in the American edition (*T. S. Eliot*, New York: Viking, 1975), pp. 251–2. Adapted in *The Little, Brown book of anecdotes*, Clifton Fadiman, general editor (Boston: Little, Brown, 1985), p. 190.

I561 William Targ. *Indecent pleasures.* New York: Macmillan, 1975.

Conversations pp. 95–7.

I562 Robert Wilson. *Auden's library.* New York: [Phoenix Book Shop,] 1975.

Pamphlet on Wilson's purchase of the library.

I563 William Meredith. One of the high ones: some recollections of W. H. Auden. *Harvard advocate*, 108. 2–3 ([1975]), 10–12.

Reprinted as 'Recollections of W. H. Auden', *Connecticut College Library bulletin*, 2 (Fall 1975), 1–5; and as 'Afterword' in Joseph the Provider, Books, *The Carter Burden collection of the works of W. H. Auden* [sales catalogue], (Santa Barbara, 1989), not paged.

I564 Dorothy Day. The poet and the pauper. *Harvard advocate*, 108. 2–3 ([1975]), 28–9.

I565 William Empson. Wartime recollections. *Harvard advocate*, 108. 2–3 ([1975]), 31.

I566 Phyllis McGinley. Tribute to an honored guest. *Harvard advocate*, 108. 2–3 ([1975]), 36.

I567 Harry Levin. Auden at Harvard. *Harvard advocate*, 108. 2–3 ([1975]), 38–40.

Reprinted in his *Memories of the moderns* (New York: New Directions, 1980), pp. 150–5.

I568 Richard Howard. Audiences. *Harvard advocate*, 108. 2–3 ([1975]), 40–1.

Recollections in verse. Reprinted in his *Fellow feelings* (New York: Atheneum, 1976), 13–15.

1569 Frances Steloff. Brief encounters with W. H. Auden at the Gotham Book Mart. *Harvard advocate*, 108. 2–3 ([1975]), 45.

Also printed as 'W. H. Auden' in *Journal of modern literature*, 4. 4 (Apr. 1975), 877–9.

1570 Elizabeth Bishop. A brief reminiscence and a brief tribute. *Harvard advocate*, 108. 2–3 ([1975]), 47–8.

1571 Anthony Hecht. Discovering Auden. *Harvard advocate*, 108. 2–3 ([1975]), 48–50.

Conversations in Italy.

1572 Tennessee Williams. W. H. Auden: a few reminiscences. *Harvard advocate*, 108. 2–3 ([1975]), 59.

1573 Hannah Arendt. Remembering Wystan H. Auden, who died in the night of the twenty-eighth of September, 1973. *New Yorker*, 50. 48 (20 Jan. 1975), 39–40, 45–6.

Recollections from 1958 and after. Reprinted in *Harvard advocate*, 108. 2–3 ([1975]), 42–5, and, as 'Remembering Wystan Auden', in *W. H. Auden, a tribute*, edited by Stephen Spender (London: Weidenfeld & Nicolson, 1975), pp. 181–7.

1574 Howard Moss. [Untitled review of *Thank you, fog.*] *New York times*, 12 Jan. 1975, section 7 (book review), pp. 1, 10, 12.

Quotes brief remarks. Reprinted as 'Goodbye to Wystan' in his *Whatever is moving* (Boston: Little, Brown, 1981), pp. 28–37, and in his *Minor monuments* (New York: Ecco, 1986), pp. 120–9.

1575 Stephen Spender. W. H. Auden—a tribute. *Index on censorship*, 4. 1 (Spring 1975), 3–4.

Spender's address at Westminster Abbey on the laying of Auden's memorial stone. Brief remarks.

1576 James Schuyler. Wystan Auden. *Times literary supplement*, 28 Mar. 1975, p. 327.

Biographical poem. Reprinted in his *The morning of the poem* (New York: Farrar, Straus & Giroux, 1980), pp. 28–30; and *Selected poems* (New York: Farrar, Straus & Giroux, 1988), pp. 169–70.

1577 Charles Osborne. The day of the funeral. *London magazine*, n.s. 15. 1 (Apr.–May 1975), 80–5.

Brief recollections. Reprinted in *Harvard advocate*, 108. 2–3 ([1975]), 62–4, and revised in *Poetry dimension*, 4 (1976), 164–9.

1578 V. S. Yanovsky. W. H. Auden. *Antaeus*, 19 (Autumn 1975), 107–35.

Extensive reports of conversations.

1579 A. Alvarez. W. H. Auden: a memoir. *American review*, 23 (Oct. 1975), 144–56.

Conversations; one sentence quoted.

1580 Loren Eiseley. PW interviews: Loren Eiseley [interviewed by John F. Baker]. *Publishers weekly*, 208. 18 (3 Nov. 1975), 10, 12.

Auden at dinner. Reprinted in *The author speaks: selected* PW *interviews 1967–1976*, by *Publishers weekly* editors and contributors (New York: R. R. Bowker, 1977), pp. 283–5.

1581 Bertolt Brecht. Encounter with the poet Auden. *Poems*, edited by John Willett and Ralph Manheim with the co-operation of Erich Fried. London: Eyre Methuen, 1976.

Brief poem, probably misremembered from 1946, pp. 418–19. First published in this translation; German text first published in **1688**, p. 70.

1582 Irving Drutman. *Good company: a memoir, mostly theatrical*. Boston: Little, Brown, 1976.

'W. H. Auden', pp. 261–8, includes reminiscences from 1947–73.

1583 David Hockney. *David Hockney*, edited by Nikos Stangos. London: Thames & Hudson, 1976.

During a sitting for a 1969 portrait Auden complains about pornography in public, pp. 194–5. Similar recollections in: William Cash, 'The sunshine state: David Hockney', *Times*, 14 Nov. 1992, Saturday Review, p. 4.

1584 A. L. Rowse. *A Cornishman abroad*. London: Jonathan Cape, 1976.

Auden as an undergraduate; brief remarks, pp. 135–7.

1585 Oliver Sacks. *Awakenings*, revised edition. Harmondsworth: Penguin, 1976.

The notion of a disease with a 'Dionysiac' potential was often discussed in the Auden household, p. 35.

1586 Christopher Isherwood. *Christopher and his kind, 1929–1939*. New York: Farrar, Straus & Giroux, 1976; London: Eyre Methuen, 1977.

Conversations quoted from Isherwood's diaries, *passim*.

1587 Paul Ferris. *Dylan Thomas*. London: Hodder & Stoughton, 1977.

Auden said to have refused an offer to adapt *Peer Gynt* for BBC Television, 1947, p. 226. Perhaps refers to an exchange by letter.

I588 Michael Wishart. *High diver*. London: Blond & Briggs, 1977.

'He [Roy Campbell] cried when, a long time after the event, W. H. Auden took his hand and conceded that Roy had been right after all in his attitude regarding the Spanish war', p. 33.

I589 [Interview with Lily Tomlin.] *Advocate*, San Mateo, California, 14 Jan. 1976, p. 25.

Auden, backstage at a broadcast interview, objects to the other participants.

I590 William Coldstream. Art: talking to Coldstream [interview with Mark Glazebrook]. *London magazine*, n.s. 16. 1 (Apr.–May 1976), 88–95.

Auden told Coldstream, *ca*. 1935 that abstract art was irrelevant and that he should paint what everyone could understand, pp. 92, 94.

I591 Margaret Gardiner. Auden: a memoir. *New review*, 3. 28 (July 1976), 9–19.

Conversations from 1929 through the late 1960s. Reprinted in Gardiner's *A scatter of memories* (London: Free Association Books, 1988), pp. 135–61. A further brief indirect quotation is on p. 117.

I592 Edward Mendelson. Editing Auden. *New statesman*, 92. 2374 (17 Sept. 1976), 376–7.

Indirect quotation on his collected works and plans for future work.

I593 [Harry Bergholz.] Auden at Kirchstetten, 1973. *South Atlantic quarterly*, 75. 1 (Winter 1976), 8–19.

I594 The New School Media Studies Program presents Akalq (a 12-tone loop) starring Michael Newman . . . at the New School Cinema, [New York], 17 & 18 Dec. 1976, 7 & 8 Jan. 1977 [program card].

'Auden called us "Mad in a good way."'

I595 James Atlas. *Delmore Schwartz: the life of an American poet*. New York: Farrar, Straus & Giroux, 1977.

Conversations about and with Schwartz, 1939 and early 1940s, pp. 129, 156–7, 237. See also I819.

I596 *Conversations with writers*, conversations, vol. 1. Detroit: Gale Research, 1977.

Interview with Robert Hayden, pp. 157–79, with an account of Auden at Michigan, 1941–2 (pp. 165–6). Reprinted as 'A certain vision' in Hayden's *Collected prose* (Ann Arbor: University of Michigan Press, 1986), pp. 90–114 (Auden discussed on pp. 99–101).

I597 Tom Driberg. *Ruling passions*. London: Jonathan Cape, 1977.

Brief indirect report of conversations, pp. 58–62.

1598 Jonathan Fryer. *Isherwood: a biography of Christopher Isherwood.* London: New English Library, 1977.
Auden in 1939, recalled by Harold Norse, p. 191. In the expanded American edition (Garden City, NY: Doubleday, 1978), pp. 186–7.

1599 T. S. Matthews. *Jacks or better: a narrative.* New York: Harper & Row, 1977.
Reply to a reported insult by Robert Graves, p. 304.

1600 Anne Valery. *The edge of a smile.* London: Peter Owen, 1977.
Vague paraphrase of remarks in postwar London, pp. 203–4.

1601 Edmund Wilson. *Letters on literature and politics 1912–1972,* edited by Elena Wilson. New York: Farrar, Straus & Giroux, 1977.
Reports on Auden's conversation, 1945–6, pp. 429–31.

1602 James Fenton. A backward love. *New review*, 3. 36 (March 1977), 41–3.
Reported comments on homosexuality, his tentative proposal of marriage to Teckla Clark, and other subjects, p. 42.

1603 W. I. Scobie. The youth that was I—a conversation in Santa Barbara with Christopher Isherwood. *London magazine*, n.s. 17. 1 (Apr.–May 1977), 23–32.
Auden admired Brian Howard's poems, p. 28.

1604 Karl Miller. Goodbye to Britain. *New York review of books*, 24. 10 (9 June 1977), 15–16.
Review of *The Auden generation*, by Samuel Hynes; second-hand report that Auden in conversation supported the war in Vietnam. A letter by John B. Myers, ibid. (4 Aug. 1977), p. 42, disputes this report.

1605 David Jackson. Three pictures of W. H. Auden. *Christopher Street*, 2. 4 (Oct. 1977), 42.
Conversations in 1965, 1972, and 1973. Reprinted in *The Christopher Street reader*, edited by Michael Denneny, Charles Ortleb, Thomas Steele (New York: Coward, McCann & Geoghegan, 1983), pp. 289–90.

1606 P. K. Walker. Auden thoughts. *Theology*, 80. 678 (Nov. 1977), 428–38.
Auden at Oxford, 1972–3; brief remarks.

1607 Susan Wood. Bards of America. *Washington post*, 11 Dec. 1977, book world, p. E1.
'Once when W. H. Auden was answering questions from his audience following a poetry reading at Princeton University, a student asked him to "name in order the ten best poets now writing in the United States." "My

god, young man," the dismayed Auden replied gruffly, "it isn't a horse-race! Next question."'

I608 Dorothy Commins. *What is an editor? Saxe Commins at work.* Chicago: University of Chicago Press, 1978.

Conversations at a New Year's party (probably in fact a birthday party), pp. 142–3.

I609 Evan Esar. *The comic encyclopedia.* Garden City, NY: Doubleday, 1978.

Reports Auden's recitation of a scatological verse that delighted him when he was six, p. 183.

I610 P. N. Furbank. *E. M. Forster: a life,* vol. 2. London: Secker & Warburg, 1978.

About his marriage to Erika Mann and at the wedding of John Simpson and Therese Giehse, p. 213.

I611 David Gascoyne. *Paris journal 1937–1939.* London: Enitharmon Press, 1978.

Brief report of Auden in Paris, Dec. 1938, pp. 103–4. Reprinted in his *Collected journals 1936–1942* (London: Skoob Books, 1991), pp. 228–30.

I612 Donald E. Hayden. *Literary studies: the poetic process.* Tulsa: University of Tulsa [monograph series, no. 15], 1978.

The essay 'Annus mirabilis: Spender, Lewis, Auden' reports on Auden's visit to Tulsa, 15 Jan. 1958, pp. 62–7.

I613 Alfred Kazin. *New York Jew.* New York: Alfred A. Knopf, 1978.

Comments on Delmore Schwartz, p. 26, and on Brooklyn Heights, p. 59 (repeated on p. 151).

I614 John Lehmann. *Thrown to the Woolfs.* London: Weidenfeld & Nicolson, 1978.

Indirect remarks on publication plans, pp. 52, 77. Also reported in his *Christopher Isherwood: a personal memoir* (London: Weidenfeld & Nicolson, 1987), p. 48; and, very briefly, in **I417**.

I615 John Pudney. *Thank goodness for cake.* London: Michael Joseph, 1978.

Auden indirectly quoted at school and after, pp. 51–3.

I616 Stephen Spender. *The thirties and after: poetry, politics, people, 1933–1970.* New York: Random House, 1978.

Remarks and conversation quoted in the essay 'Background to the thirties' (pp. 3–20); British edition: London: Macmillan, 1978 (pp. 54–61). Also reprints **I480**.

I617 Vera Stravinsky and Robert Craft. *Stravinsky in pictures and documents*. New York: Simon & Schuster, 1978.

Conversations, pp. 204–5, 396–416 *passim*, 490–1, 538, 650 (Auden lecturing at Barnard, 1946), 653, and 654.

I618 Peter Sutcliffe. *The Oxford University Press, an informal history*. Oxford: Clarendon Press, 1978.

Auden proposes an *Oxford book of light verse* to Charles Williams, 1938, pp. 244–5.

I619 Gore Vidal. Rich kids. *New York review of books*, 25. 1 (9 Feb. 1978), 9–10, 12–13.

Quotes a brief remark on Auden's social class, p. 10. Reprinted in Vidal's *Second American Revolution and other essays (1976–1982)* (New York: Random House, 1982), pp. 197–208 (Auden on p. 203); and his *United States: essays 1952–1992* (New York: Random House, 1993), pp. 629–40 (Auden on p. 635).

I620 Leif Sjöberg. A sketch of W. H. Auden. *Upstart*, Columbia University, Spring 1978, pp. 17–18.

I621 Dale Wasserman. Tilting with 'Man of La Mancha'. *Los Angeles times*, 5 Mar. 1978, Calendar section, p. 60.

A conversation about Auden's lyrics that were written for, but not used in, the musical version of the play, 1962.

I622 W. I. Scobie. W. H. Auden: in faithless arms, in faithful love. *Advocate*, San Mateo, California, 14 June 1978, pp. 24–7.

Remarks reported by Auden's friends.

I623 Anthony Holden. The great dark blue poetry punch-up. *Sunday times*, 16 July 1978, pp. 33–4.

Brief remarks on the Oxford Professorship of Poetry.

I624 Robert L. Chapman. Auden in Ann Arbor. *Michigan quarterly review*, 17. 4 (Fall 1978), 507–20.

Remarks from Auden's classes and elsewhere, 1941–2.

I625 Katie Louchheim. The truth is not the proper thing to tell. *Washington post*, 5 Nov. 1978, magazine, pp. 20–1, 23–4.

Auden's visit to the Louchheims, 1939.

I626 Brian Finney. *Christopher Isherwood: a critical biography*. London: Faber & Faber, 1979.

Quotes Isherwood's letter to Spender about Auden in China, p. 139; other brief remarks reported, pp. 62, 76.

I627 Naomi Mitchison. *You may well ask: a memoir, 1920–1940*. London: Victor Gollancz, 1979.

Conversations briefly recalled in the chapter 'The bright star', pp. 117–26.

I628 Charles Osborne. *W. H. Auden: the life of a poet*. London: Eyre Methuen, 1979.

Conversations and remarks, *passim*.

I629 Peter H. Salus. Englishing the Edda. *Comparative criticism*, 1 (1979), 141–51.

Remarks on Icelandic poetry.

I630 Leif Sjöberg. Translating with W. H. Auden: Gunnar Ekelöf's last poems. *Comparative criticism*, 1 (1979), 185–97.

Remarks on translation, publishing, etc.

I631 Milo Keynes. Auden [letter to the editor]. *Times literary supplement*, 3 Apr. 1979, p. 379.

One sentence on Britten's librettists.

I632 David Roberts. W. H. Auden's mountain. *Horizon*, Tuscaloosa, Alabama, 22. 5 (May 1979), 56–61.

Conversation on mountaineering during a visit in 1969.

I633 Stephen Spender. Foreword. [Programme of] *Cambridge Mummers present W. H. Auden's* The orators *in a stage version by Mark Vessey*, at the Reid Concert Hall, Teviot Row, [Edinburgh,] 4 and 6 September 1979, p. [2].

'Auden told me at the time that he wrote *The Orators* in "sweat and blood". . . . Another thing I remember Auden saying while he was writing it, was something to the effect that poetry ought now to be funny.'

I634 Sean Day-Lewis. *C. Day-Lewis, an English literary life*. London: Weidenfeld & Nicolson, 1980.

Auden visits Cecil Day-Lewis, pp. 75, 103, 179, 217, 239, and 297; talks with Sean Day-Lewis, p. 264.

I635 Christopher Isherwood. *My guru and his disciple*. New York: Farrar, Straus & Giroux, 1980.

Auden in New York, 1939, pp. 3–5, 8; and later, pp. 203–4.

I636 Thomas Mann. *Tagebücher 1937 bis 1939*, herausgegeben von Peter de Mendelssohn. Frankfurt am Main: S. Fischer, 1980.

Sketchy references to conversations and visits, 1939, pp. 354–5, 399, 480, 503, 504.

1637 J. M. Richards. *Memoirs of an unjust fella*. London: Hamish Hamilton, 1980.

Auden at Gresham's School, p. 36.

1638 A. L. Rowse. *Memories of men and women*. London: Eyre Methuen, 1980.

'The poet Auden', brief remarks, pp. 240–58.

1639 Stephen Spender. *Letters to Christopher*, edited by Lee Bartlett. Santa Barbara: Black Sparrow, 1980.

Spender's letter of 7 Sept. 1933 reports a brief conversation about Auden's driving, p. 63.

1640 Stephen Spender. The art of poetry XXV [interview with Peter Stitt]. *Paris review*, 77 (Winter–Spring 1980), 119–54.

Reprinted in *Writers at work: The* Paris review *interviews, sixth series*, edited by George Plimpton (New York: Viking, 1984), pp. 39–73.

1641 Bryan Kelly. W. H. Auden, a musical guest. *Royal College of Music magazine*, 86. 1 (Spring Term, 1980), 15–19.

Conversations in the 1950s on music.

1642 Richard Hoggart. Auden's life-music. *Listener*, 103. 2652 (6 Mar. 1980), 314–15.

Report of Auden's reason for disapproving of Brecht, Yeats, and Frost, his reaction to his father's death, and other subjects.

1643 Anthony Curtis. Look, stranger. *Financial times*, 8 Mar. 1980.

Auden 'talked fascinatingly about the poetry of St. John Perse which he had just discovered and for which he had the highest admiration.'

1644 Nigel Dennis. How Auden was let down by his friends. *Sunday telegraph*, 9 Mar. 1980, p. 16.

Report of Auden's comments on biography and on earlier writings about him.

1645 Stephen Spender. W. H. Auden [letter to the editor]. *Times literary supplement*, 14 Mar. 1980, p. 294.

Auden's complaint when told of a telephone call from Guy Burgess.

1646 'Pendennis' [Tom Davies]. My glimpse of Auden's wisdom. *Observer*, 16 Mar. 1980, p. 44.

Brief recollections of a conversation in 1972.

1647 Moira Hodgson. Host to the art world keeps his meals simple and unpretentious. *New York times*, 19 Mar. 1980, p. C6.

Interview with John Bernard Myers, at whose apartment Auden lived briefly in the 1950s: 'When he woke up in the middle of the night Wystan liked to console himself with a cold spud'.

I648 Walter Allen. *As I walked down New Grub Street: memoirs of a writing life*. London: Heinemann, 1981.

Miscellaneous remarks, pp. 51–8 *passim*. Excerpted as 'Wystan at the wedding', *Times*, 28 Nov. 1981, p. 9.

I649 John Malcolm Brinnin. *Sextet: T. S. Eliot, Truman Capote & others*. New York: Delacorte Press/Seymour Lawrence, 1981.

Remarks on leaving a party given by Truman Capote, Dec. 1948, p. 38. Reprinted in Brinnin's *Truman Capote: dear heart, old buddy* (New York: Delacorte Press/Seymour Lawrence, 1986), p. 53. See also Brinnin's 'On first meeting W. H. Auden', *Ploughshares*, 2. 4 (1975), 31–5.

I650 Humphrey Carpenter. *W. H. Auden: a biography*. London: George Allen & Unwin, 1981.

Conversations reported by others, including many reports from otherwise unpublished interviews and memoirs, *passim*.

I651 Millicent Dillon. *A little original sin: the life and work of Jane Bowles*. New York: Holt, Rinehart, and Winston, 1981.

Auden and Jane and Paul Bowles, around 1941, pp. 94–5.

I652 Victoria Glendinning. *Edith Sitwell: a unicorn among lions*. London: Weidenfeld & Nicolson, 1981.

Brief reports of conversations, pp. 271 and 300.

I653 Howard Griffin. *Conversations with Auden*, edited by Donald Allen. San Francisco: Grey Fox, 1981.

Reprinted from I392, I395, I398, I399, I401, I405, I400, and I410, some in corrected or expanded texts.

I654 Edward Mendelson. *Early Auden*. New York: Viking, 1981.

Indirect quotations of remarks to friends, *passim*.

I655 Donald Mitchell. *Britten and Auden in the thirties: the year 1936*. London: Faber & Faber, 1981.

Conversations with Auden reported in Britten's letters and journals, *passim*.

I656 Richard Crossman. *The backbench diaries of Richard Crossman*, edited by Janet Morgan. London: Hamish Hamilton & Jonathan Cape, 1981.

Vague account of a dinner with Auden given by Spender, 1956, pp. 498–9.

I657 Richard Stern. Extracts from a journal. *Tri-quarterly*, 50 (Winter 1981), 261–73.

Conversations in Chicago, 14–15 Feb. 1967 (misdated 1965), pp. 267–8.

I658 Robert Medley. The Group Theatre 1932–39: Rupert Doone and Wystan Auden. *London magazine*, n.s. 20. 10 (Jan. 1981), 47–60.

Similar material appears in different form in I682.

1659 Robert Medley. Poet and composer. *Financial times*, 9 Feb. 1981, p. 13.

Brief remark on education.

1660 Maréki Saito. Auden in Kirchstetten. *Research reports of Ube Technical College*, 27 (Mar. 1981), 129–46.

Reports of recollections by Auden's Austrian housekeeper.

1661 Jane Kramer. A reporter in Europe: London. *New Yorker*, 57. 12 (11 May 1981), 91–124.

'W. H. Auden, who spent five years as a schoolmaster to some of the children of England's old money, liked to describe them as the real cream— "rich and thick"', p. 108.

1662 Peter Porter. The laureate of ambiguity. *Times literary supplement*, 3 July 1981, pp. 745–6.

'I know from many reminiscences of his friends that he would enquire avidly of people what their fathers did and what they felt for them.' Reprinted in *The modern movement: a TLS companion*, edited by John Gross (London: Harvill, 1992), pp. 139–47.

1663 Ned Rorem. W. H. Auden: the remarkable life of a poet. *Chicago tribune*, 23 Aug. 1981, Book World, pp. 1, 5.

Review of Humphrey Carpenter, *W. H. Auden: a biography*. Brief remark to Frank O'Hara on poetic style: 'You've got to be an Auden to get away with lines like that.' Expanded as 'An Auden', *Christopher Street*, 5. 9 (Sept.–Oct. 1981), 40–5, and reprinted in Rorem's *Setting the tone* (New York: Coward-McCann, 1983), pp. 200–8. A different version of the remark appears elsewhere in *Setting the tone*, p. 33; and a comment on Auden's relations with composers who set his poems appears on p. 302.

1664 Lincoln Kirstein. Uncle Wiz the wizard. *New York review of books*, 28. 20 (17 Dec. 1981), 53–6.

Brief remarks and indirect reports. Reprinted as 'W. H. Auden—Uncle Wiz' in Kirstein's *By with to & from: a Lincoln Kirstein reader*, edited by Nicholas Jenkins (New York: Farrar, Straus & Giroux, 1991), pp. 309–22.

1665 John Haffenden. *The life of John Berryman*. London: Routledge & Kegan Paul, 1982.

Brief conversation with Berryman, 1936, pp. 83–4. Berryman recalls the event in his poem 'Transit', in *Love & fame* (New York: Farrar, Straus & Giroux, 1970), p. 47. Similar report in: Paul Mariani, *Dream song: the life of John Berryman* (New York: William Morrow, 1990), p. 64.

1666 *Snobs*, compiled by Jasper Griffin. Oxford: Oxford University Press, 1982.

Remark on Canada, p. 77.

I667 Ian Hamilton. *Robert Lowell: a biography*. New York: Random House, 1982.

Brief remarks on Lowell, pp. 344 and 425; a remark by Kallman is misattributed to Auden on p. 438.

I668 Thomas Mann. *Tagebücher 1940 bis 1943*, herausgegeben von Peter de Mendelssohn. Frankfurt am Main: S. Fischer, 1982.

Sketchy references to conversations and visits, 1940–1, pp. 125, 126, 176, 368.

I669 *Creators and disturbers: reminiscences of Jewish intellectuals of New York*, drawn from conversations with Bernard Rosenberg and Ernest Goldstein. New York: Columbia University Press, 1982.

'Grace Paley: the writer in Greenwich Village', pp. 288–98, includes remarks by Auden when teaching at the New School, 1946, pp. 291–2. This account is incorporated in: Judith Arcana, *Grace Paley's life stories: a literary biography* (Urbana: University of Illinois Press, 1993), pp. 43–4.

I670 Elisabeth Young-Bruehl. *Hannah Arendt: for love of the world*. New Haven, Conn.: Yale University Press, 1982.

Auden praises Arendt's *The human condition*, 1958, p. 371, and proposes marriage, 1970, p. 372. Mary McCarthy confirms the story and tells a reporter, 'I think Auden was slightly put up to it by Stephen Spender', in: Deirdre Carmody, 'Mary McCarthy, '33, sends papers to Vassar', *New York times*, 1 May 1985, section B, p. 1.

I671 Carol B. Schoen. *Anzia Yezierska*. Boston: Twayne, 1982.

Auden encourages Yezierska, p. 82. A further account, in which Auden agrees to cut his introduction to Yezierska's *Red ribbon on a white horse*, appears in: Louise Levitas Henriksen, *Anzia Yezierska: a writer's life* (New Brunswick: Rutgers University Press, 1988), pp. 268, 271.

I672 Martin Seymour-Smith. *Robert Graves: his life and work*. London: Hutchinson, 1982.

Auden meets Graves at a party, p. 507; see also p. 468.

I673 Igor Stravinsky. *Selected correspondence*, vol. 1, edited and with commentaries by Robert Craft. New York: Alfred A. Knopf, 1982.

Letters with reports of Auden's conversation, pp. 269–70, 271, 279, 281, 285, 292, and 354.

I674 Hans Egon Holthusen. W. H. Auden 75 Jahre (21. 2. 1982). *Neue deutsche Hefte*, 29. 1 (1982), 212–17.

Remark on Churchill from a conversation in Munich, May 1966, when Auden was recording a Bayerischer Rundfunk broadcast talk.

I675 Joseph Brodsky. The art of poetry XXVII [interview with Sven Birkerts]. *Paris review*, 83 (Spring 1982), 82–126.

Brief encounters with Auden, pp. 103 and 107–9. Reprinted in *Writers at work: the* Paris review *interviews, eighth series*, edited by George Plimpton (New York: Viking, 1988), pp. 375–412 (Auden on pp. 392 and 404–5).

I676 Robert Robinson. The Auden landscape. *Listener*, 107. 2750 (4 Mar. 1982), 9–11.

Partial transcript of a BBC Television portrait of Auden broadcast 27 Feb. 1982, with brief reports of conversation. Further quotations appear in: Humphrey Carpenter, 'Leading a generation', *TLS*, 12 Mar. 1982, p. 280.

I677 Philip Larkin. The art of poetry XXX [interview with Robert Phillips]. *Paris review*, 84 (Summer 1982), 42–72.

Brief rebuke to Larkin's sense of unhappiness, p. 59. Reprinted in Larkin's *Required writing* (London: Faber & Faber, 1983), pp. 57–76 (Auden's remark on p. 67), and in *Writers at work: the* Paris review *interviews, seventh series*, edited by George Plimpton (New York: Viking, 1986), pp. 149–75 (Auden's remark on p. 164).

I678 Ruthven Todd. Memoirs: Auden in London. *Malahat review*, 62 (July 1982), 36–41.

Brief remarks.

I679 Edward Callan. *Auden: a carnival of intellect*. New York: Oxford University Press, 1983.

Remark about Ischia, p. 239.

I680 Max Hayward. *Writers in Russia, 1917–1978*. San Diego: Harcourt Brace Jovanovich, 1983.

Introduction by Patricia Blake quotes from conversations during a visit by Hayward and Blake to Austria, July 1963, and a later visit in New York, pp. lxiv–lxvi.

I681 Yousuf Karsh. *Karsh: a fifty-year retrospective*. Boston: Little, Brown, A New York Graphic Society Book, 1983.

Remarks during a portrait photography session, 1972, p. 67.

I682 Robert Medley. *Drawn from the life: a memoir*. London: Faber & Faber, 1983.

Conversations, *passim*.

I683 Charles H. Miller. *Auden: an American friendship*. New York: Charles Scribner's Sons, 1983.

Conversations at the University of Michigan, 1941–2, and after, *passim*.

I684 John Bernard Myers. *Tracking the marvelous: a life in the New York art world*. New York: Random House, 1983.

Reported remarks on surrealism, p. 38.

1685 Frederic Prokosch. *Voices: a memoir*. New York: Farrar, Straus & Giroux, 1983.

Highly unreliable reports of Auden in New York, 1939, pp. 110–13, and in Italy, 1948, pp. 213–15, 271–3.

1686 Michael Straight. *After long silence*. New York: W. W. Norton, 1983.

Quotes Auden's reason for being in America, Feb. 1940, p. 140.

1687 A. J. P. Taylor. *A personal history*. London: Hamish Hamilton, 1983.

Indirect report of Auden's correction of an anecdote about him: it took him two days, not a week, to drive G. N. Clark's car from Old Marston to Oxford during the 1926 General Strike, and he did not smash up the car, pp. 81–2.

1688 John Willett. *Brecht in context: comparative approaches*. London: Methuen, 1983.

The essay 'The case of Auden', pp. 58–72, includes remarks on Brecht recalled by Charles Monteith, p. 71. Reprinted as 'Auden and Brecht' in *Transformations in modern European drama*, edited by Ian Donaldson (London: Macmillan, 1983), pp. 162–76 (recalled on p. 174).

1689 Edmund Wilson. *The forties: from notebooks and diaries of the period*, edited with an introduction by Leon Edel. New York: Farrar, Straus & Giroux, 1983.

Indirect report of a remark on priests, p. 48.

1690 Charles Miller. Auden in Ann Arbor. *Ann Arbor observer*, 7. 7 (Mar. 1983), 31, 33–9.

Not identical to the account in **1683**.

1691 Joseph Brodsky. To please a shadow. *Vanity fair*, 46. 8 (Oct. 1983), 83–90.

Remarks on poets and poetry. Reprinted in his *Less than one: selected essays* (New York: Farrar, Straus & Giroux, 1986), pp. 357–83.

1692 [Anthony Curtis.] Elderly schoolboy shows promise. *Financial times*, 8 Oct. 1983, p. 17.

Indirect quotation of remarks to William Golding on *Lord of the flies*.

1693 *W. H. Auden a Forio*, scritti di Aurora Ciliberti [*et al.*]. Forio d'Ischia: Circolo Georges Sadoul, 1984.

Remembered conversations quoted in Ettore Settanni, 'Un pomeriggio a Forio con Auden', pp. 34–6; R. M. de Angelis, 'Où sont les neiges d'antan?', p. 37; Giocondo Sacchetti [interview], 'Gli "anni di Auden"', pp. 38–9; 'Testimonianze di Pietro Verde e Giovanni Maresca', pp. 40–1; and Nino d'Ambra, 'Gli anni cinquanta a Forio e l'insegnamento di Auden', pp. 42–7.

I694 Dorothy J. Farnan. *Auden in love*. New York: Simon & Schuster, 1984.

Conversations, *passim*.

I695 Robert M. Farnsworth. *Melvin B. Tolson, 1898–1966: plain talk and poetic prophecy*. Columbia: University of Missouri Press, 1984.

Auden told Tolson he never read book reviews of his poetry, p. 223. A very brief report of this conversation appears in Joy Flasch, *Melvin B. Tolson* (New York: Twayne, 1972), p. 44.

I696 Geoffrey Grigson. *Recollections, mainly of artists and writers*. London: Chatto & Windus/The Hogarth Press, 1984.

Auden hands Grigson a book dedicated to him, p. 69; see also pp. 109–10.

I697 *Portrait of Mr. B: photographs of George Balanchine*, with an essay by Lincoln Kirstein. New York: Viking, 1984.

Kirstein's essay 'A ballet master's belief' includes Auden's brief reported criticism of Balanchine's *Prodigal son*, p. 28. Also printed as 'Beliefs of a master' in *The New York review of books*, 31. 4 (15 Mar. 1984), 17–23; reprinted as 'A ballet master's belief' in Kirstein's *By with tò & from: a Lincoln Kirstein reader*, edited by Nicholas Jenkins (New York: Farrar, Straus & Giroux, 1991), pp. 198–219.

I698 Lincoln Kirstein. *Paul Cadmus*. New York: Imago Books, 1984.

Auden suggests that Cadmus paint a series about the Christian virtues, and tells him that Pride can be represented only by a mirror, p. 55. Excerpted in Kirstein's *By with to & from: a Lincoln Kirstein reader*, edited by Nicholas Jenkins (New York: Farrar, Straus & Giroux, 1991), p. 267.

I699 Arthur and Cynthia Koestler. *Stranger on the square*, edited and with an introduction and epilogue by Harold Harris. London: Hutchinson, 1984.

Notebook entry from Ischia, June 1954: 'Saw a lot of Auden. More sex-obsessed than anybody I know. Said: you ought to write autobiography—not novels', p. 182.

I700 Erika Mann. *Briefe und Antworten*, herausgegeben von Anna Zanco Prestel, Band I 1922–1950. München: Edition Spangenberg, 1984.

Erika Mann reports from London to her mother, May 1936: 'Mein Mann ist ein Tyrann', p. 92.

I701 Hugh MacDiarmid. *The thistle rises: an anthology of poetry and prose*, edited by Alan Bold. London: Hamish Hamilton, 1984.

Reports a phrase on communism from a conversation with MacDiarmid, probably at the Poetry International festival, London, 1967, p. 257.

I702 Oliver Sacks. *A leg to stand on*. New York: Summit Books, 1984.
Brief conversation on victims of Parkinson's disease, p. 219. This passage is not in the British edition (London: Duckworth, 1984).

I703 Michael J. Sidnell. *Dances of death: the Group Theatre of London in the thirties*. London: Faber & Faber, 1984.
Indirect reports of Auden's views, *passim*.

I704 Flora Solomon. *Baku to Baker Street: the memoirs of Flora Solomon*, by herself and Barnet Litvinoff. London: Collins, 1984.
Auden as tutor to Peter Benenson, 1930, pp. 143–6. The American edition of the book was titled *A woman's way* (New York: Simon & Schuster, 1984). See also untitled interview with Benenson by Craig Raine, *New review*, 4. 47 (Feb. 1978), 28.

I705 Amos N. Wilder. W. H. Auden: cartographer of the modern. *Wirklichkeit und Dichtung: Studien zur englishen und amerikanischen Literatur: Festschrift zum 60. Geburtstag von Franz Link*, herausgegeben von Ulrich Halfmann, Kurt Müller und Klaus Weiss (Berlin: Duncker & Humblot, 1984), pp. 155–67.
Miscellaneous remarks on Milton, censorship, popular art, and other topics.

I706 Virginia Woolf. *The diary of Virginia Woolf*, edited by Anne Olivier Bell, assisted by Andrew McNeillie, vol. 5, 1936–1941. London: Hogarth Press, 1984.
General account of a meeting at the Albert Hall, 24 June 1937, pp. 98–9.

I707 Harold Norse. Making it with Auden. *Advocate*, 387 (7 Feb. 1984), 26–7, 30–2, 48.
Conversations, mostly in 1939–40. Substantially reprinted in I762.

I708 Michael Davie. Auden's heiress from Winona. *Observer*, 19 Feb. 1984, p. 52.
Interview with Dorothy Farnan, with brief reports of Auden.

I709 Bertram Rota Ltd. Catalogue no. 235, London, Spring 1984.
Nevill Coghill's annotation in a copy of Auden's *Poems* (1930) quotes Auden's explanation of excisions he made in the book around 1945: 'The influence of Mr. Bridges did not agree with me', p. 3.

I710 D. J. R. Bruckner. A candid talk with Saul Bellow. *New York times*, 15 Apr. 1984, section 6 (magazine), pp. 52–62.
Bellow quotes Auden's remark on *Herzog*: 'Don't you think it might be *too* well written?'

I711 Harold Norse. The honeymoon. *No apologies*, 3 (Fall 1984), 111–22.

Kallman's letters to Norse on travels with Auden, 1939. Continued in 'The honeymoon: part two', ibid., 4 (Spring 1985), 7–22. Not included in **I762**.

I712 Robert Craft. Lives of the poets. *New York review of books*, 31. 14 (27 Sept. 1984), 7–8, 10.

Miscellaneous recollections in a review of Dorothy J. Farnan, *Auden in love* (**I694**). Reprinted as part of 'Wystan in and out of love' in Craft's *Small Craft advisories* (London: Thames & Hudson, 1989), pp. 63–70.

I713 Elizabeth Frank. *Louise Bogan, a portrait*. New York: Alfred A. Knopf, 1985.

Auden introduces Bogan and Elizabeth Mayer, pp. 349–50. Also includes quotations from **I478**.

I714 Laurence Grobel. *Conversations with Capote*. New York: New American Library, 1985.

Auden assumed to have insulted Tennessee Williams on Ischia, 1949, p. 144. A similarly vague report of a snub appears in Jack Dunphy, *'Dear genius . . .': a memoir of my life with Truman Capote* (New York: McGraw-Hill, 1987), pp. 207–8.

I715 Kevin Ingram. *Rebel: the short life of Esmond Romilly*. London: Weidenfeld & Nicolson, 1985.

Perhaps apocryphal account of a meeting with Auden, mid-1930s, p. 113. See also **I418**.

I716 *Randall Jarrell's letters: an autobiographical and literary selection*, edited by Mary Jarrell. Boston: Houghton Mifflin, 1985.

Auden praises Jarrell's poems, 1951, pp. 286–7.

I717 Edward Upward. At the Ferry Inn. *London magazine*, 25. 4 (July 1985), 3–13.

Short story with Auden represented as Walter Selwyn. Reprinted in Upward's *The night walk and other stories* (London: Heinemann, 1987), pp. 123–37.

I718 Donald Pearce. Fortunate fall: W. H. Auden at Michigan. *W. H. Auden: the far interior*, edited by Alan Bold (London: Vision; Totowa, NJ: Barnes & Noble, 1985), pp. 129–57.

Auden's classroom lectures, 1941. Reprinted in his *Para/worlds: entanglements of art and history* (University Park: Pennsylvania State University Press, 1989), pp. 151–74.

I719 Jane Rule. *A hot-eyed moderate*. Tallahassee: Naiad Press, 1985.

'"Silly like us," a recollection', pp. 205–14, an account of a weekend visit to Auden in Kirchstetten, 1962.

I720   Stephen   Spender.   *Journals   1939–1983*,   edited   by   John Goldsmith. London: Faber & Faber, 1985.
Conversations, *passim.*

I721   Igor Stravinsky. *Selected correspondence*, vol. 3, edited and with commentaries by Robert Craft. New York: Alfred A. Knopf, 1985.
Letters with reports of Auden's conversation, pp. 320 and 354.

I722   Laurence Whistler. *The laughter and the urn: the life of Rex Whistler*. London: Weidenfeld & Nicolson, 1985.
'Later [in the 1930s?] I met Auden . . . "I've seen you in the *Tatler*", was his only remark', p. 215.

I723   Wendell Stacy Johnson. Auden in order: a memoir and commentary. *Confrontation*, 29 (Winter 1985), 70–9.

I724   Hertha Staub. Merlin in Österreich: Erinnerungen an W. H. Audens Kirchstettner Jahre. *Wiener Zeitung*, 25 Jan. 1985, Extra Section, p. 3.

I725   Ruth Nanda Anshen. *Biography of an idea*. Mt. Kisco, NY: Moyer Bell, 1986.
Conversations on religion, pp. 119–25.

I726   Weldon Kees. *Weldon Kees and the midcentury generation: letters, 1935–1955*, edited by Robert E. Knoll. Lincoln: University of Nebraska Press, 1986.
Letters from Kees report on Auden at Olivet College, 1941, p. 54, and on Auden's affair with Rhoda Jaffe, 1946, p. 101.

I727   Bruce Laughton. *The Euston Road school: a study in objective painting*. Aldershot: Scolar, 1986.
Indirect reports of conversations with William Coldstream, pp. 115–19.

I728   Elizabeth Longford. *The pebbled shore: the memoirs of Elizabeth Longford*. London: Weidenfeld & Nicolson, 1986.
Auden and Gabriel Carritt at Oxford, pp. 74–5.

I729   Joe Orton. *The Orton diaries*, edited by John Lahr. London: Methuen, 1986.
Auden embarrassed by the King when he receives the Gold Medal for Poetry, as told by George Greeves, p. 168.

I730   Charles Osborne. *Giving it away: the memoirs of an uncivil servant*. London: Secker & Warburg, 1986.
Remarks on various subjects, pp. 140, 142, 144, 199, 202, 243, and 247.

1731 Delmore Schwartz. *Portrait of Delmore: journals and notes of Delmore Schwartz 1939–1959*, edited and introduced by Elizabeth Pollet. New York: Farrar, Straus & Giroux, 1986.

Notes on conversations with Auden, July 1943, pp. 122–5, 129; and 1949, pp. 306 and 312.

1732 Edmund Wilson. *The fifties: from notebooks and diaries of the period*, edited with an introduction by Leon Edel. New York: Farrar, Straus & Giroux, 1986.

Conversations quoted and reported, pp. 291–301, 347–50, 386–7, 526–8, 604.

1733 Robert Fitzgerald. From the notebooks of Robert Fitzgerald. *Erato*, Poetry and Farnsworth Rooms, Harvard College Library, 2–3 (Fall–Winter 1986), 1.

Conversations from Fitzgerald's diaries, 1939.

1734 Alan Ansen. *The vigilantes: a fragment*. Sudbury, Mass.: Water Row Press, 1987.

Fragment of a novel, with Auden thinly disguised as the silent character Von der Goltz.

1735 E. J. Brown. *The first five: the story of a school*. [Colwall, Malvern: E. J. Brown, 1987.]

Anonymous reminiscence of Auden at the Downs School, p. 50; see also p. 40.

1736 John Catlin. *Family quartet*. London: Hamish Hamilton, 1987.

Auden visits the Downs School to talk about China, p. 135.

1737 Sidney Hook. *Out of step: an unquiet life in the 20th century*. New York: Harper & Row, 1987.

Auden as director of and speaker at the American Committee for Cultural Freedom, pp. 425–7.

1738 Mervyn Jones. *Chances: an autobiography*. London: Verso, 1987.

Auden's poetry-writing seminar for the League of American Writers, 1940 (i.e., 1939), p. 51. Some of the contents similar to Jones's letter to the editor, 'Auden's collected poems', *New statesman*, 92. 2376 (1 Oct. 1976), 449.

1739 Ned Rorem. *The Nantucket diary of Ned Rorem*. San Francisco: North Point Press, 1987.

Reported remark, p. 71; see also pp. 150, 265.

1740 A. L. Rowse. *The poet Auden*. London: Methuen, 1987.

Conversations, *passim*.

1741 Junius Irving Scales and Richard Nickson. *Cause at heart: a former Communist remembers*. Athens: University of Georgia Press, 1987.

Conversation after a lecture at the University of North Carolina, Apr. 1939, pp. 65–6.

I742 Eva Haraszti Taylor. *A life with Alan: the diary of A. J. P. Taylor's wife Eva, from 1978 to 1985*. London: Hamish Hamilton, 1987.
Brief account of Auden as Professor of Poetry at Oxford, pp. 102–3.

I743 Ann Waldron. *Close connections: Caroline Gordon and the Southern renaissance*. New York: G. P. Putnam's Sons, 1987.
Auden warned his friends to keep their wives away from Allen Tate, *ca.* 1952, p. 292.

I744 Beth Britten. *My brother Benjamin*. Abbotsbrook, Bourne End, Bucks.: Kensal, 1988.
Reports on Auden in letters from Britten and Peter Pears.

I745 Gerald Clarke. *Capote: a biography*. New York: Simon & Schuster, 1988.
'W. H. Auden called him [George Davis] the wittiest person he had ever known', p. 88. See also pp. 197, 199.

I746 Samuel R. Delany. *The motion of light in water: sex and science fiction writing in the East Village 1957–1965*. New York: Arbor House, 1988.
Detailed account of visits with Auden, 1959, pp. 79–81, 84–93. Includes a passage from an interview with Marilyn Hacker not otherwise located.

I747 Richard Hoggart. *A local habitation (life and times, volume I: 1918–40)*. London: Chatto & Windus, 1988.
A favourite story reported, p. 4; see also p. 175 (apparently a misremembered paraphrase of an essay).

I748 James Kirkup. *I, of all people: an autobiography of youth*. London: Weidenfeld & Nicolson, 1988.
Auden, at the Downs School, affirms that one may read others' postcards, but not their letters, p. 119.

I749 Ted Morgan. *Literary outlaw: the life and times of William S. Burroughs*. New York: Henry Holt, 1988.
Brief report of Auden's style of conversation, 1940–1, p. 72.

I750 Frances Spalding. *Stevie Smith, a critical biography*. London: Faber & Faber, 1988.
Auden trades memories of Germany, and sings ditties, with Stevie Smith after a reading at the Edinburgh Festival, 1965, p. 278.

I751 Stephen Spender. *The temple*. London: Faber & Faber, 1988.
Revised text of an unpublished novel written in 1929. Auden is caricatured as 'Simon Wilmot'; see introduction, p. xi.

I752 Stephen Spender. W. H. Auden as I first knew him. *W. H. Auden 1907–1973: Ergebnisse eines Symposions*, Redaktion: Michael O'Sullivan. [Wien:] Niederösterreich-Gesellschaft für Kunst und Kultur, [1988], pp. 13–16.

I753 Susana Walton. *William Walton: behind the façade.* Oxford: Oxford University Press, 1988.

Auden on Ischia, pp. 112–16.

I754 Edward Upward. Remembering Mortmere. *London magazine,* n.s. 27. 11 (Feb. 1988), 54–9.

Auden read the unexpurgated 'The railway accident' to academic audiences, and an indirect quotation about the story. See also I300.

I755 Anthony Hecht. The art of poetry XXXX [interview with J. D. McClatchy]. *Paris Review,* 108 (Fall 1988), 161–205.

Auden on Ischia, pp. 176–9.

I756 John Hollander. W. H. Auden. *Yale review,* 77. 4 (Oct. 1988), 501–11.

Reprinted in *Encounters,* edited by Kai Eriksson (New Haven, Conn.: Yale University Press, 1989), pp. 140–9.

I757 Donald MacLeod. Recollections that throw an ironic light on Auden. *Scotsman,* 21 June 1988, p. 13.

Auden at Helensburgh, 1930–2.

I758 Peter F. Alexander. *William Plomer: a biography.* Oxford: Oxford University Press, 1989.

Auden, Isherwood, Plomer, and Spender go to a Garbo movie, p. 186.

I759 Alan Ansen. *The table talk of W. H. Auden,* edited by Nicholas Jenkins with an introduction by Richard Howard. New York: Sea Cliff Press, 1989.

Ansen's conversations with Auden, 1946–8. Transcribed contemporaneously by Ansen; edited and arranged, with notes, by Jenkins. Excerpts appeared as '*From* The table talk of W. H. Auden', *Ontario review,* 30 (Spring–Summer 1989), 7–18. The book was reprinted with minor corrections in trade editions (Princeton: Ontario Review Press, 1990; London: Faber & Faber, 1991). Howard's introduction and Ansen's afterword also report Auden's remarks.

I760 Michael Meyer. *Not Prince Hamlet.* London: Secker & Warburg, 1989.

Conversation in Stockholm, 1963, pp. 200–1. American edition titled *Words through a window-pane* (New York: Grove Weidenfeld, 1989).

I761 Barry Miles. *Ginsberg.* New York: Simon & Schuster, 1989.

Quotations of remarks to Allen Ginsberg and Gregory Corso, pp. 230, 242, and 452–3.

I762 Harold Norse. *Memoirs of a bastard angel.* New York: William Morrow, 1989.

Conversations, mostly 1939–41, *passim*.

I763 Michael Kennedy. *Portrait of Walton.* Oxford: Oxford University Press, 1989.

William Walton's letters to Christopher Hassall report Auden's suggestions for Walton's *Troilus and Cressida*, pp. 161–2, 168–9.

I764 Peter Parker. *Ackerley: a life of J. R. Ackerley.* London: Constable, 1989.

Auden reportedly made Ackerley pay for the gin he drank, and marked the bottle, p. 372.

I765 Oliver Sacks. *Seeing voices: a journey into the world of the deaf.* Berkeley: University of California Press, 1989.

Auden recommends David Wright's *Deafness*, 1969, pp. 2–3.

I766 Daniel J. Boorstin. The civility of American politics. *U. S. News and world report*, 106. 3 (23 Jan. 1989), 68.

On the American presidential election, 1952: 'You probably wouldn't even notice it, but neither candidate is packing his bags to leave the country if he doesn't win.'

I767 Gurney Thomas. Recollections of Auden at the Downs School. *W. H. Auden Society newsletter*, 3 (Apr. 1989), 1–2.

I768 John Bridgen. Auden on Christianity—a memoir. *W. H. Auden Society newsletter*, 3 (Apr. 1989), 3–4.

Extensive report of a conversation in 1971.

I769 Jill Benton. *Naomi Mitchison: a century of experiment in life and letters.* London: Pandora, 1990.

Mitchison noted in the margin of her novel *We have been warned* (begun 1932): 'this elephant part is in a way the genesis of the book—Wystan telling me to write a book about an elephant at a garden party', p. 90.

I770 John Bridgen. Frank McEachran (1900–1975): an unrecognized influence on W. H. Auden. *W. H. Auden, 'The map of all my youth': early works, friends and influences*, Auden Studies 1, edited by Katherine Bucknell and Nicholas Jenkins. Oxford: Clarendon Press, 1990, pp. 117–33.

Indirect report of Auden's admiration for McEachran, p. 118.

I771 Anthony Burgess. *You've had your time: the second part of the confessions.* London: Heinemann, 1990.

In 1966 Auden reportedly turned down an offer to translate Berlioz's *L'enfance du Christ* for the BBC, p. 122. Perhaps refers to an exchange by letter.

I772 Lawrence Gowing and David Sylvester. *The paintings of William Coldstream 1908–1987*. London: Tate Gallery, 1990.

Coldstream's notebook reports a conversation with Auden, Jan. 1939, p. 31.

I773 Philip Hoare. *Serious pleasures: the life of Stephen Tennant*. London: Hamish Hamilton, 1990.

Indirect quotation from a visit by Auden, 1950, p. 310.

I774 Richard Hoggart. *A sort of clowning (life and times, volume I: 1940–59)*. London: Chatto & Windus, 1990.

Brief report of Auden's response to Hoggart's book about him, p. 89.

I775 Anthony Howard. *Crossman: the pursuit of power*. London: Jonathan Cape, 1990.

Auden rebuffs Crossman's (accurate) claim that Crossman had written poetry at Oxford, 1970, p. 321.

I776 Wendell Stacy Johnson. *W. H. Auden*. New York: Continuum, A Frederick Ungar Book, 1990.

Miscellaneous remarks and reported conversations, *passim*.

I777 Klaus Mann. *Tagebücher 1938 bis 1939*, herausgegeben von Joachim Heimannsberg, Peter Laemmle und Wilfried F. Schoeller. München: Spangenberg, 1990.

Conversations reported briefly, pp. 84–5, 101, 114, 125, 144.

I778 *Letters of Katherine Anne Porter*, selected and edited and with an introduction by Isabel Bayley. New York: Atlantic Monthly Press, 1990.

Porter indirectly quotes conversations with Auden, pp. 169–70 and 174.

I779 Karl Shapiro. *Reports of my death*. Chapel Hill, NC: Algonquin Books of Chapel Hill, 1990.

Miscellaneous remarks, some second-hand, pp. 42, 263, 266, 268, 273, 274.

I780 Glenway Wescott. *Continual lessons: the journals of Glenway Wescott, 1937–1955*, edited by Robert Phelps with Jerry Rosco. New York: Farrar, Straus & Giroux, 1990.

Remarks indirectly reported, pp. 303, 307, and (on a broadcast) 331.

I781 Charles H. Miller. 'Auden was here for three days and we are still dazed'. *Diarist's journal*, 26 (Feb. 1990), 1, 4.

Excerpts from Miller's journals, 1940–1.

I782 Alan Ansen. [Review of *Memoirs of a bastard angel*, by Harold Norse.] *Review of contemporary fiction*, 10. 2 (Summer 1990), 283–4.
Ansen and Kallman bring Auden to tears by objecting to his revisions.

I783 Christopher Niebuhr. Some memories of Auden. *W. H. Auden Society newsletter*, 6 (Dec. 1990), 8–9.
Brief personal remarks.

I784 Kingsley Amis. *Memoirs*. London: Hutchinson, 1991.
Brief indirect report of Auden at a café in Paris in the late 1930s, p. 246.

I785 Benjamin Britten. *Letters from a life: the selected letters and diaries of Benjamin Britten 1913–1976*, vol. 1, 1923–1939 [*and* vol. 2, 1939–1945], edited by Donald Mitchell, assistant editor Philip Reed. London: Faber & Faber, 1991.
Conversations with Auden reported in Britten's letters and journals, *passim*.

I786 Klaus Mann. *Tagebücher 1940 bis 1943*, herausgegeben von Joachim Heimannsberg, Peter Laemmle und Wilfried F. Schoeller. München: Spangenberg, 1991.
Conversations reported briefly, pp. 18, 52, 67, 72, 75, 77.

I787 David Marr. *Patrick White: a life*. London: Jonathan Cape, 1991.
Brief recollection by Peggy Garland of conversations with Auden before his visit to Spain, pp. 173, 672–3.

I788 Diane Wood Middlebrook. *Anne Sexton: a biography*. Boston: Houghton Mifflin, A Peter Davison Book, 1991.
Auden was cross with Sexton for reading far beyond her allotted time at Poetry International, 1967, p. 278.

I789 *Remembering Reinhold Niebuhr: letters of Reinhold and Ursula M. Niebuhr*, edited by Ursula M. Niebuhr. San Francisco: Harper-SanFrancisco, 1991.
Brief quotations, pp. 4, 409.

I790 Andrew Sinclair. Fable of paper mountain. *Times*, 28 Mar. 1991, p. 20.
'Auden also used to say, if he thought of two perfect lines to open or conclude a poem, he eliminated them, or there was no point in writing the poem at all.'

I791 Harold Norse. Awed by Auden: sacred monster redux. *Lambda book report*, 2. 9 (Mar.–Apr. 1991), 18–19.
Brief personal remarks.

1792 Nicholas Jenkins. A conversation with Lincoln Kirstein. *W. H. Auden Society newsletter*, 7 (Oct. 1991), 2–8.
Brief remarks.

1793 Michael Hope. Remembering Wystan Auden. *W. H. Auden Society newsletter*, 7 (Oct. 1991), 8–9.
Auden at Oxford, 1927–8.

1794 [James] Schuyler in conversation with Raymond Foye. *XXIst century*, 1. 1 (Winter 1991–2), 44–9.
Indirect quotations from Auden on Ischia, pp. 46–7.

1795 Isaiah Berlin and Rahan Jahanbegloo. *Conversations with Isaiah Berlin*. London: Peter Halban, 1992.
Auden changed the subject when asked why he admired Hannah Arendt, pp. 83–4. (The edition published in New York by Scribner's, Maxwell Macmillan International, dated 1991, in fact followed the London edition.)

1796 Humphrey Carpenter. *Benjamin Britten: a biography*. London: Faber & Faber, 1992.
Conversations reported in Britten's diaries, pp. 69–70 and *passim*.

1797 Robert Craft. *Stravinsky: glimpses of a life*. London: Lime Tree, 1992.
One sentence about Dylan Thomas, p. 53; see also pp. 28 and 57.

1798 Barbara B. Heyman. *Samuel Barber: the composer and his music*. New York: Oxford University Press, 1992.
Barber met Auden in 1940 and discussed a possible text for an aria, p. 337.

1799 Richard Hoggart. *An imagined life (life and times, volume II: 1959–91)*. London: Chatto & Windus, 1992.
Detailed report of Auden's visit to Birmingham, 1967, pp. 100–8; how to kill kittens, p. 275.

1800 Rolfe Humphries. *Poets, poetics, and politics: America's literary community viewed from the letters of Rolfe Humphries*, edited by Richard Gillman and Michael Paul Novak. Lawrence: University of Kansas Press, 1992.
Reports that Auden called Frederic Prokosch his best critic, p. 171, and a vague account of dinner with Auden, 1941, p. 175.

1801 Philip Larkin. *Selected letters of Philip Larkin*, edited by Anthony Thwaite. London: Faber & Faber, 1993.
Vague report of an evening with Auden, 1972, p. 460; Larkin thanks Charles Monteith for the news that Auden is willing to nominate him for Professor

of Poetry at Oxford, 1973, p. 470. See also p. 524. The letter to Monteith is described in Andrew Motion, *Philip Larkin: a writer's life* (London: Faber & Faber, 1993), p. 429; Motion also repeats the remark quoted in **1677**.

1802 Robert Manning. *The swamp root chronicle: adventures in the word trade*. New York: Norton, 1992.
One sentence to Theodore Spencer, p. 89.

1803 Larry Rivers, with Arnold Weinstein. *What did I do? the unauthorized autobiography*. New York: HarperCollins, Aaron Asher Books, 1992.
Remark to Kallman, p. 110.

1804 Michael Schumacher. *Dharma lion: a biography of Allen Ginsberg*. New York: St. Martin's Press, 1992.
Conversations with Ginsberg, pp. 267–78 and 578–9.

1805 Martin Stannard. *Evelyn Waugh: no abiding city 1939–1966*. London: J. M. Dent & Sons, 1992.
Letter from John B. Auden to Waugh, 1951, reports that Auden 'had decided by August 1938, when I was staying with him in Bruxelles, to become an American citizen', p. 299, note 114.

1806 Duncan Fallowell. The spies who loved me. *Sunday times*, 7 Apr. 1992, magazine, pp. 18, 20, 22.
Profile of Jack Hewit, with brief quotation from Auden's visits to Isherwood in the 1930s, p. 20.

1807 Rebecca Fowler. Catholicism turns to computers as the saints go marching in. *Sunday times*, 10 May 1992, section 2, p. 6.
'W. H. Auden said of him: [Cardinal] "Manning would have been canonised years ago, but thought it too campy to do a miracle."' The source of the quotation is unidentified.

1808 Joel Lewis. Dylan Thomas in his own voice. *San Francisco chronicle*, 13 Sept. 1992, Sunday Review, p. 4.
'W. H. Auden privately referred to Thomas as "a professional Welshman"'. A different quotation from that in **1797**. The author reports that he can no longer remember where he learned of Auden's remark.

1809 Margaret Lefranc. Auden in the southwest. *Palacio*, Museum of New Mexico, 98. 1 (Winter 1992–3), 32–5, 49–53.
A journey from New Mexico to California in 1939.

1810 Christopher Andersen. *Jagger unauthorized*. New York: Delacorte, 1993.
A question to Marianne Faithfull on drug smuggling, p. 182.

I811 Anatole Broyard. *Kafka was the rage: a Greenwich Village memoir*. New York: Crown, 1993.

Auden's inarticulate response when Broyard's girlfriend accidentally fell on him, pp. 9–10.

I812 William S. Burroughs. *The letters of William S. Burroughs, 1945–1959*, edited and with an introduction by Oliver Harris. New York: Viking, 1993.

Brief second-hand report of Auden's view of Burroughs and Jack Kerouac, p. 247.

I813 Brad Gooch. *City poet: the life and times of Frank O'Hara*. New York: Alfred A. Knopf, 1993.

Brief remarks to O'Hara and to an audience, pp. 120 (from **I663**), 260, 365.

I814 James V. Hatch. *Sorrow is the only faithful one: the life of Owen Dodson*. Urbana: University of Illinois Press, 1993.

Accounts of a meeting with Auden and a visit with him, 1939 and 1942, pp. 58, 116.

I815 John Heath-Stubbs. *Hindsights: an autobiography*. London: Hodder & Stoughton, 1993.

Reports of remarks following two public readings, probably 1970–3; he 'spoke of Edwardian virtues and how his mother would punish him if he ever lolled about in an easy chair', pp. 68–9.

I816 Anthony Hecht. *The hidden law: the poetry of W. H. Auden*. Cambridge, Mass.: Harvard University Press, 1993.

Remark on Freud's cancer, p. 21; on the diction of 'In memory of W. B. Yeats', p. 141; Auden on Ischia (excerpted from **I755**), pp. 175–6; on 'Under which lyre', p. 358.

I817 James Merrill. *A different person: a memoir*. New York: Alfred A. Knopf, 1993.

Auden on Mediterranean men, 1965, pp. 230–1.

I818 Anne Rouse. *Sunset grill*. Newcastle-upon-Tyne: Bloodaxe, 1993.

Poem 'Memo to Auden' quotes Auden in Oxford *ca.* 1973 telling a tourist who asked about an unidentified poem, 'I scrapped it' p. 62.

I819 Delmore Schwartz and James Laughlin. *Selected letters*, edited by Robert Phillips. New York: Norton, 1993.

Auden visits Cambridge in the early 1940s, pp. 66, 213, 333.

I820 David Sweetman. *Mary Renault: a biography*. London: Chatto & Windus, 1993.

Auden, who attended Gilbert Murray's lectures at Oxford, thought him a 'mythopoeic' person, p. 76 (no source cited).

1821 Marcella Comès Winslow. *Brushes with the literary: letters of a Washington artist 1943–1959*. Baton Rouge: Louisiana State University Press, 1993.

Brief impressions of Auden at dinner in Washington, November 1948, pp. 254–5.

1822 Reed Whittemore. *Six literary lives: the shared impiety of Adams, London, Sinclair, Williams, Dos Passos, and Tate*. Columbia: University of Missouri Press, 1993.

Indirect report of remarks on the endings of 'In memory of W. B. Yeats' and 'September 1, 1939', from around 1959–60, pp. 8–9.

1823 Edmund Wilson. *The sixties: the last journal, 1960–1972*, edited with an introduction by Lewis M. Dabney. New York: Farrar, Straus & Giroux, 1993.

Reported conversations, 1960–70, *passim*. Briefly excerpted as 'A man of the 20's in his 70's', *New York times*, 16 May 1973, section 7 (book review), pp. 1, 37.

1824 A. H. Barken. Ageing, anxiety, & Auden. *Oxford today*, 5. 3 (Trinity Issue, 1993), 30–1.

Detailed report of a conversation, 1967.

1825 Anthony Curtis. William Golding—lord of the sea. *Financial times*, 21 June 1993, p. 15.

Indirect quotation of remarks to William Golding on *Lord of the flies*. Similar to **1692**.

1826 Raymond Sokolov. Why spill vitriol on such a squalid screed? *Wall Street journal*, 12 Aug. 1993, p. A10.

'I can well remember when W. H. Auden told me how shocked he was by David Halberstam's long, seamless [fabricated] quotations in "The Best and the Brightest," many sounding like the author's own voice.'

1827 Paul Driver. Upstaging. *London review of books*, 15. 16 (19 Aug. 1993), 22–3.

Auden proposed writing librettos for Michael Tippett and Harrison Birtwistle, who both refused.

ADDENDA

1828 Louis MacNeice. Letter to Graham and Anne Shepard. *Letters from Iceland*, by W. H. Auden and Louis MacNeice (London: Faber & Faber, 1937), pp. 31–5.

Reports Auden's invitation to join him on the trip to Iceland, p. 33.

1829 W. H. Auden. Address on Henry James. *Gazette of the Grolier Club*, 2.7 (Feb. 1947), 208–25.

The introductory remarks by Monroe Wheeler report a story about James that Auden told at dinner before his speech, p. 210.

1830 Stephen Spender. Guy Burgess [letter to the editor]. *Sunday times*, 13 Jan. 1957, p. 2.

Auden's reply when told of a telephone call from Guy Burgess. Auden amplifies the story in a letter to the editor, ibid., 20 Jan. 1957, p. 4.

1831 Paul William Driver. Back in time. *Cherwell*, Oxford, 145. 7 (8 Mar. 1973), 9.

Brief general interview with no direct quotations.

1832 Sotheby & Co. Catalogue of nineteenth century & modern first editions . . . London, 15–16 July 1974.

A. L. Snodgrass 'tells us that he read proofs of this book [*The orators*] with Auden at his parents' house and that Auden then told him that he changed his mind about the colour of the binding [yellow in a trial binding, black as issued].'

1833 Lawrance Thompson and R. H. Winnick. *Robert Frost: the later years, 1938–1963*. New York: Holt, Rinehart and Winston, 1976.

In 1957, when Frost addressed Rhodes Scholars in Oxford Auden relayed questions from the floor, p. 239.

1834 *W. H. Auden: the critical heritage*, edited by John Haffenden. London: Routledge & Kegan Paul, 1983.

Auden's opinion of Geoffrey Grigson, reported by Lincoln Kirstein, pp. 55–6, and his opinion of F. R. Leavis, reported by Stephen Spender, p. 67.

1835 Brian Urquhart. *A life in peace and war*. New York: Harper & Row, 1987.

Auden, after saying he was too busy, agrees to supervise the translation of Hammarskjöld's *Markings*, p. 177.

1836 Robert Skidelsky. *John Maynard Keynes, a biography, volume 2: the economist as saviour, 1920–1937*. London: Macmillan, 1992.

Keynes reports a conversation with Auden, November 1936, p. 628.

1837 James Broughton. *Coming unbuttoned: a memoir*. San Francisco: City Lights, 1993.

Miscellaneous remarks during Broughton's visit to Ischia, pp. 117–18.

1838 Ved Mehta. *Up at Oxford*. London: John Murray, 1993.

Remarks during and about his meeting in Oxford with Allen Ginsberg and Gregory Corso, pp. 218–19; compare **1450**.

1839 Diana Trilling. *The beginning of the journey: the marriage of Diana and Lionel Trilling*. New York: Harcourt Brace, 1993.

Indirect report of Auden's opinion of the management of the book clubs he edited with Lionel Trilling and Jacques Barzun, p. 266; his exclamation when Diana Trilling praised Allen Ginsberg, p. 362 (similar to **I341**).

1840 David Ansen. Avedon. *Newsweek*, 122. 11 (13 Sept. 1993), 66.

Auden grumpily agrees to an invitation to be photographed by Richard Avedon, 3 March 1960.

1841 Ann Chisholm. Paris Spring with le grand Sam. Obituary: James Stern. *Guardian*, 24 Nov. 1993, p. 41.

'Brian Howard . . . said, "the one man who might just persuade Wystan to alter one word in a poem, my dear, is Jimmy Stern."'

1842 Derwent May. Callas and offal. *Times*, 19 Jan. 1994.

Brief excerpts from a BBC World Service radio interview with Kevin Byrne, recorded in 1971, and broadcast by the BBC Radio 3 in 1994. This review, on the authority of newspaper listings of the broadcast, incorrectly describes the interview as dating from 1962; the listings were prepared before the BBC's producer, and Peter Porter who introduced the broadcast, decided to use the 1971 interview with Byrne instead of a 1962 interview with A. Alvarez.

1843 Amy Gamerman. Rhyme and reason: editing the poet of the century. *Wall Street journal*, 20 Jan. 1994, p. A12.

Interview with Edward Mendelson, reporting brief remarks by Auden.

NOTES ON CONTRIBUTORS

RICHARD BOZORTH is a graduate of Princeton University and a doctoral candidate in English at the University of Virginia. He is currently completing his dissertation, 'The Angler's Lie: Auden and the Meanings of Homosexuality'.

KATHERINE BUCKNELL edited *Juvenilia: Poems 1922–1928* by W. H. Auden (1994). She is now preparing Christopher Isherwood's *American Journals*.

RICHARD DAVENPORT-HINES is writing a biography of Auden which will be published in 1995. His recent books include *Sex, Death and Punishment* (1990), *The Macmillans* (1992), and *Vice: An Anthology* (1993).

NICHOLAS JENKINS, a Harkness Fellow from 1986 to 1988, is the editor of *The Table Talk of W. H. Auden* (1990) and *By With To & From: A Lincoln Kirstein Reader* (1991). He is completing a D.Phil. on Auden.

DAVID LUKE is an Emeritus Student (Emeritus Fellow) of Christ Church, Oxford, where he was Tutor in German from 1959 to 1988. He has published various translations, most accompanied by critical essays, from Goethe's poetry and dramatic works and from other German writers (Thomas Mann, Kleist, the Grimm brothers).

EDWARD MENDELSON, who teaches English and Comparative Literature at Columbia University, is Auden's literary executor. His edition of the Auden–Kallman libretti, the second volume in *The Complete Works of W. H. Auden*, was published in 1993.

DONALD MITCHELL is the foremost authority on Benjamin Britten. His extensive commentary includes *Britten and Auden in the Thirties* (The T. S. Eliot Memorial Lectures) as well as radio features and television documentaries. The first two volumes of Britten's diaries and letters, edited by him with Philip Reed, appeared in 1991; the remaining volumes are in preparation. Dr Mitchell is also writing the fourth and final volume of his study of Mahler.

DAVID PASCOE is Lecturer in English at Oriel College, Oxford. He was awarded a D.Phil. for research into C. Day-Lewis and is currently working on a study of Auden's addictions.

PHILIP REED has been Staff Musicologist at the Britten–Pears Library, Aldeburgh, since 1986. His publications include the first two volumes of *Letters from a Life: The Selected Letters and Diaries of Benjamin Britten* (with Donald Mitchell) and a Cambridge Opera Handbook on *Billy Budd* (with Mervyn Cooke). At present he is preparing an edition of Peter Pears's diaries.

STAN SMITH is Professor and Head of English at Dundee University and has published widely on modern poets, including Auden. His *The Origins of Modernism: Eliot, Pound, Yeats and the Rhetorics of Renewal* appeared in 1994. He is general editor of the Longman Critical Reader series.

INDEX